"Do not go where the path may lead, go instead where there is no path and leave your mark."

Quote from Ralph Waldo Emerson posted on a Facebook page dedicated to the memory of Samia Yusuf Omar

An Olympic Dream

The Story of Samia Yusuf Omar

First published 2016
by SelfMadeHero
139-141 Pancras Road
London NW1 1UN
www.selfmadehero.com

Copyright text and illustrations © 2015
by CARLSEN Verlag GmbH, Hamburg, Germany
First published in Germany under the title
"Der Traum von Olympia – Die Geschichte von Samia Yusuf Omar"

Written & Illustrated by: Reinhard Kleist
Translated from German to English by Ivanka Hahnenberger

Publishing Assistant: Guillaume Rater
Sales & Marketing Manager: Sam Humphrey
Publishing Director: Emma Hayley
UK Publicist: Paul Smith
US Publicist: Maya Bradford
Designer: Kate McLauchlan
With thanks to: Dan Lockwood

Other acknowledgements:
Michael Groenewald, Sabine Witkowski, Mustaf Hajj Adem and his friends,
Rechtsanwälte Dominik Bender and Maria Bethke, Klaus Schikowski,
Andreas Platthaus, Judith Gleitze and Maria from Borderline Europe,
The Goethe-Institut, and especially Roman Maruhn, Christina Hasenau,
Ulrich Fügender, Miriam Jesske, Atelier Kastanienallee 77, Claudia
Jerusalem Groenewald, Karen Kollmetz, everyone at Carlsen Verlag,
Teresa Krug, Hodan Omar, Abdi Warsame, Heli Gerlach, Susanne Hellweg,
Andreas Löhlein, Anne Jung, Elias Bierdel, Ralf Liebe and Jochen Matthes

A CIP record for this book is available from the British Library

ISBN: 978-1-910593-09-7

10 9 8 7 6 5 4 3 2 1

Printed and bound in China

An Olympic Dream

The Story of Samia Yusuf Omar

BY REINHARD KLEIST

SELF MADE HERO

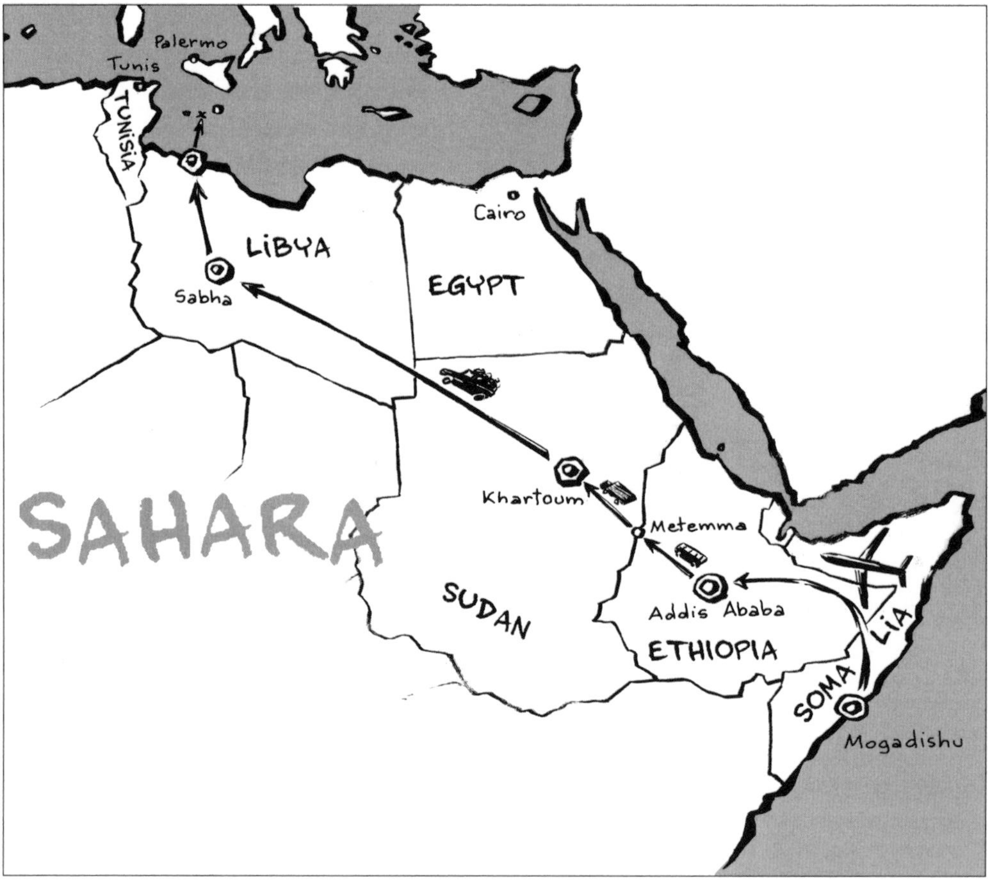
Palermo
Tunis
TUNISIA
LIBYA
Sabha
Cairo
EGYPT
Khartoum
Metemma
SAHARA
SUDAN
Addis Ababa
ETHIOPIA
SOMALIA
Mogadishu

PREFACE

Every day, we see images of people trying to reach Europe by boat, but we are usually unaware of the traumatic odysseys – taking weeks, months, sometimes years – that lead up to these desperate, often fatal, crossings. We don't even take notice of the numbers any more, whether there were ten, twenty or even hundreds of deaths involved. So why does the story of Samia Yusuf Omar stick with us and not one of the many thousands of others about those who died such cruel deaths?

Since I read Elias Bierdel's book *Ende einer Rettungsfahrt (The End of a Rescue Mission)*, I have not stopped thinking about the refugee policy issue. In October 2012, I spent a month in Palermo researching this topic. What I discovered there shocked me deeply. It ranged from government systems failures to downright slavery – so that we, in the rest of Europe, can have cheap fruit and vegetables.

When I heard Samia Yusuf Omar's story, the tragic force of it all overwhelmed me. Thanks to the help of the journalist Teresa Krug, who had befriended her, I was able to speak personally with her sister Hodan Yusuf Omar, who in 2006 had fled to Helsinki.

She gave me insight into the lives of their relatives in Mogadishu and the tragedy that had torn the family apart. Although the wound left by the death of her sister was still fresh, she supported my project to tell her story in a graphic novel. Her support was very important to me. Through Facebook, Samia Yusuf Omar was able to keep in contact with her friends and family almost all the time during her odyssey. Her entries have, in the meantime, been deleted. The Facebook messages in this book are used to disseminate information to the reader, and for this reason I have fictionalised most of them, except for one: her desperate call for help from Tripoli, which she had addressed to Teresa Krug.

Many descriptions of the events during Samia Yusuf Omar's nearly year-long journey were incomplete or not fully comprehensible, so I used pieces of reports by other refugees and in some cases filled in the blanks myself. I used my imagination to depict how people would handle such a situation, how they would think and feel, how they would react. And many of the real events related here are, for a European like me, quite incomprehensible.

I hope that this book will justly portray Samia Yusuf Omar and that her story will raise our consciousness to the fact that behind the news stories there is a refugee issue that needs to be addressed – and that the abstract numbers represent human lives.

REINHARD KLEIST

Al-Shabaab is a militant Islamist movement in Somalia whose goal is the establishment of an Islamic state and a global jihad. In the south and the centre of the country, there have been decades of civil war – armed clashes with government troops – that continue even today. In the areas controlled by the Al-Shabaab militia, Sharia law is strictly imposed.

Hawala is a worldwide informal money transfer system. In countries where the banking system has broken down, it is often the only way to send money. If someone wants to send money to anyone anywhere, they rely on and trust the Hawala dealers. One dealer relays a message to another in the recipient's location, telling them to pay that person the agreed sum. The dealers arrange their fees between themselves.

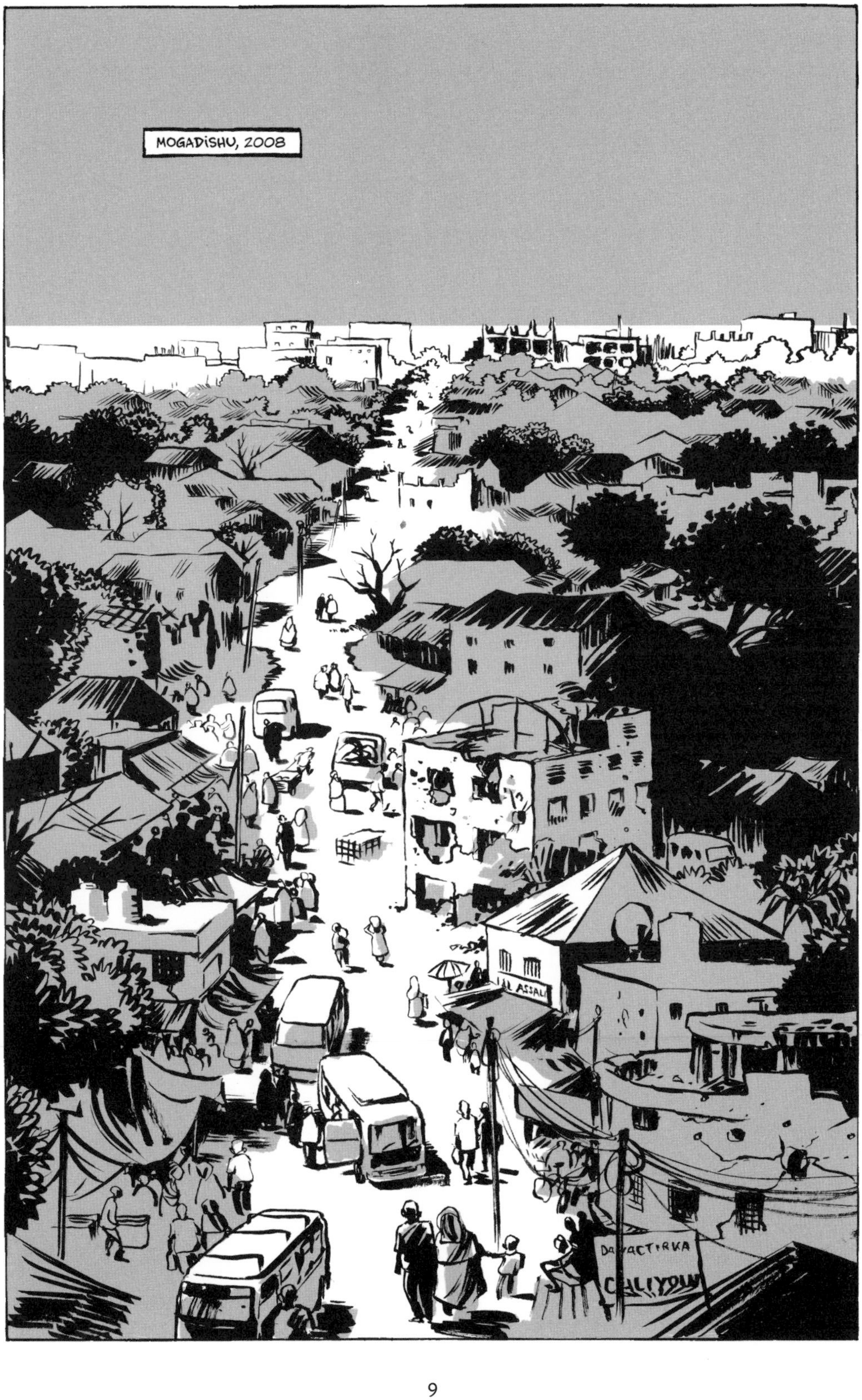
MOGADISHU, 2008
ASSALI

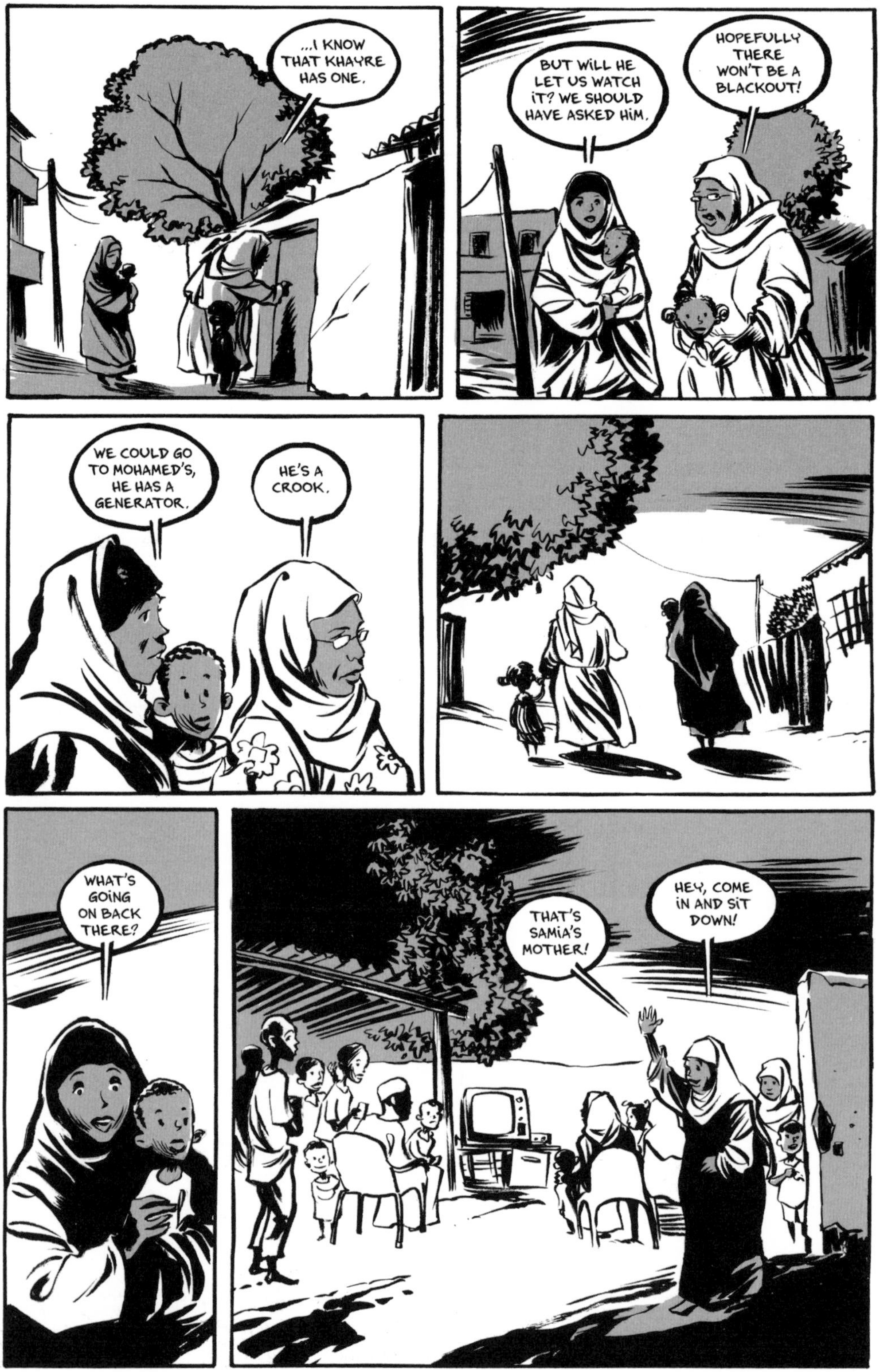
...I KNOW THAT KHAYRE HAS ONE.
BUT WILL HE LET US WATCH IT? WE SHOULD HAVE ASKED HIM.
HOPEFULLY THERE WON'T BE A BLACKOUT!
WE COULD GO TO MOHAMED'S, HE HAS A GENERATOR.
HE'S A CROOK.
WHAT'S GOING ON BACK THERE?
THAT'S SAMIA'S MOTHER!
HEY, COME IN AND SIT DOWN!

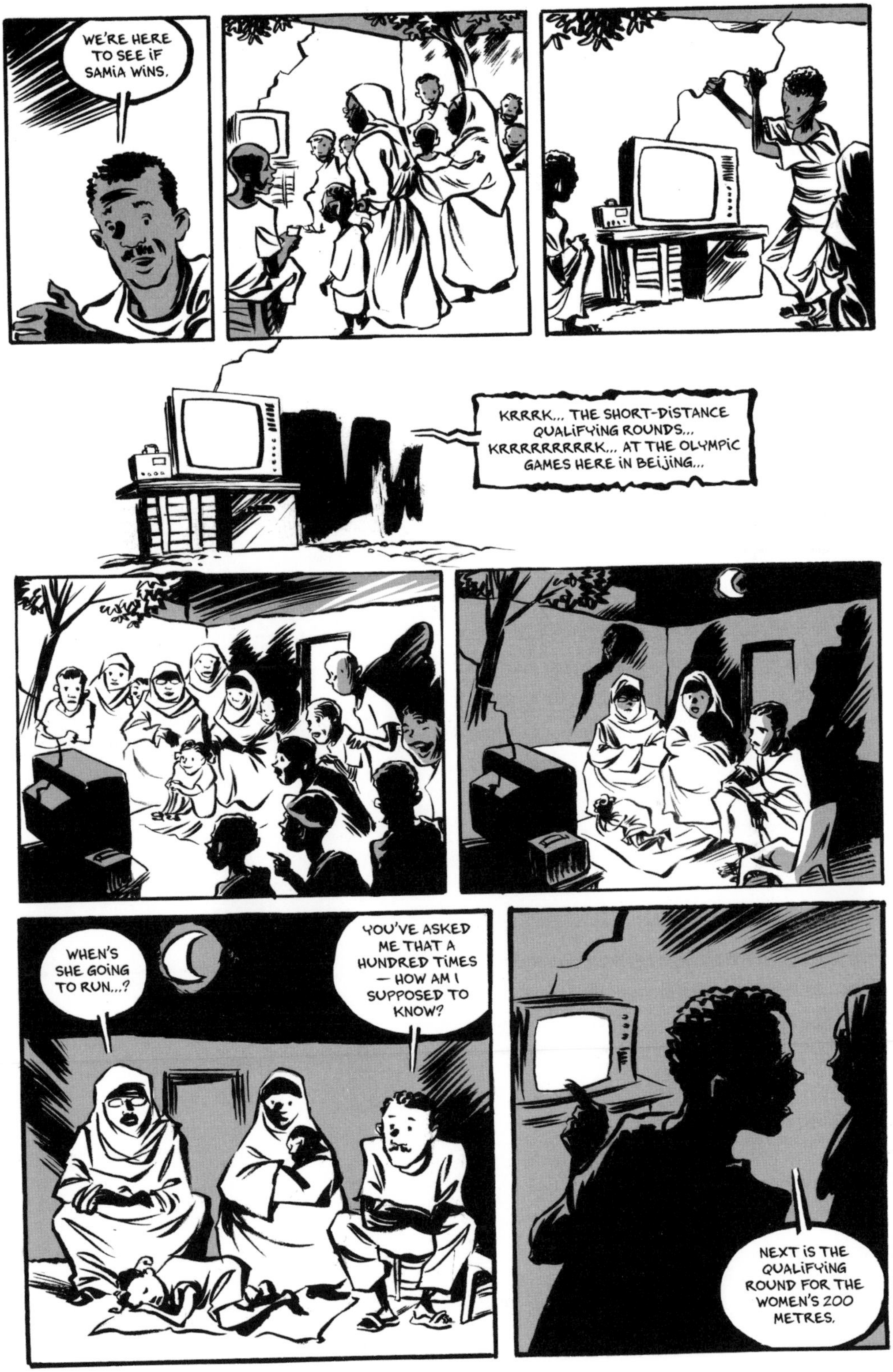
WE'RE HERE TO SEE IF SAMIA WINS.
KRRRK... THE SHORT-DISTANCE QUALIFYING ROUNDS... KRRRRRRRRRK... AT THE OLYMPIC GAMES HERE IN BEIJING...
WHEN'S SHE GOING TO RUN...?
YOU'VE ASKED ME THAT A HUNDRED TIMES — HOW AM I SUPPOSED TO KNOW?
NEXT IS THE QUALIFYING ROUND FOR THE WOMEN'S 200 METRES.

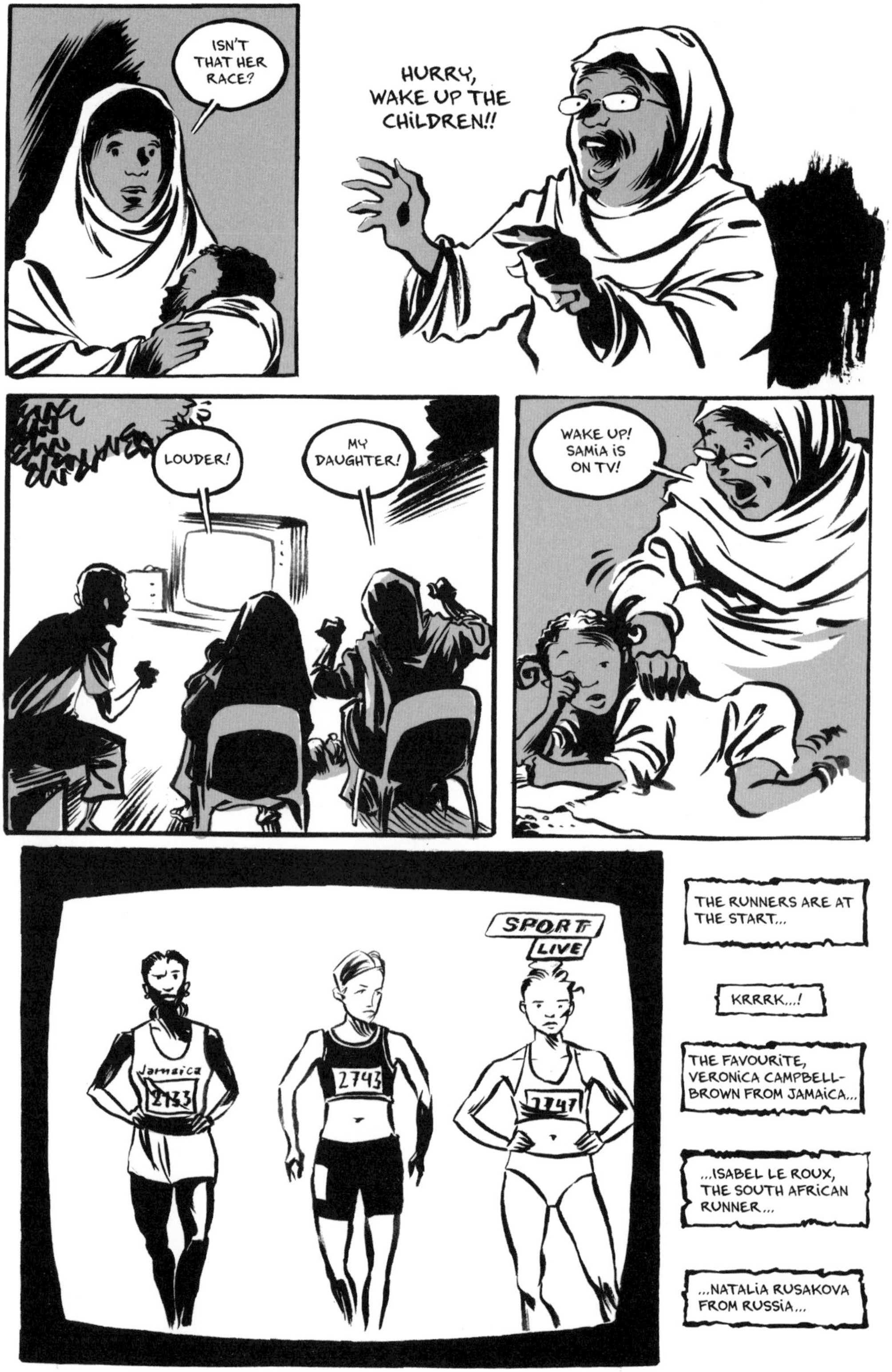

ISN'T THAT HER RACE?
HURRY, WAKE UP THE CHILDREN!!
LOUDER!
MY DAUGHTER!
WAKE UP! SAMIA IS ON TV!
SPORT
LIVE
Jamaica
2133
2743
2747
THE RUNNERS ARE AT THE START...
KRRRK...!
THE FAVOURITE, VERONICA CAMPBELL-BROWN FROM JAMAICA...
...ISABEL LE ROUX, THE SOUTH AFRICAN RUNNER...
...NATALIA RUSAKOVA FROM RUSSIA...

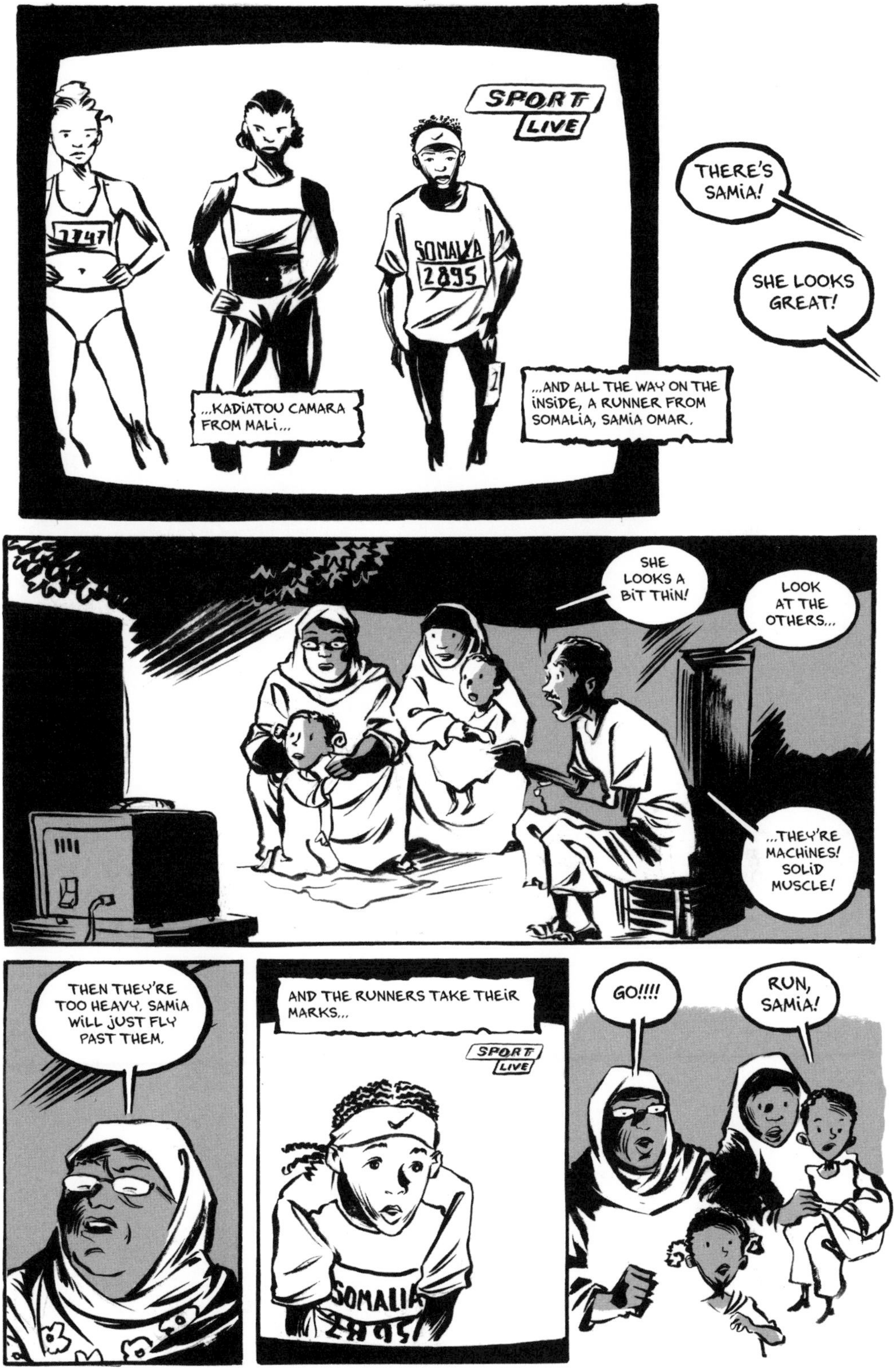
SPORT LIVE
...KADIATOU CAMARA FROM MALI...
...AND ALL THE WAY ON THE INSIDE, A RUNNER FROM SOMALIA, SAMIA OMAR.
THERE'S SAMIA!
SHE LOOKS GREAT!
SHE LOOKS A BIT THIN!
LOOK AT THE OTHERS...
...THEY'RE MACHINES! SOLID MUSCLE!
THEN THEY'RE TOO HEAVY. SAMIA WILL JUST FLY PAST THEM.
AND THE RUNNERS TAKE THEIR MARKS...
SPORT LIVE
GO!!!!
RUN, SAMIA!

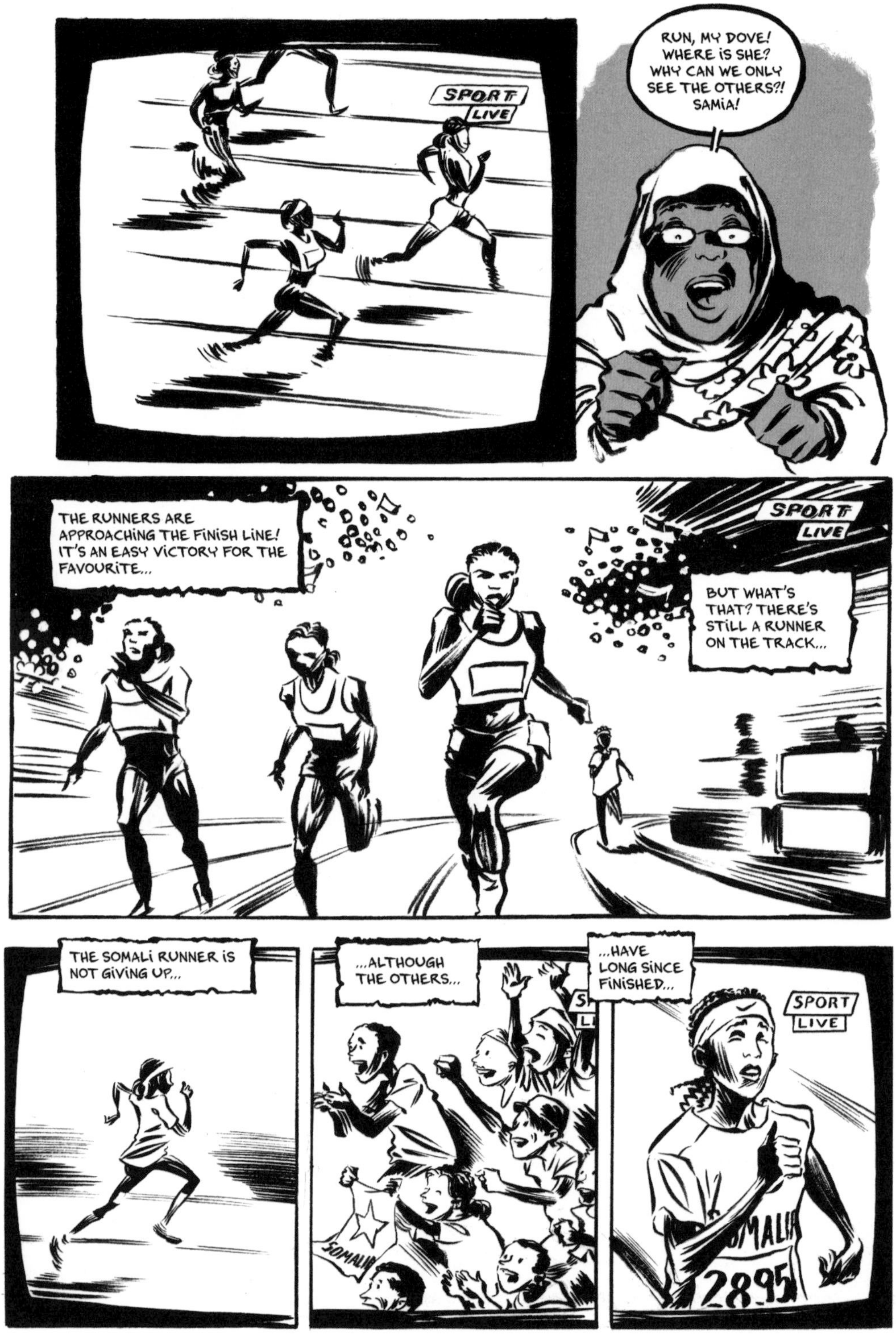
SPORT
LIVE
RUN, MY DOVE! WHERE IS SHE? WHY CAN WE ONLY SEE THE OTHERS?! SAMIA!
THE RUNNERS ARE APPROACHING THE FINISH LINE! IT'S AN EASY VICTORY FOR THE FAVOURITE...
SPORT
LIVE
BUT WHAT'S THAT? THERE'S STILL A RUNNER ON THE TRACK...
THE SOMALI RUNNER IS NOT GIVING UP...
...ALTHOUGH THE OTHERS...
SOMALIA
...HAVE LONG SINCE FINISHED...
SPORT
LIVE
2895

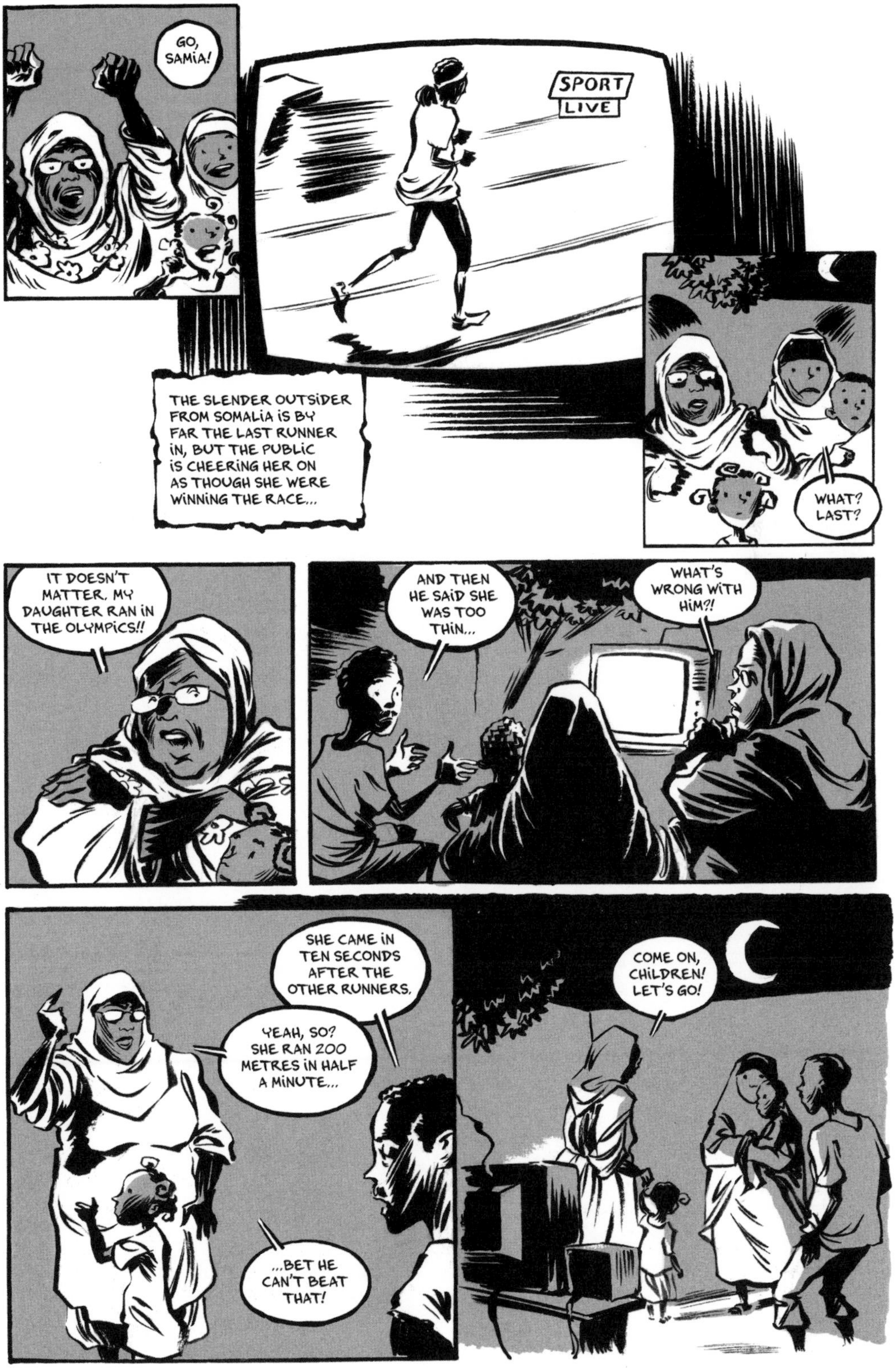
GO, SAMIA!
SPORT LIVE
THE SLENDER OUTSIDER FROM SOMALIA IS BY FAR THE LAST RUNNER IN, BUT THE PUBLIC IS CHEERING HER ON AS THOUGH SHE WERE WINNING THE RACE...
WHAT? LAST?
IT DOESN'T MATTER. MY DAUGHTER RAN IN THE OLYMPICS!!
AND THEN HE SAID SHE WAS TOO THIN...
WHAT'S WRONG WITH HIM?!
SHE CAME IN TEN SECONDS AFTER THE OTHER RUNNERS.
YEAH, SO? SHE RAN 200 METRES IN HALF A MINUTE...
...BET HE CAN'T BEAT THAT!
COME ON, CHILDREN! LET'S GO!

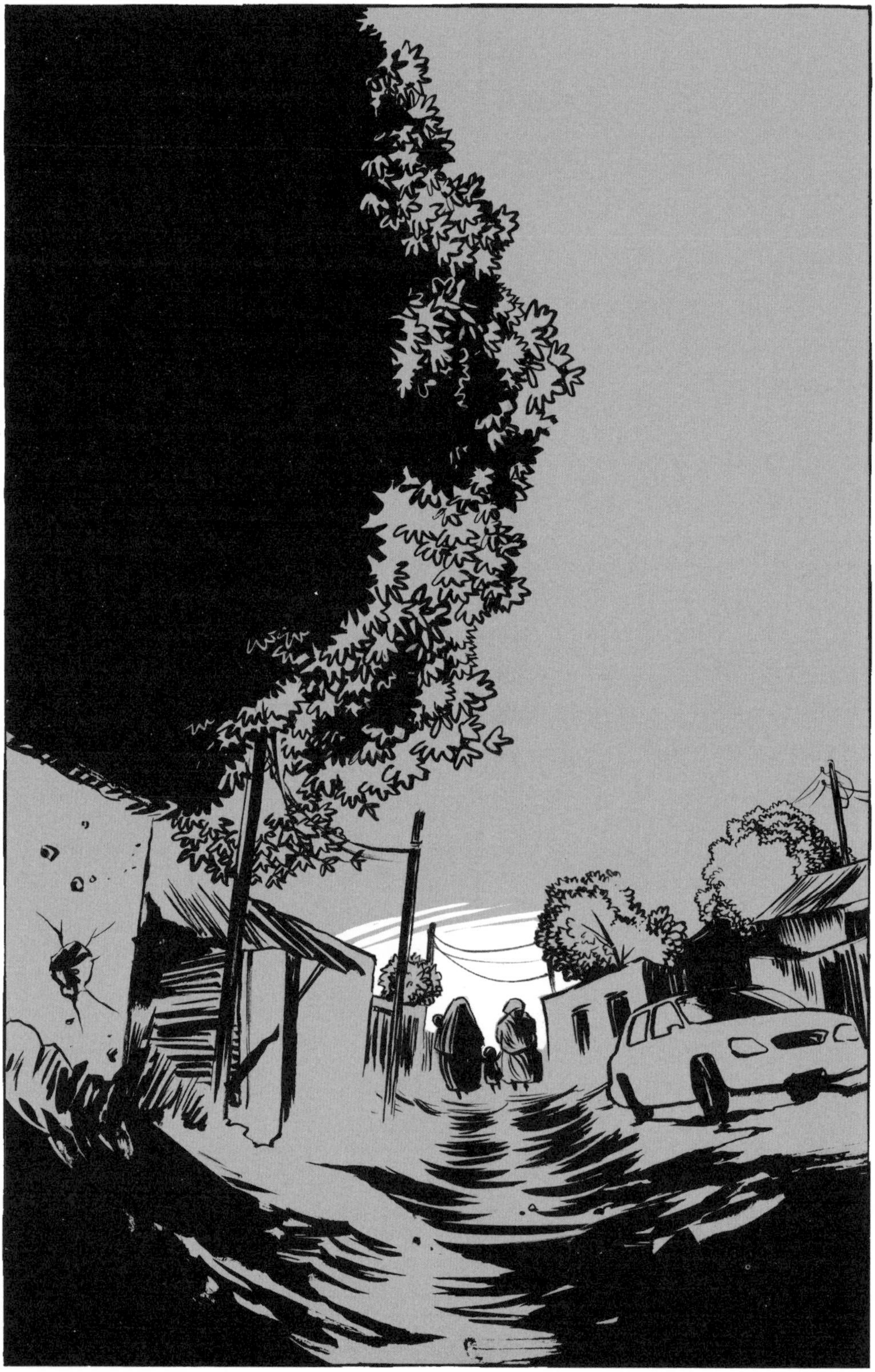

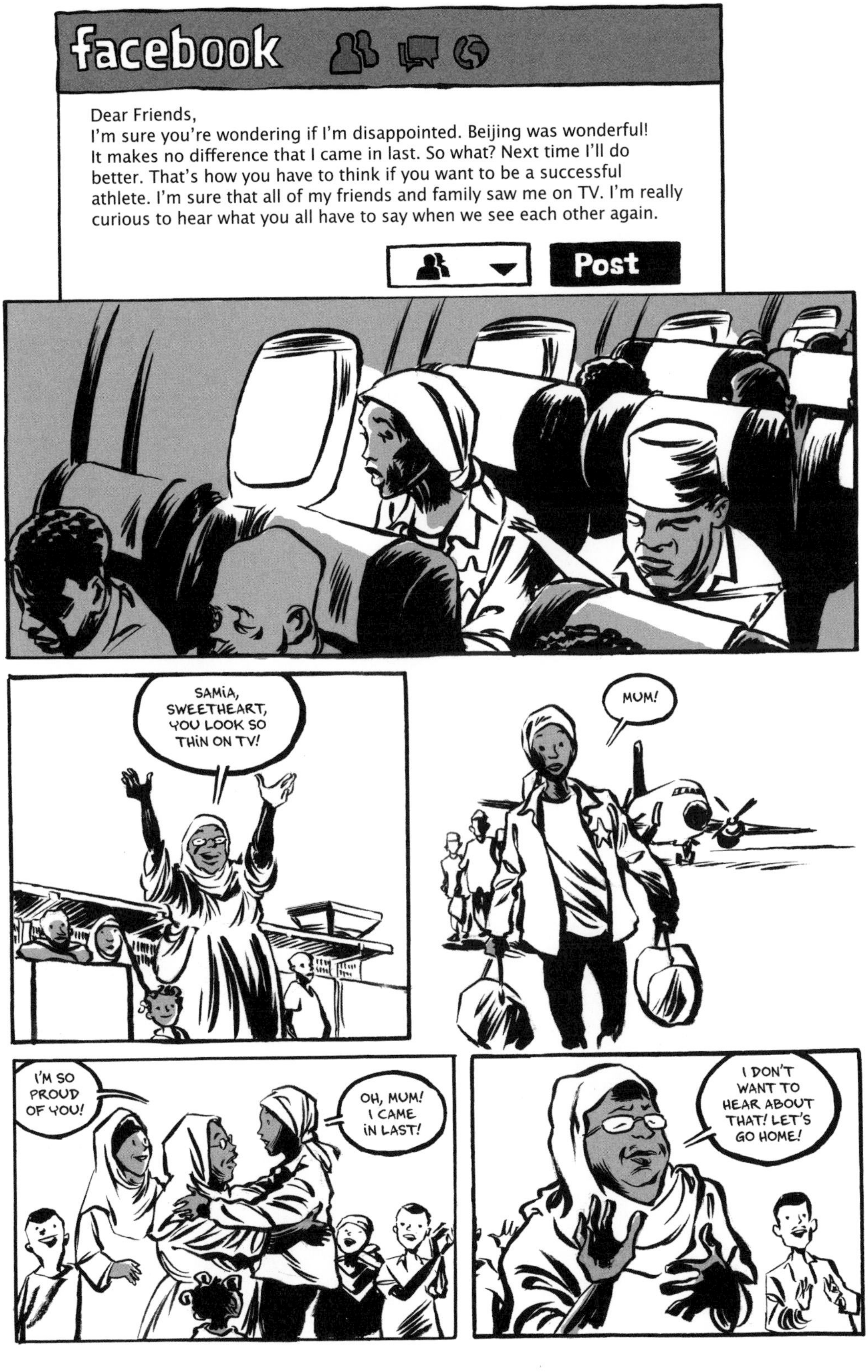
facebook
Dear Friends,
I'm sure you're wondering if I'm disappointed. Beijing was wonderful! It makes no difference that I came in last. So what? Next time I'll do better. That's how you have to think if you want to be a successful athlete. I'm sure that all of my friends and family saw me on TV. I'm really curious to hear what you all have to say when we see each other again.
Post
SAMIA, SWEETHEART, YOU LOOK SO THIN ON TV!
MUM!
I'M SO PROUD OF YOU!
OH, MUM! I CAME IN LAST!
I DON'T WANT TO HEAR ABOUT THAT! LET'S GO HOME!

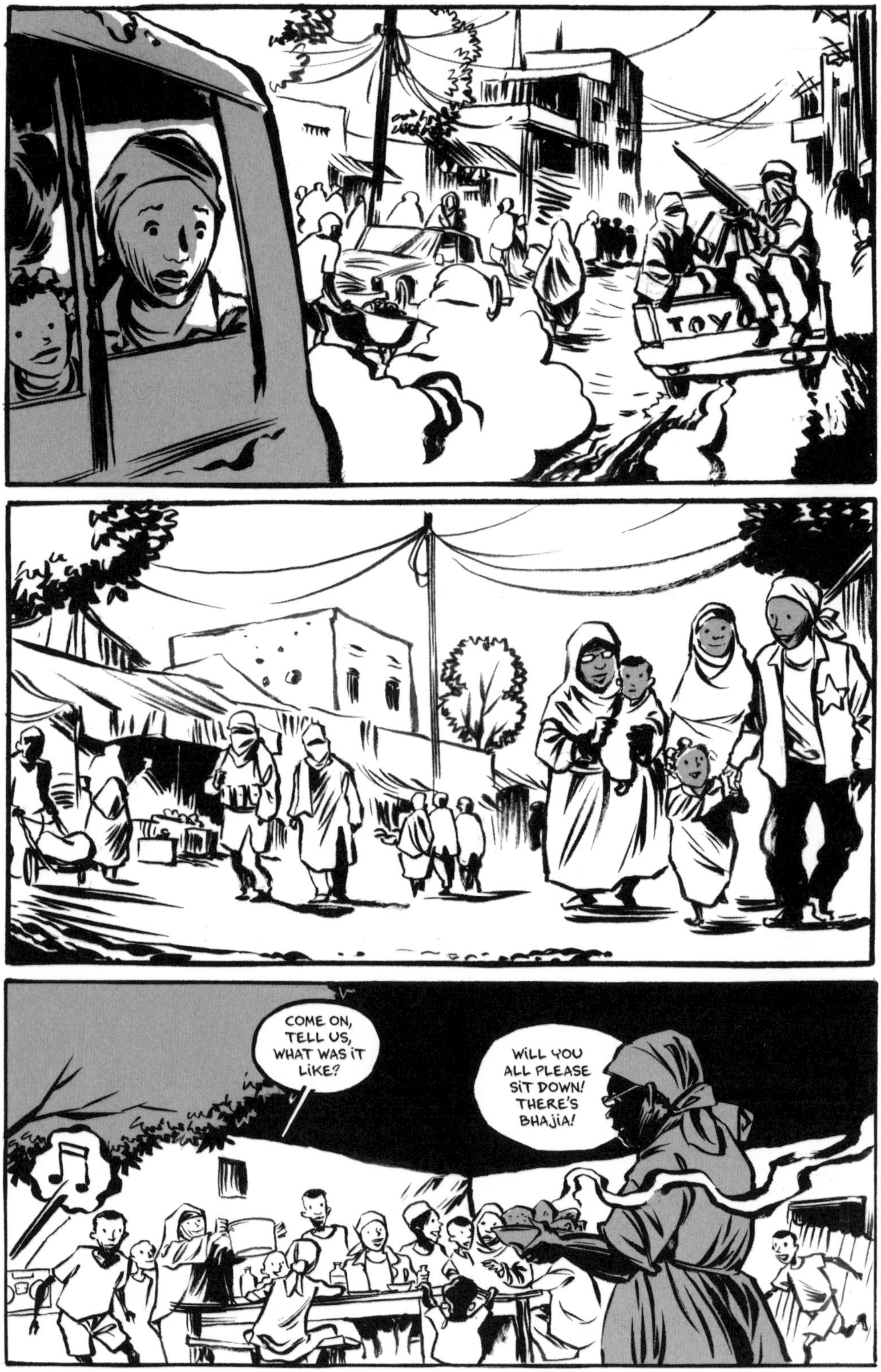
TOY
COME ON, TELL US, WHAT WAS IT LIKE?
WILL YOU ALL PLEASE SIT DOWN! THERE'S BHAJIA!

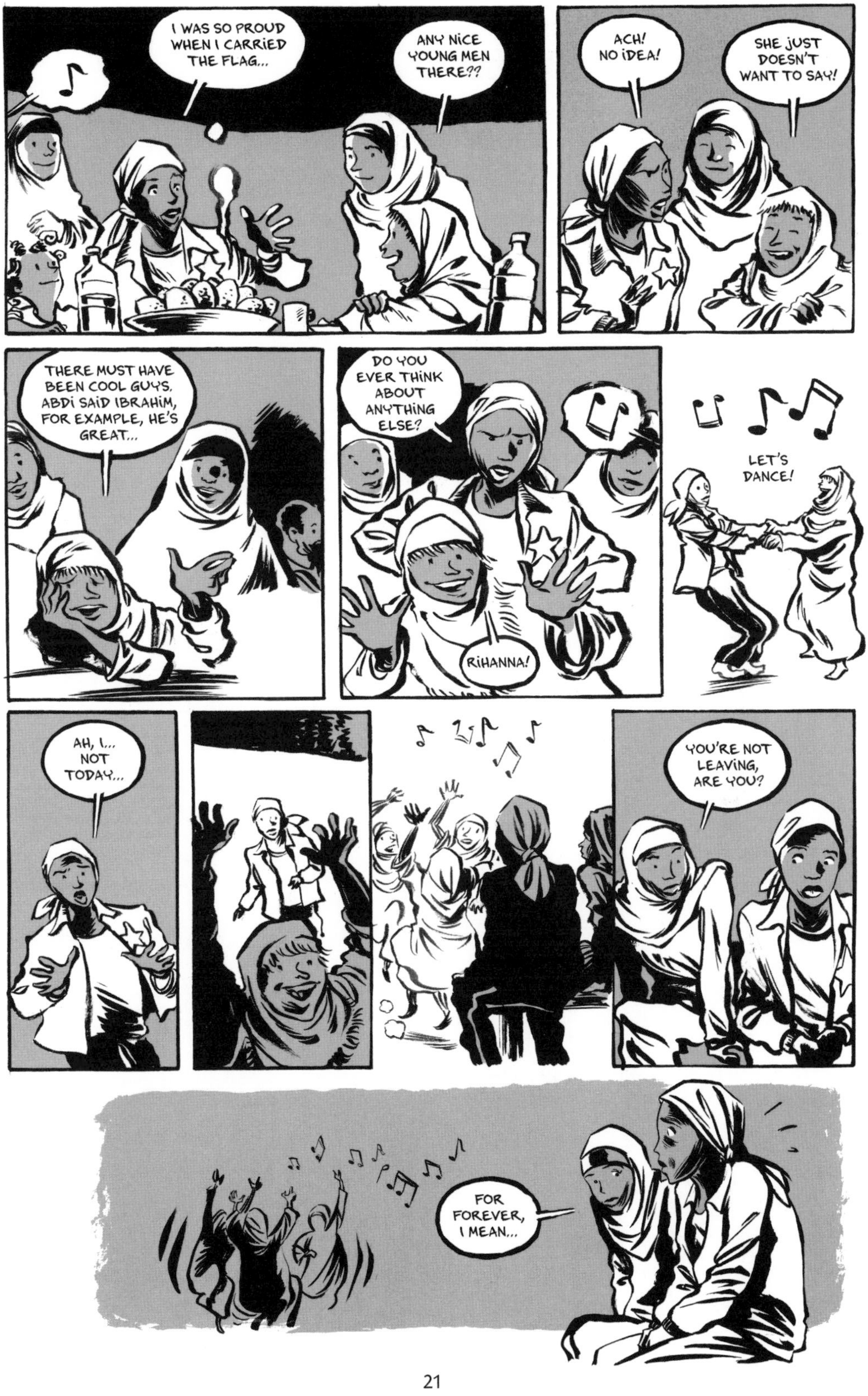
I WAS SO PROUD WHEN I CARRIED THE FLAG...
ANY NICE YOUNG MEN THERE??
ACH! NO IDEA!
SHE JUST DOESN'T WANT TO SAY!
THERE MUST HAVE BEEN COOL GUYS. ABDI SAID IBRAHIM, FOR EXAMPLE, HE'S GREAT...
DO YOU EVER THINK ABOUT ANYTHING ELSE?
RIHANNA!
LET'S DANCE!
AH, I... NOT TODAY...
YOU'RE NOT LEAVING, ARE YOU?
FOR FOREVER, I MEAN...

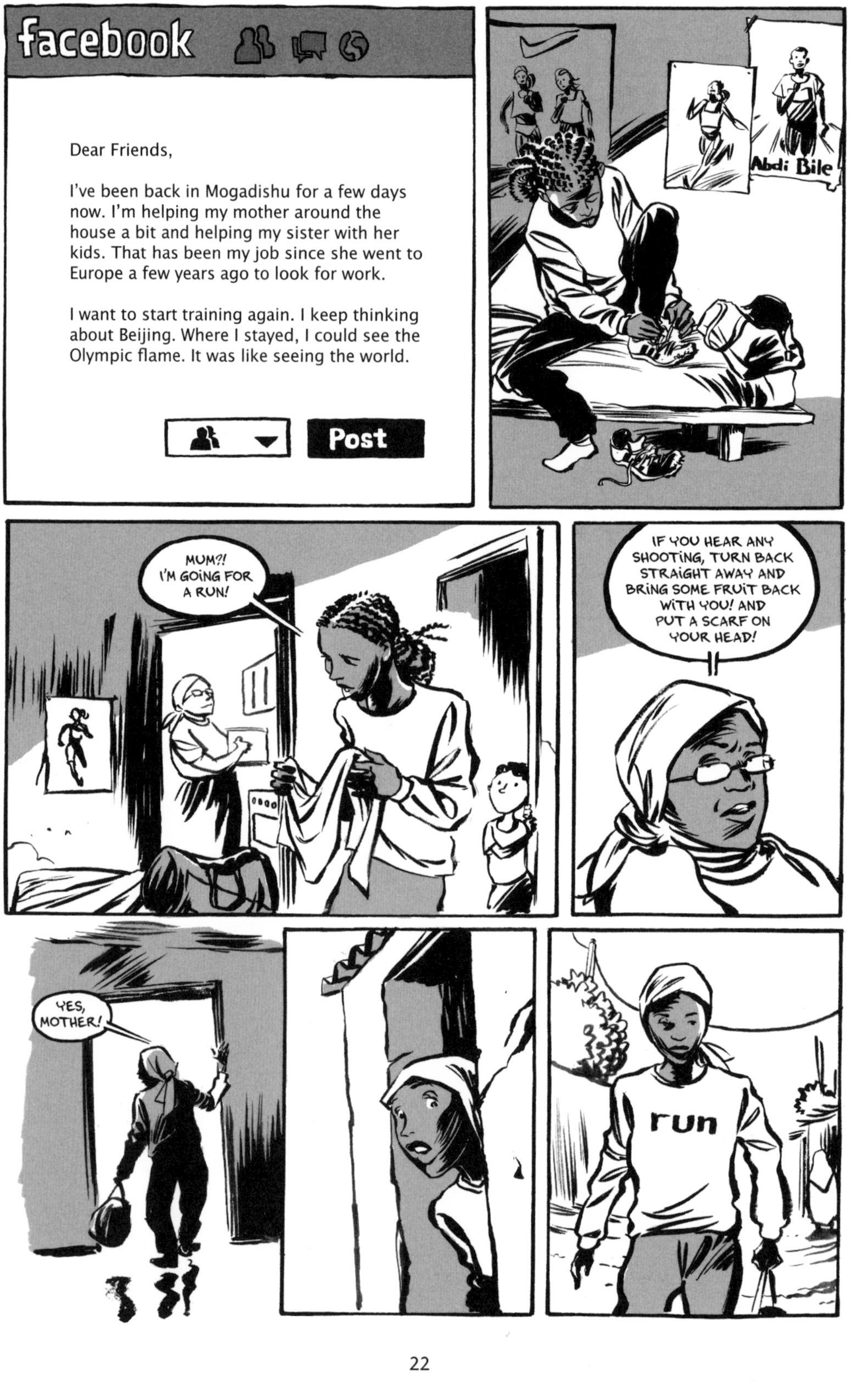
facebook
Dear Friends,
I've been back in Mogadishu for a few days now. I'm helping my mother around the house a bit and helping my sister with her kids. That has been my job since she went to Europe a few years ago to look for work.
I want to start training again. I keep thinking about Beijing. Where I stayed, I could see the Olympic flame. It was like seeing the world.
Post
Abdi Bile
MUM?! I'M GOING FOR A RUN!
IF YOU HEAR ANY SHOOTING, TURN BACK STRAIGHT AWAY AND BRING SOME FRUIT BACK WITH YOU! AND PUT A SCARF ON YOUR HEAD!
YES, MOTHER!
run

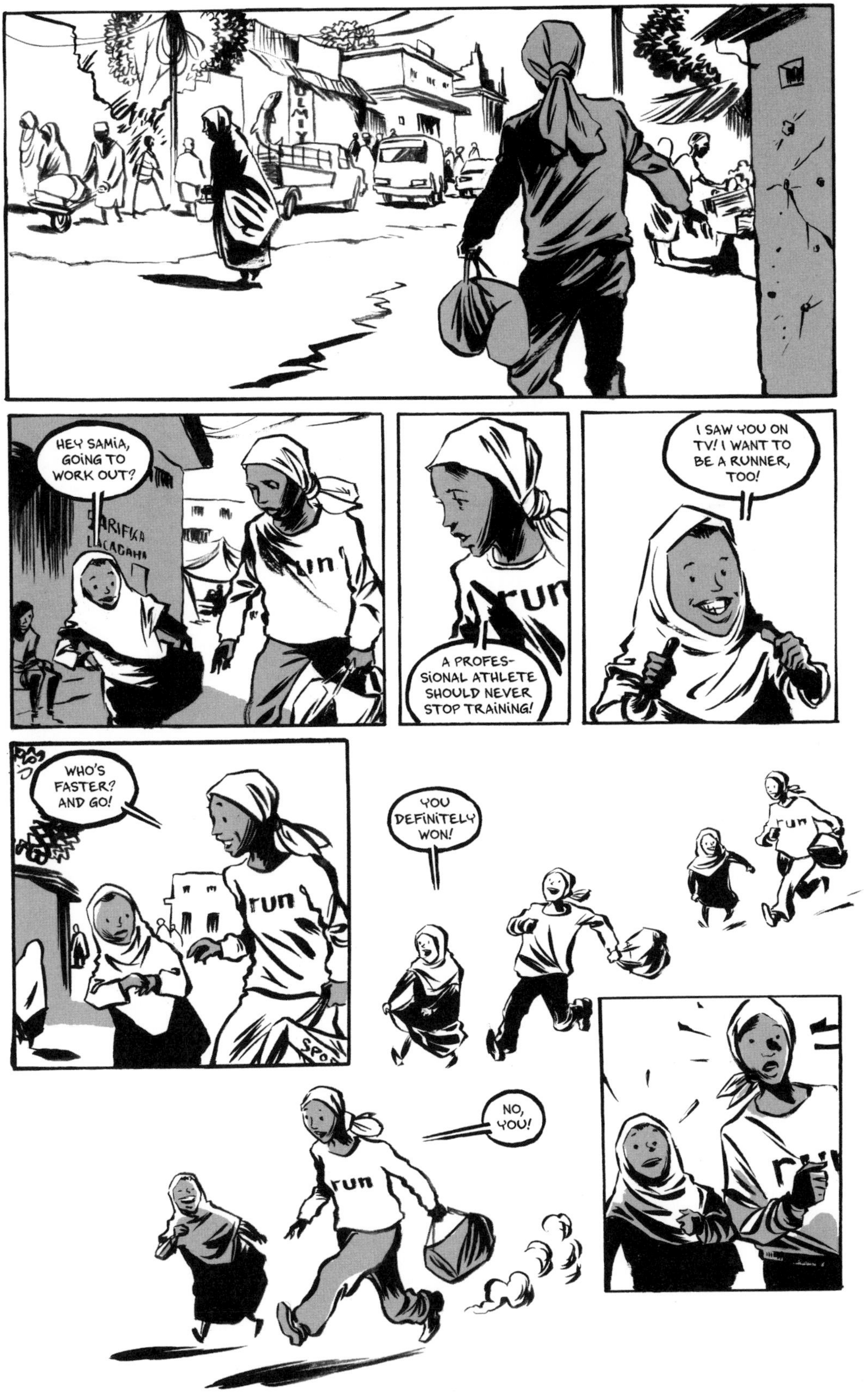
HEY SAMIA, GOING TO WORK OUT?
A PROFESSIONAL ATHLETE SHOULD NEVER STOP TRAINING!
I SAW YOU ON TV! I WANT TO BE A RUNNER, TOO!
WHO'S FASTER? AND GO!
YOU DEFINITELY WON!
NO, YOU!

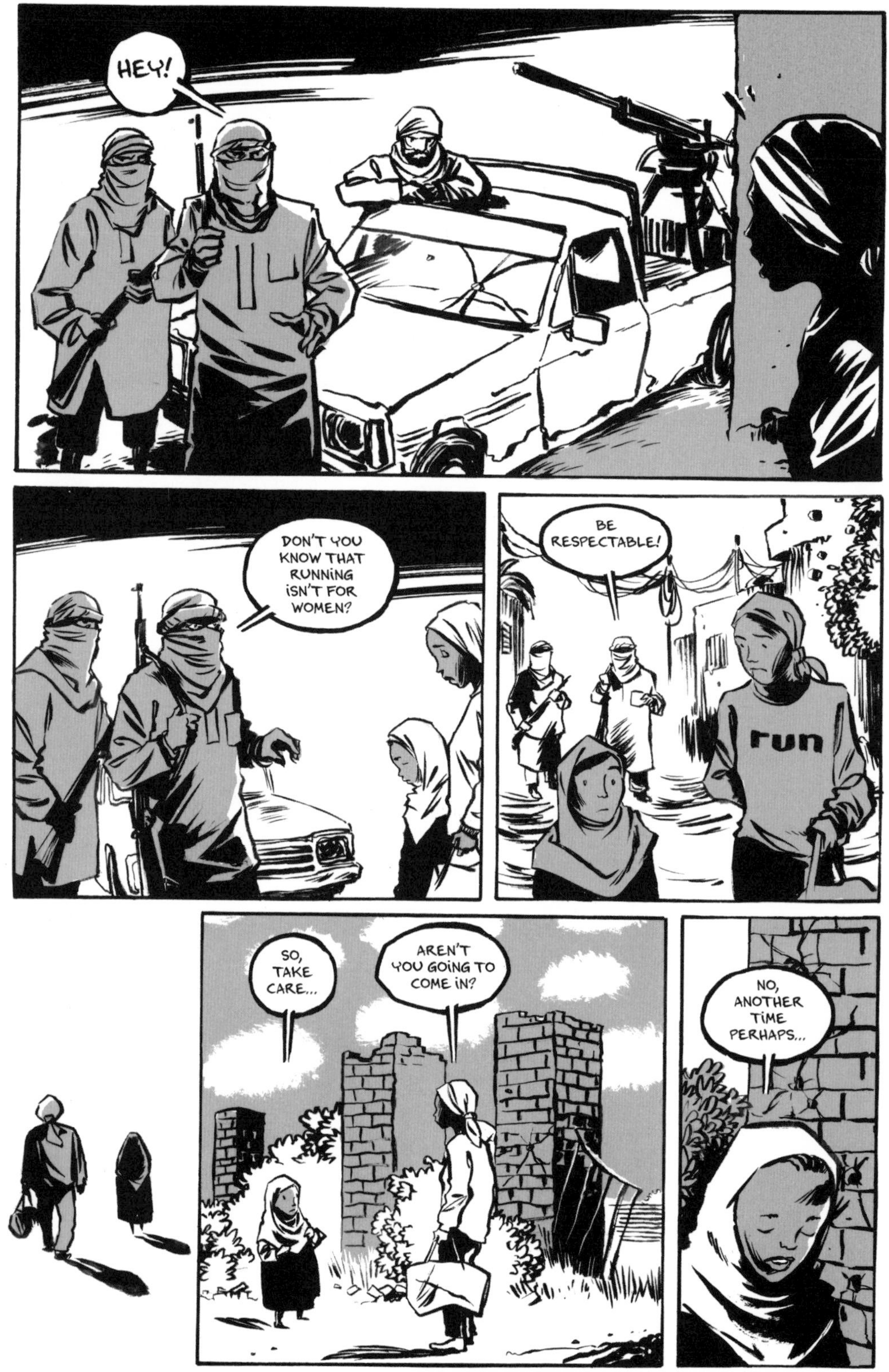
HEY!
DON'T YOU KNOW THAT RUNNING ISN'T FOR WOMEN?
BE RESPECTABLE!
RUN
SO, TAKE CARE...
AREN'T YOU GOING TO COME IN?
NO, ANOTHER TIME PERHAPS...

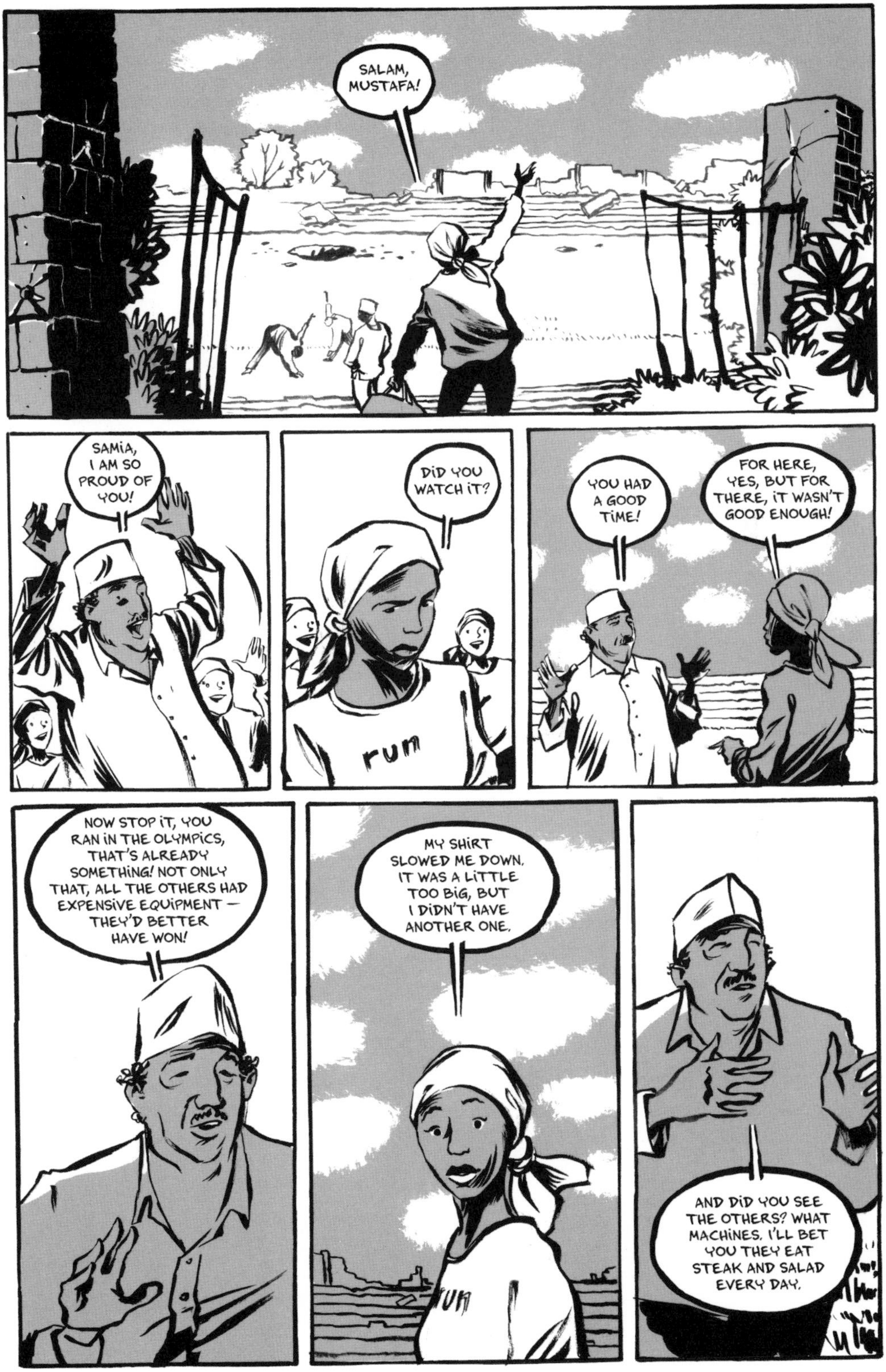
SALAM, MUSTAFA!
SAMIA, I AM SO PROUD OF YOU!
DID YOU WATCH IT?
YOU HAD A GOOD TIME!
FOR HERE, YES, BUT FOR THERE, IT WASN'T GOOD ENOUGH!
NOW STOP IT, YOU RAN IN THE OLYMPICS, THAT'S ALREADY SOMETHING! NOT ONLY THAT, ALL THE OTHERS HAD EXPENSIVE EQUIPMENT — THEY'D BETTER HAVE WON!
MY SHIRT SLOWED ME DOWN. IT WAS A LITTLE TOO BIG, BUT I DIDN'T HAVE ANOTHER ONE.
AND DID YOU SEE THE OTHERS? WHAT MACHINES. I'LL BET YOU THEY EAT STEAK AND SALAD EVERY DAY.
run

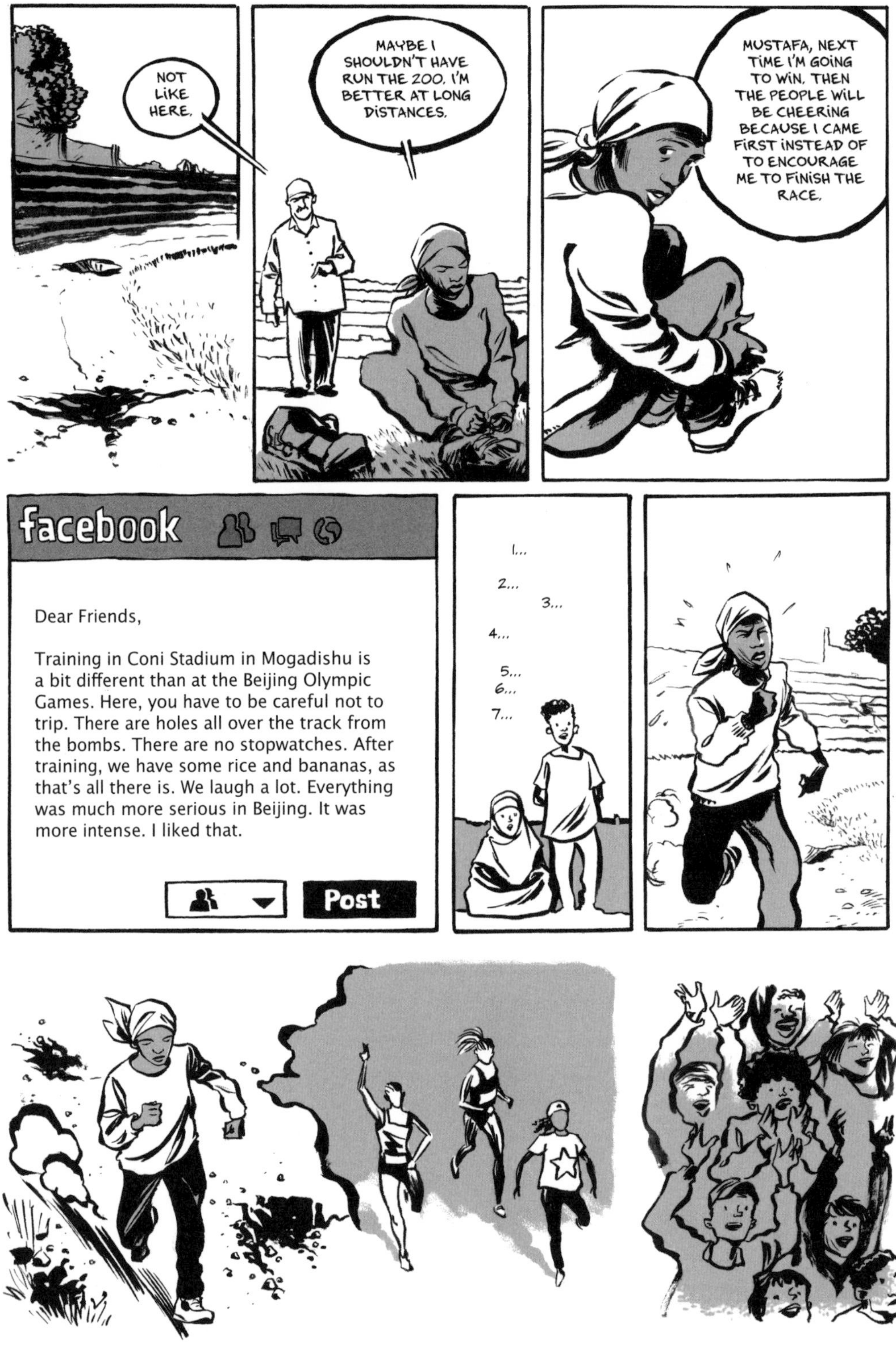
NOT LIKE HERE.
MAYBE I SHOULDN'T HAVE RUN THE 200. I'M BETTER AT LONG DISTANCES.
MUSTAFA, NEXT TIME I'M GOING TO WIN. THEN THE PEOPLE WILL BE CHEERING BECAUSE I CAME FIRST INSTEAD OF TO ENCOURAGE ME TO FINISH THE RACE.
facebook
Dear Friends,
Training in Coni Stadium in Mogadishu is a bit different than at the Beijing Olympic Games. Here, you have to be careful not to trip. There are holes all over the track from the bombs. There are no stopwatches. After training, we have some rice and bananas, as that's all there is. We laugh a lot. Everything was much more serious in Beijing. It was more intense. I liked that.
Post
1...
2...
3...
4...
5...
6...
7...

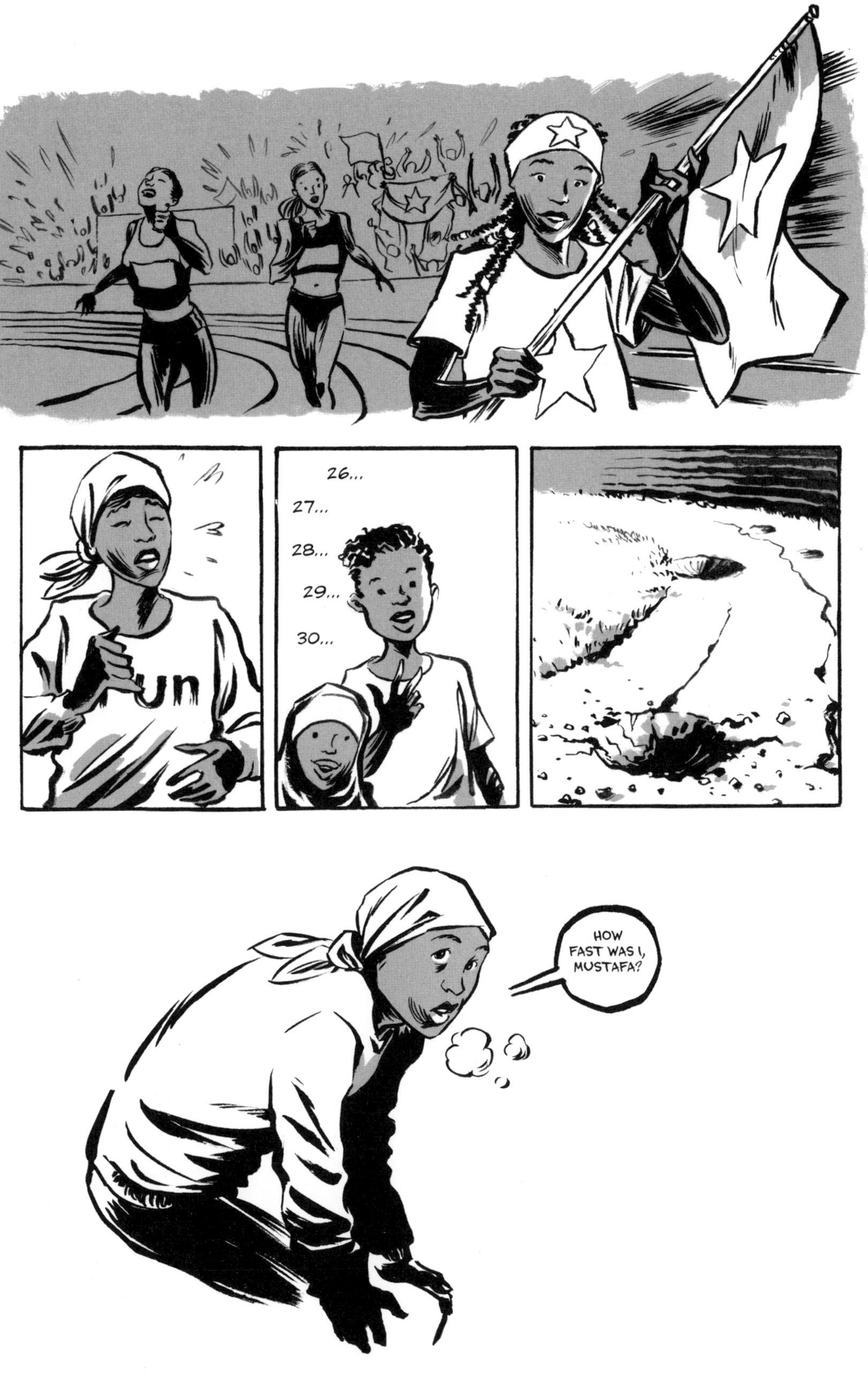
UN
26...
27...
28...
29...
30...
HOW FAST WAS I, MUSTAFA?

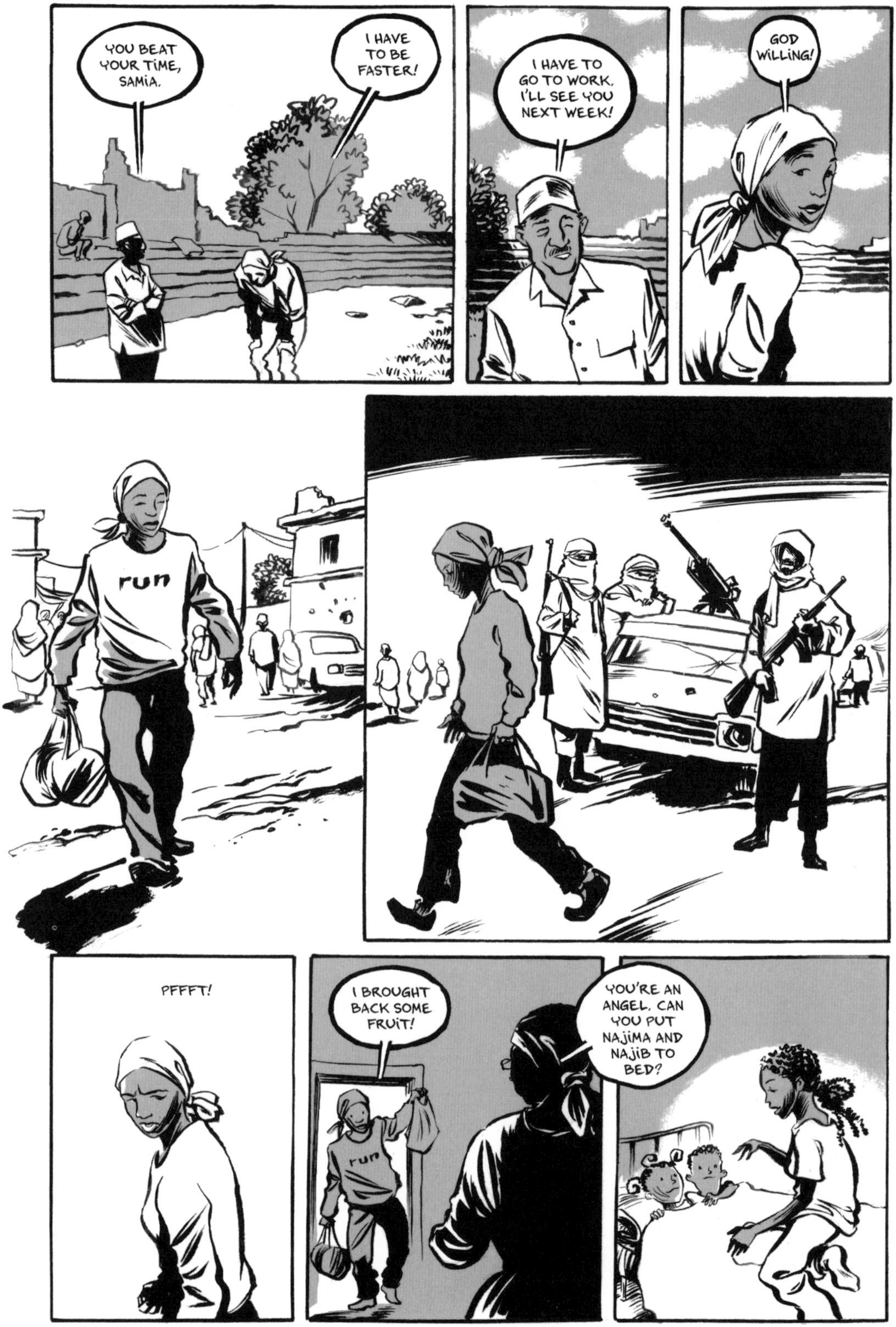
YOU BEAT YOUR TIME, SAMIA.
I HAVE TO BE FASTER!
I HAVE TO GO TO WORK, I'LL SEE YOU NEXT WEEK!
GOD WILLING!
run
PFFFT!
I BROUGHT BACK SOME FRUIT!
run
YOU'RE AN ANGEL. CAN YOU PUT NAJIMA AND NAJIB TO BED?

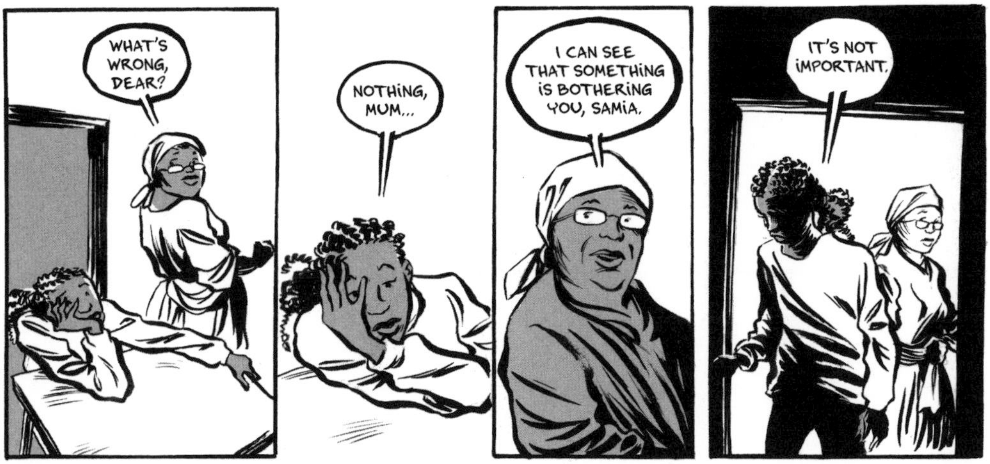
WHAT'S WRONG, DEAR?
NOTHING, MUM...
I CAN SEE THAT SOMETHING IS BOTHERING YOU, SAMIA.
IT'S NOT IMPORTANT.

facebook

Dear Friends,

I'm really motivated. I've bettered my 200 time.

After I train, I try to hide my sports stuff in my bag as well as I can. When I see Al-Shabaab, I try to avoid them. They are patrolling the streets and I have had a few run-ins with them because they don't think that running is for women.

Sometimes, when I leave the house, I wonder if I'm going to come home in one piece. But I have to run. I don't know how to do anything else.

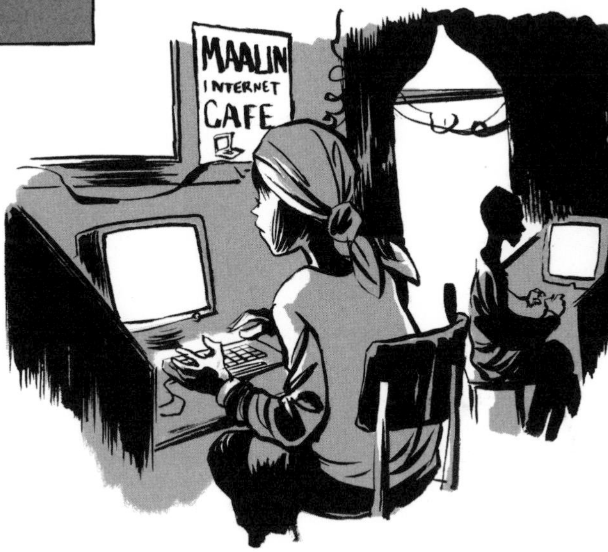
MAALIN
INTERNET
CAFE

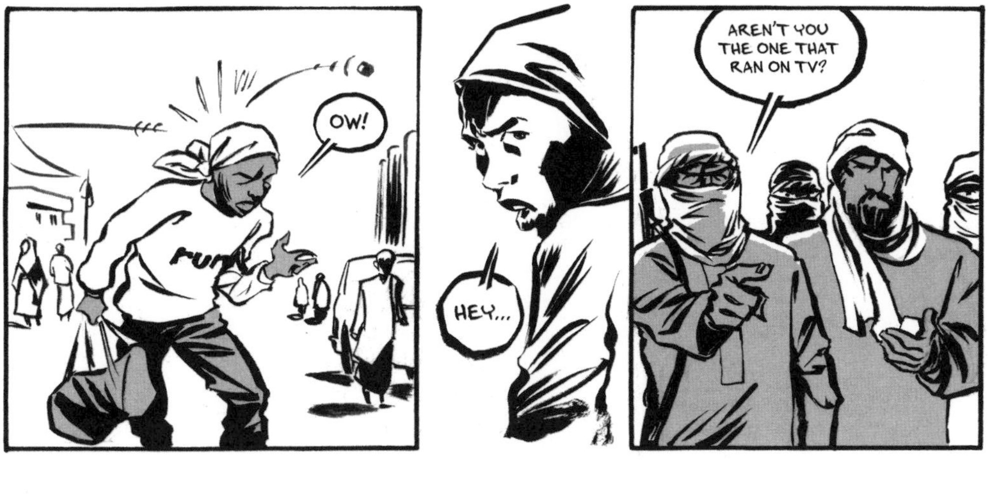
OW!
HEY...
AREN'T YOU THE ONE THAT RAN ON TV?

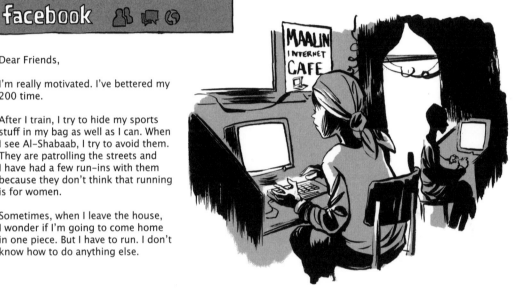

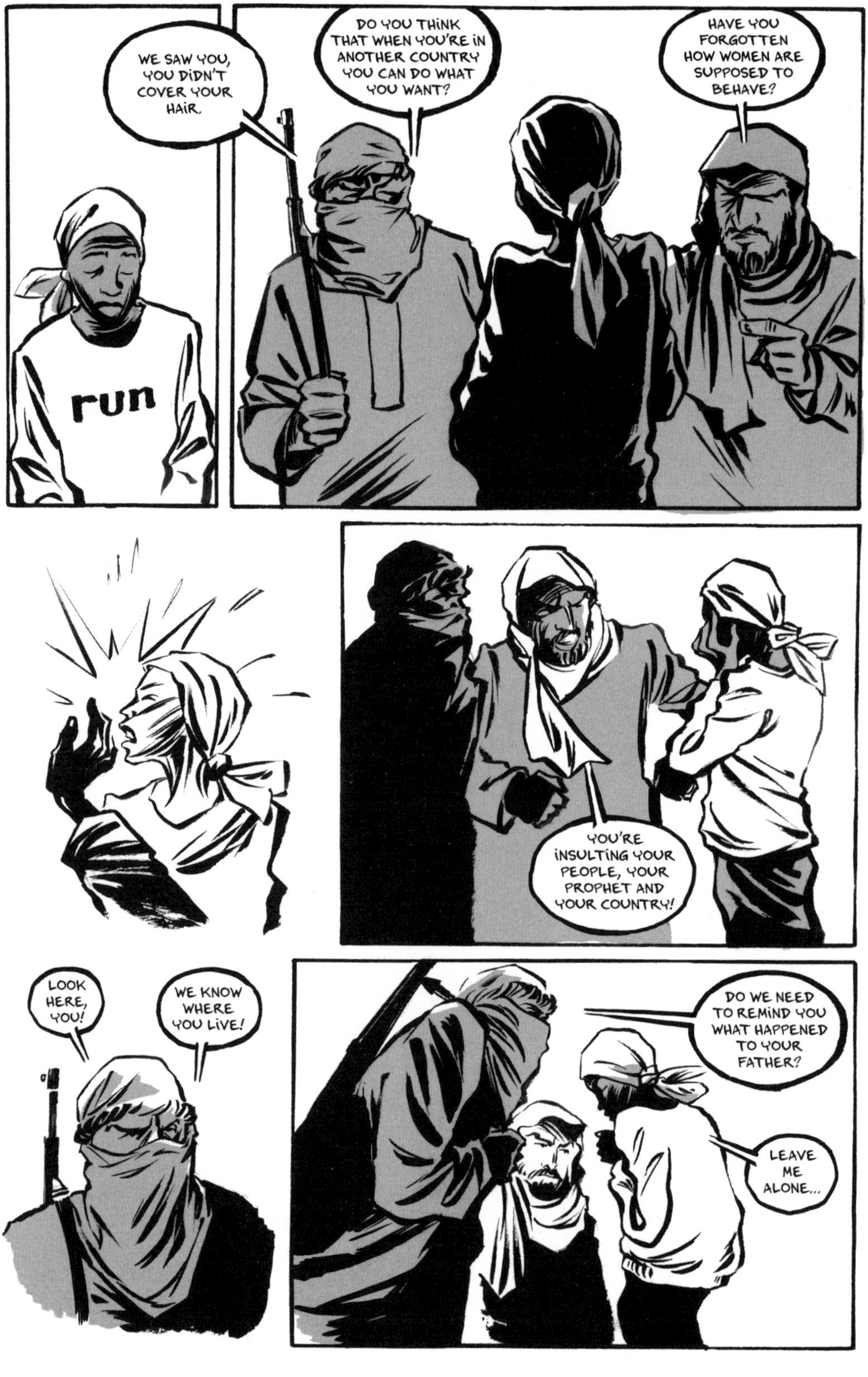

run
WE SAW YOU, YOU DIDN'T COVER YOUR HAIR.
DO YOU THINK THAT WHEN YOU'RE IN ANOTHER COUNTRY YOU CAN DO WHAT YOU WANT?
HAVE YOU FORGOTTEN HOW WOMEN ARE SUPPOSED TO BEHAVE?
YOU'RE INSULTING YOUR PEOPLE, YOUR PROPHET AND YOUR COUNTRY!
LOOK HERE, YOU!
WE KNOW WHERE YOU LIVE!
DO WE NEED TO REMIND YOU WHAT HAPPENED TO YOUR FATHER?
LEAVE ME ALONE...

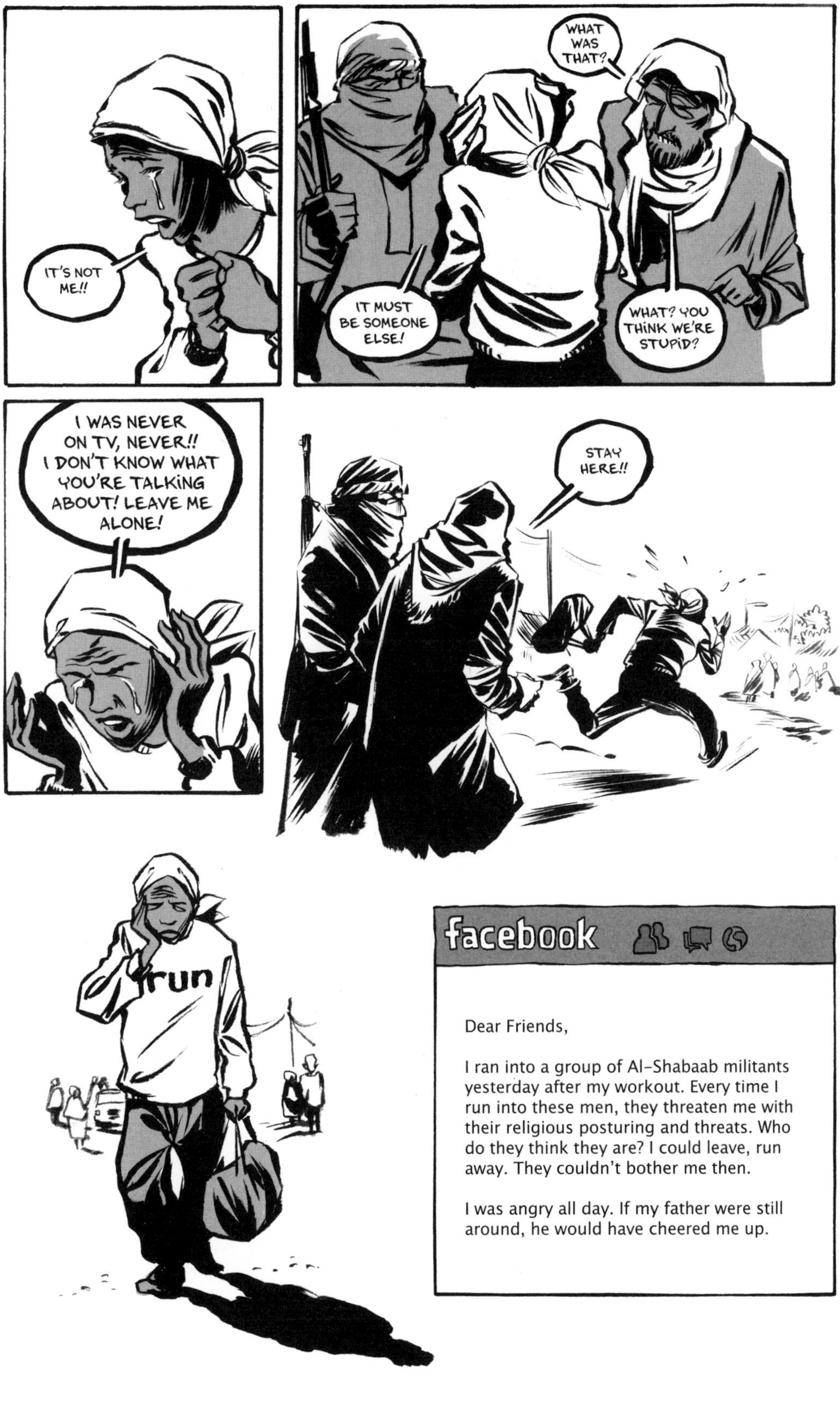

IT'S NOT ME!!
WHAT WAS THAT?
IT MUST BE SOMEONE ELSE!
WHAT? YOU THINK WE'RE STUPID?
I WAS NEVER ON TV, NEVER!! I DON'T KNOW WHAT YOU'RE TALKING ABOUT! LEAVE ME ALONE!
STAY HERE!!
run
facebook
Dear Friends,
I ran into a group of Al-Shabaab militants yesterday after my workout. Every time I run into these men, they threaten me with their religious posturing and threats. Who do they think they are? I could leave, run away. They couldn't bother me then.
I was angry all day. If my father were still around, he would have cheered me up.

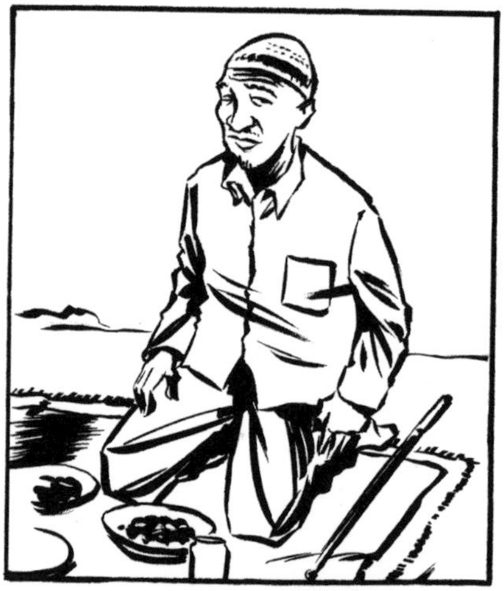

One time I forgot to make dinner for Najima while my mother was at the market getting some fresh vegetables. When she got home, she was furious...

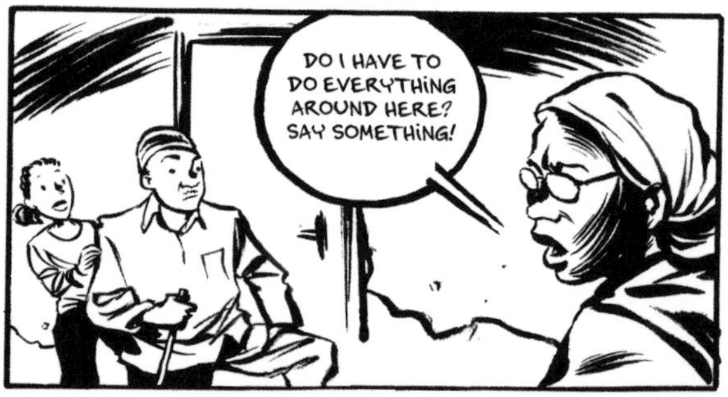
DO I HAVE TO DO EVERYTHING AROUND HERE? SAY SOMETHING!

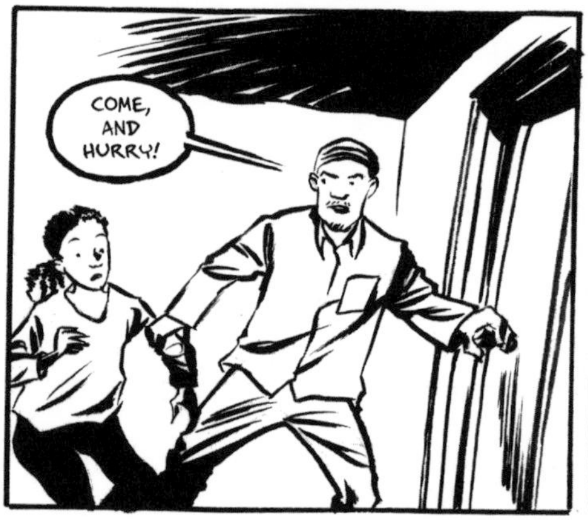
COME, AND HURRY!

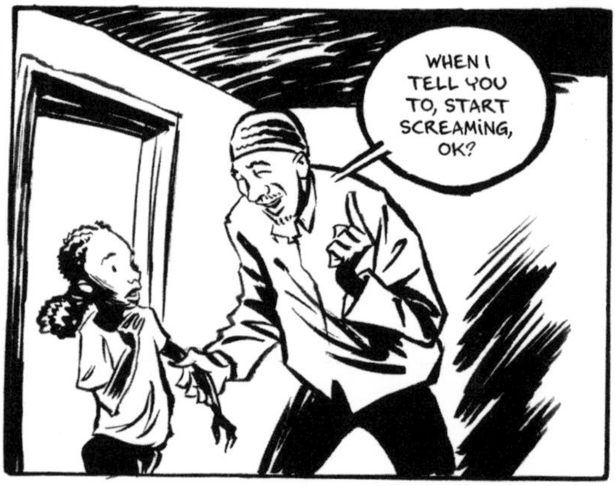
WHEN I TELL YOU TO, START SCREAMING, OK?

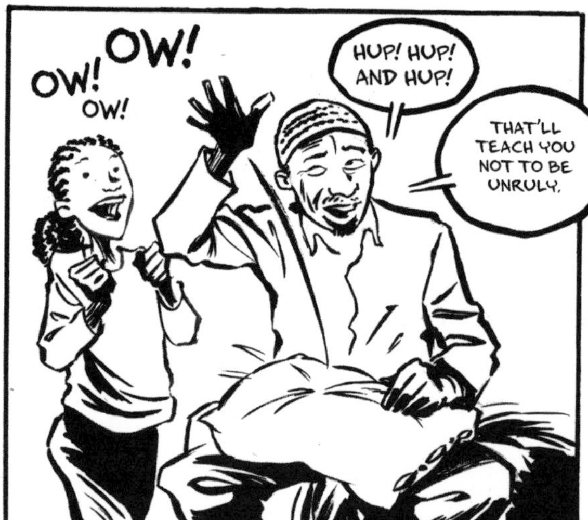
OW! OW!
OW!
HUP! HUP! AND HUP!
THAT'LL TEACH YOU NOT TO BE UNRULY.

facebook

I miss my father all the time. And I can't help remembering that awful day when he went to the market for the last time.

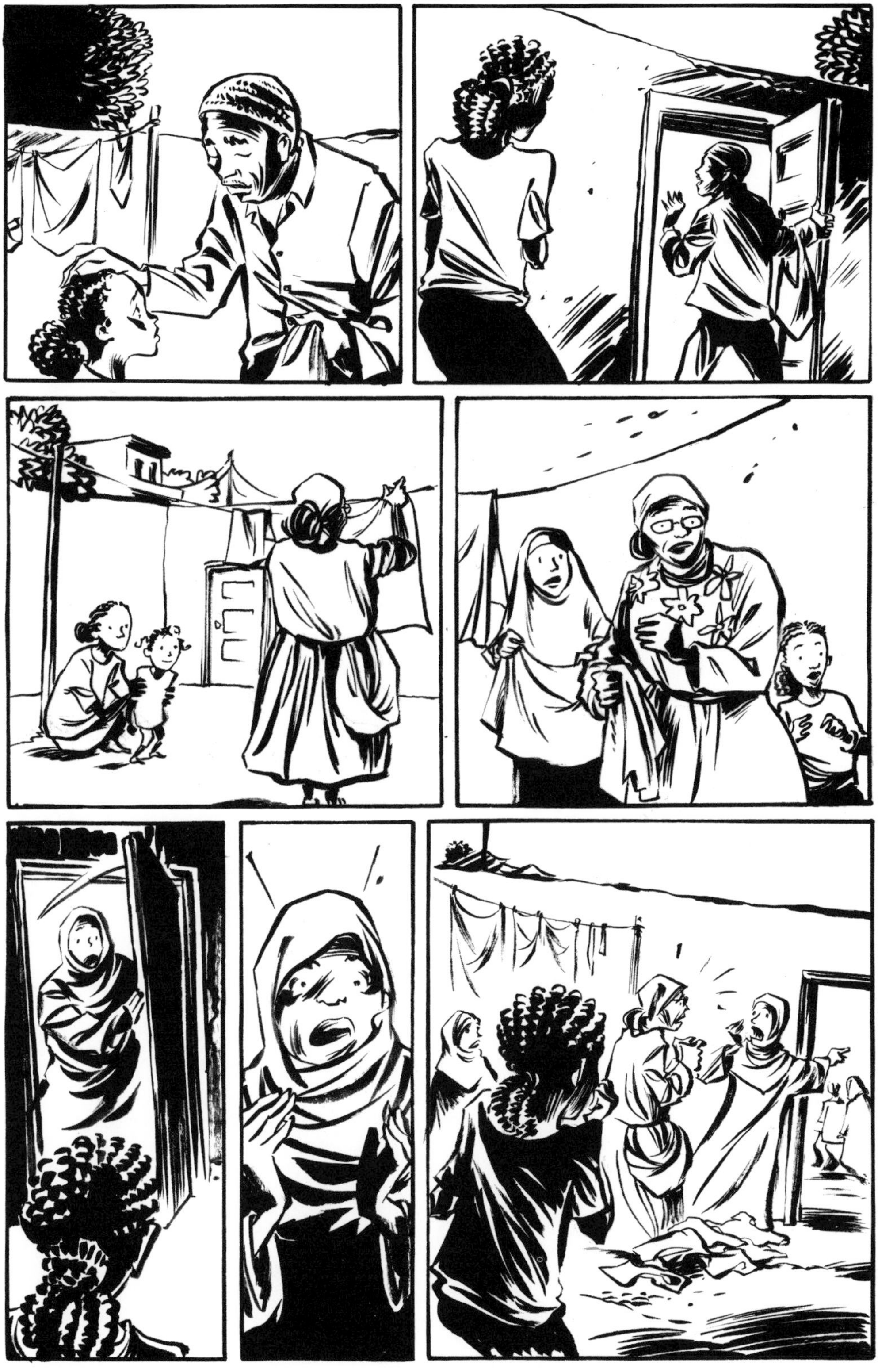
!
!

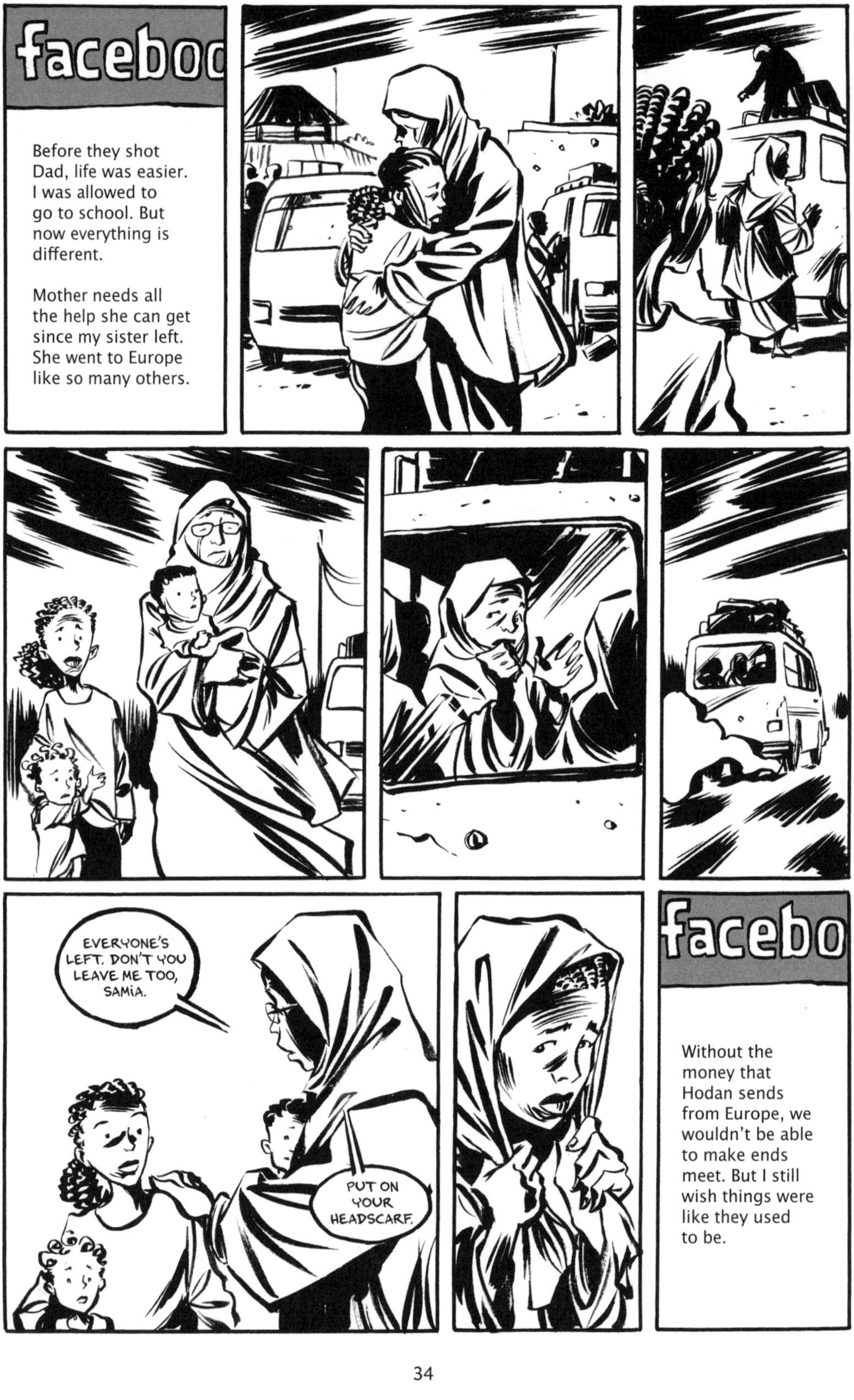
faceboo
Before they shot Dad, life was easier. I was allowed to go to school. But now everything is different.
Mother needs all the help she can get since my sister left. She went to Europe like so many others.
EVERYONE'S LEFT. DON'T YOU LEAVE ME TOO, SAMIA.
PUT ON YOUR HEADSCARF.
facebo
Without the money that Hodan sends from Europe, we wouldn't be able to make ends meet. But I still wish things were like they used to be.

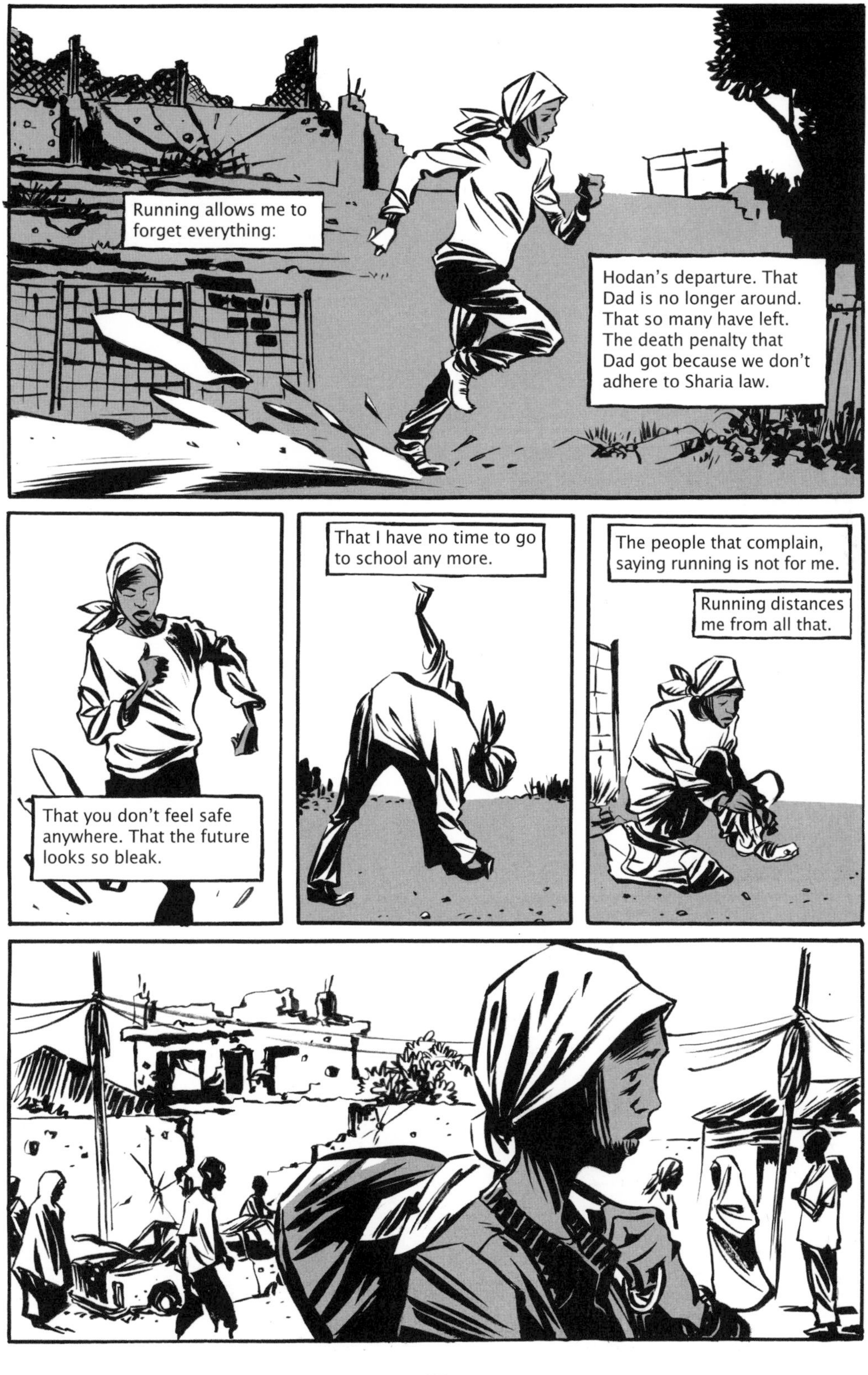

Running allows me to forget everything:
Hodan's departure. That Dad is no longer around. That so many have left. The death penalty that Dad got because we don't adhere to Sharia law.
That you don't feel safe anywhere. That the future looks so bleak.
That I have no time to go to school any more.
The people that complain, saying running is not for me.
Running distances me from all that.

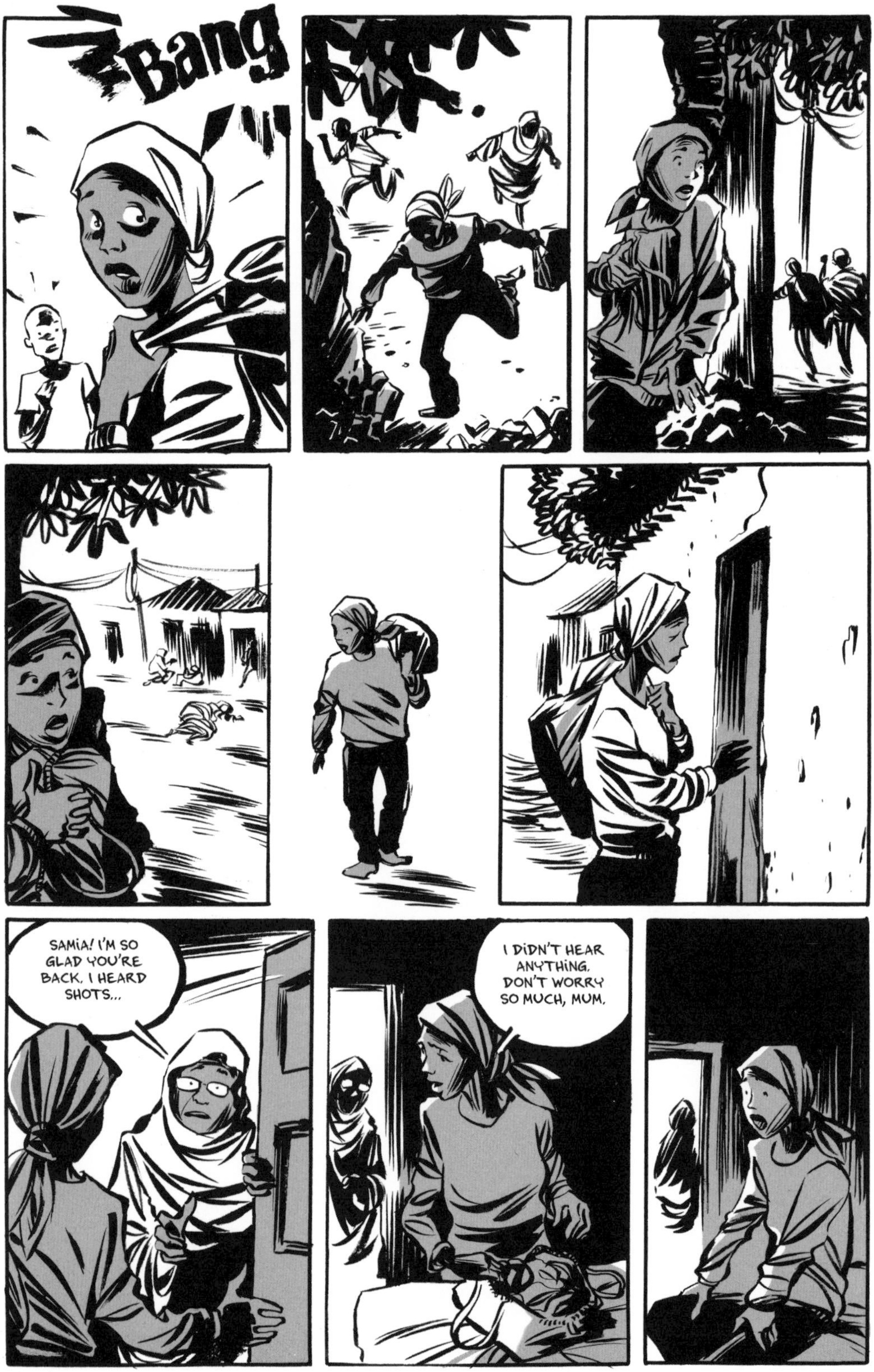
Bang
SAMIA! I'M SO GLAD YOU'RE BACK. I HEARD SHOTS...
I DIDN'T HEAR ANYTHING. DON'T WORRY SO MUCH, MUM.

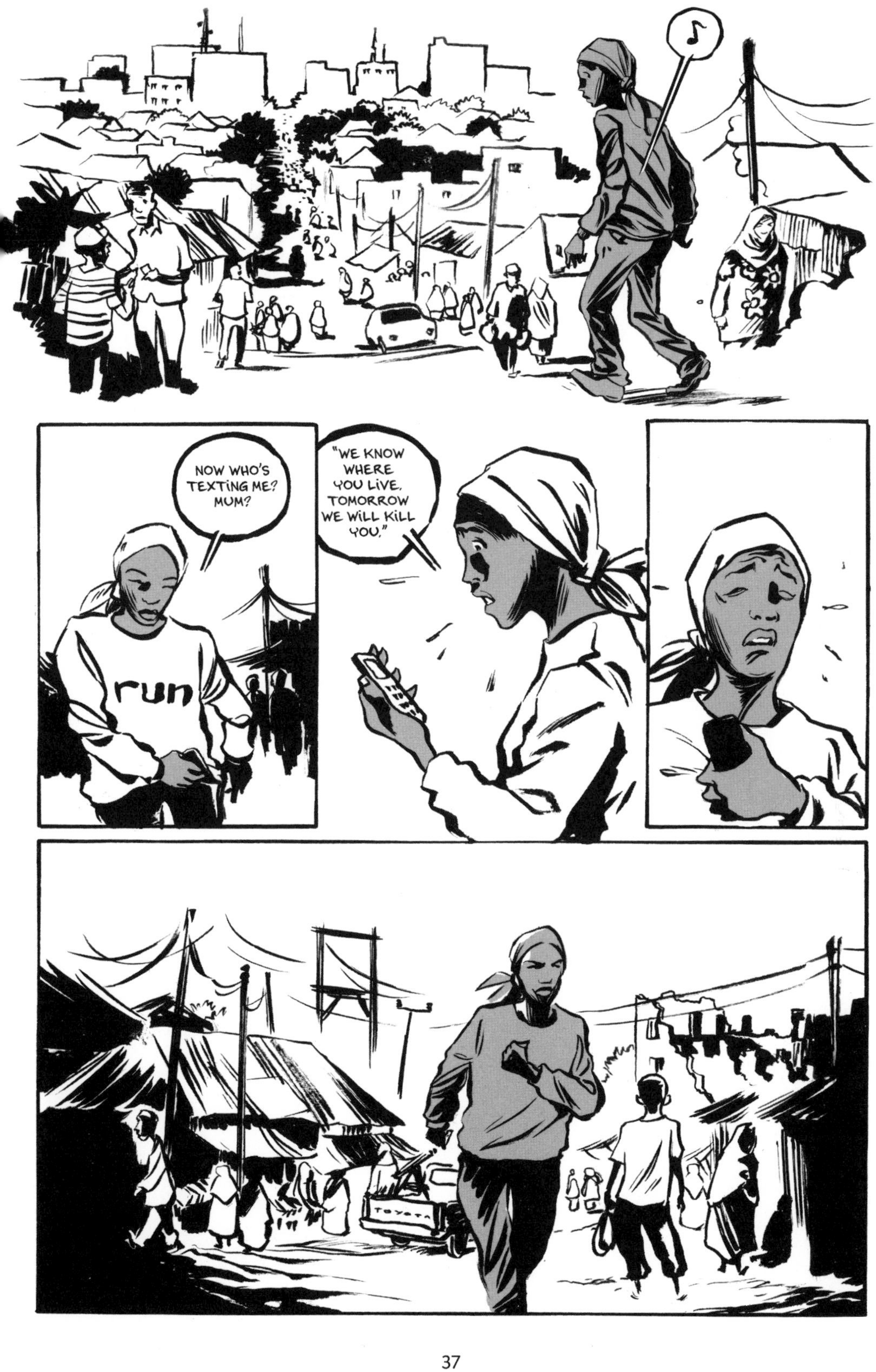
♪
NOW WHO'S TEXTING ME? MUM?
"WE KNOW WHERE YOU LIVE. TOMORROW WE WILL KILL YOU."
run
TOYOTA

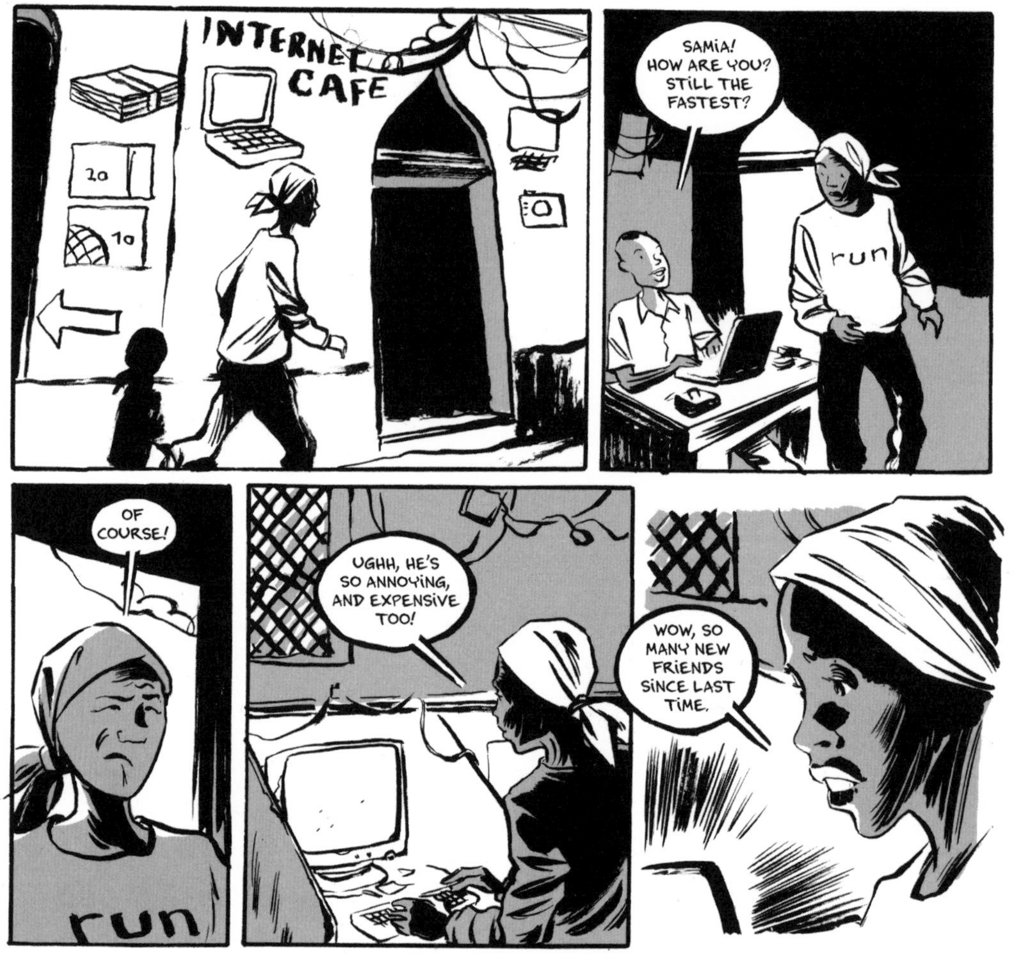
INTERNET CAFE
20
10
SAMIA! HOW ARE YOU? STILL THE FASTEST?
run
OF COURSE!
run
UGHH, HE'S SO ANNOYING, AND EXPENSIVE TOO!
WOW, SO MANY NEW FRIENDS SINCE LAST TIME.

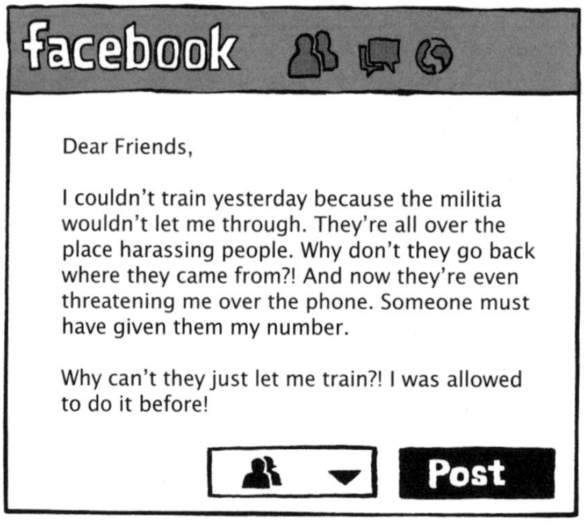
facebook
Dear Friends,
I couldn't train yesterday because the militia wouldn't let me through. They're all over the place harassing people. Why don't they go back where they came from?! And now they're even threatening me over the phone. Someone must have given them my number.
Why can't they just let me train?! I was allowed to do it before!
Post

facebook

My mother told me that Mogadishu was great when she was young and played basketball. That was when the stadium we train in was built. There were international competitions in all kinds of sports, even women's athletics.

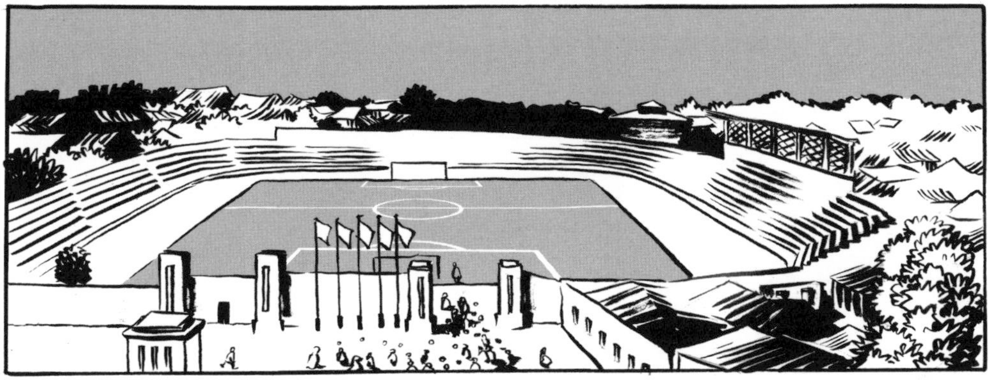

Then there was the revolution and civil war broke out. Since then, we haven't had a government. It's every man for himself. The streets are patrolled by the Al-Shabaab. They recently shot some people in the stadium for not adhering to their unjust rules.

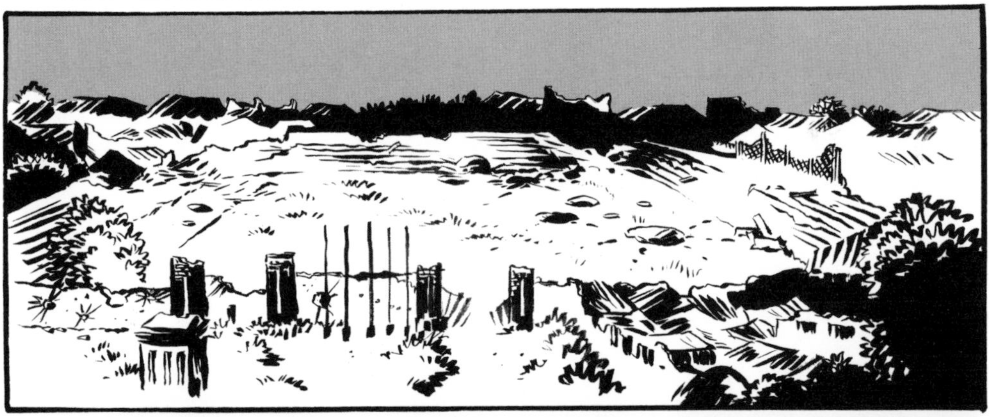

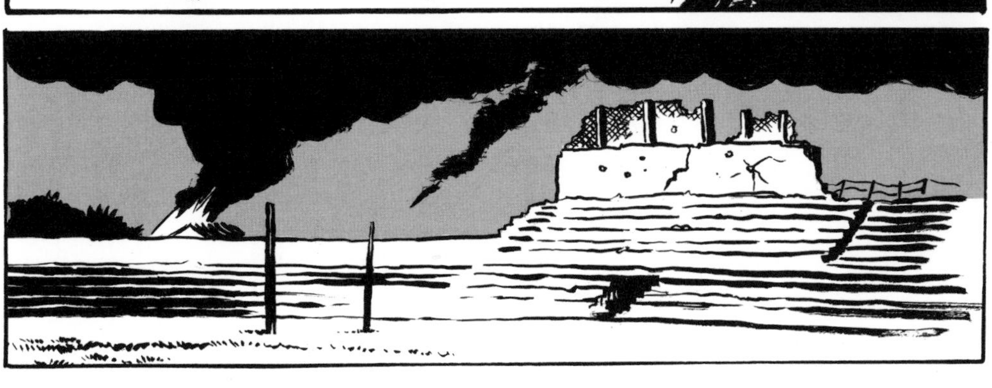

Two years ago, it got really bad and my mother had us leave the city and hide someplace outside of it.

But I came back. What was I going to do out there? I have to train.

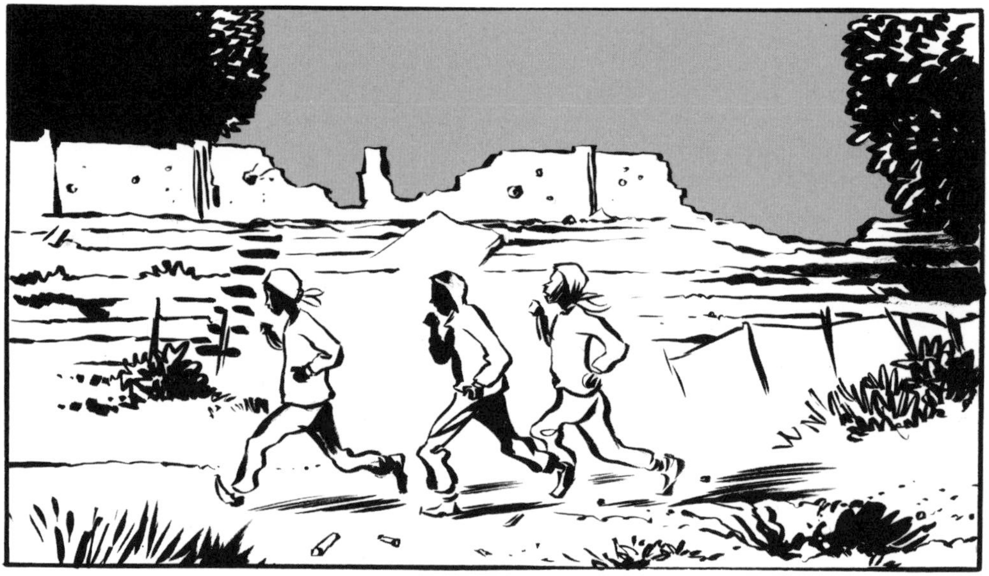

Now there's no money to fix the stadium.

Maybe one day it'll be like it was and we'll be able to train like they do in other countries.

I've been training in the stadium as often as I can anyway. When I managed to shave a second off my time, I was really happy.

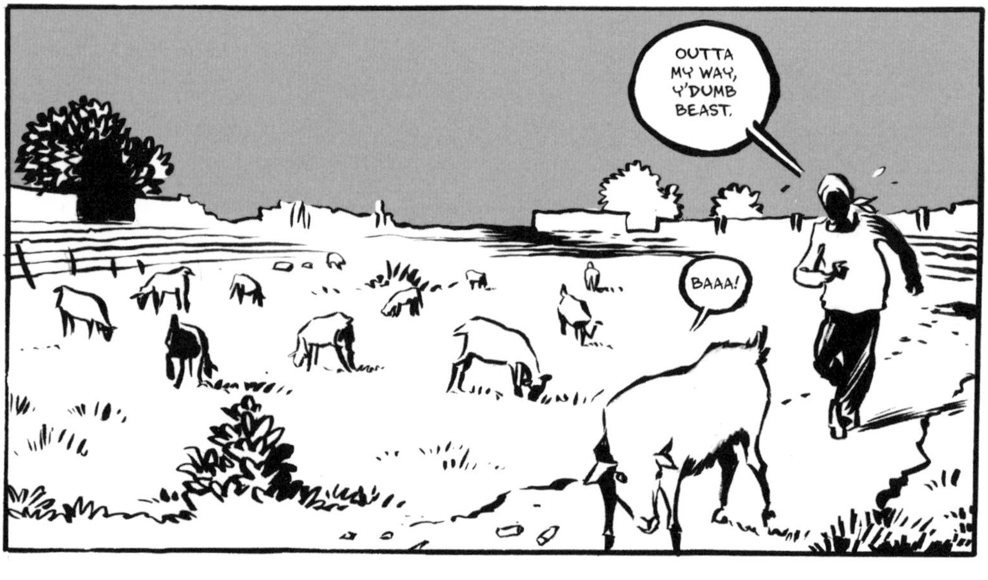
OUTTA MY WAY, Y'DUMB BEAST.
BAAA!

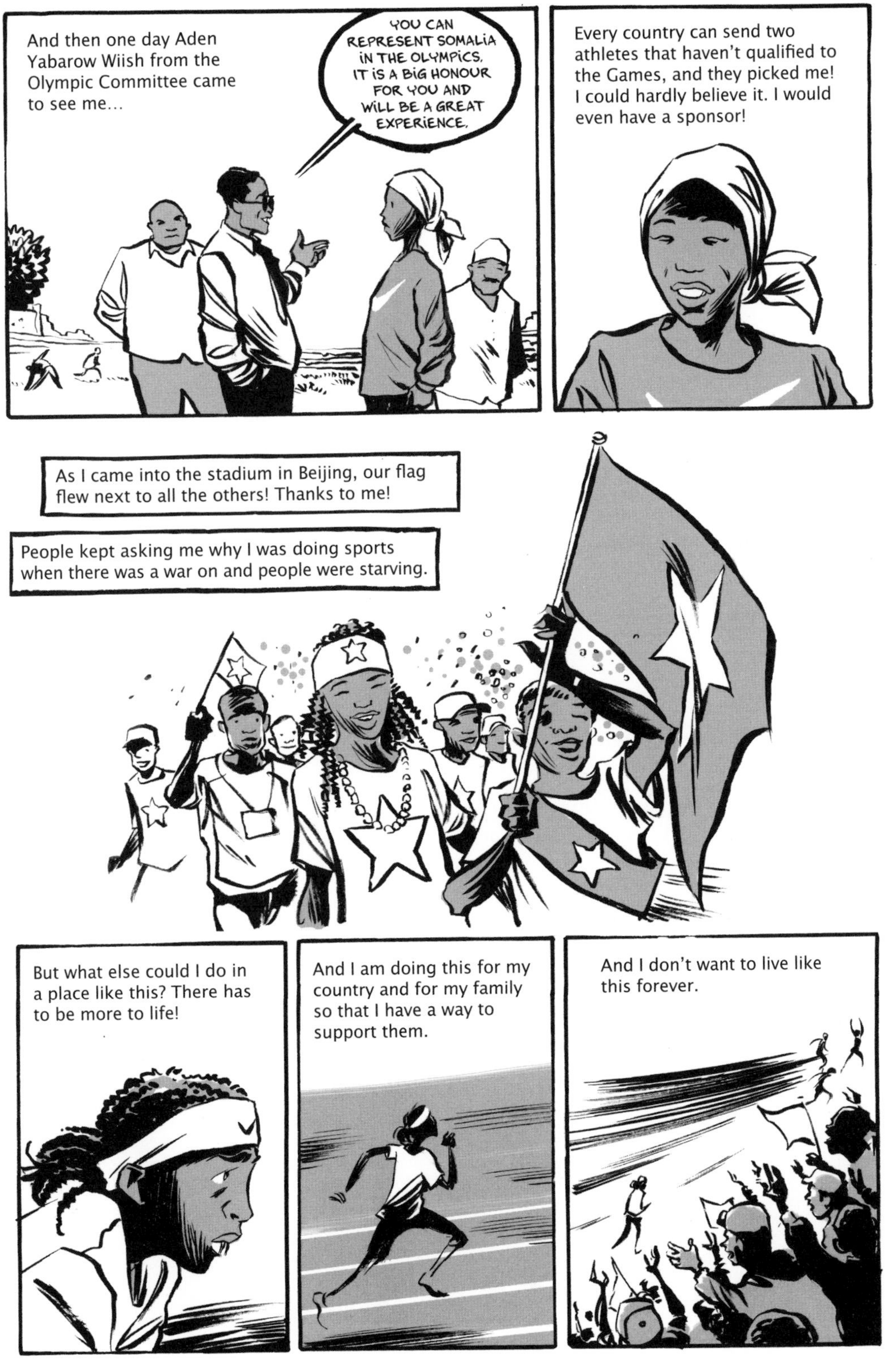

And then one day Aden Yabarow Wiish from the Olympic Committee came to see me...
YOU CAN REPRESENT SOMALIA IN THE OLYMPICS. IT IS A BIG HONOUR FOR YOU AND WILL BE A GREAT EXPERIENCE.
Every country can send two athletes that haven't qualified to the Games, and they picked me! I could hardly believe it. I would even have a sponsor!
As I came into the stadium in Beijing, our flag flew next to all the others! Thanks to me!
People kept asking me why I was doing sports when there was a war on and people were starving.
But what else could I do in a place like this? There has to be more to life!
And I am doing this for my country and for my family so that I have a way to support them.
And I don't want to live like this forever.

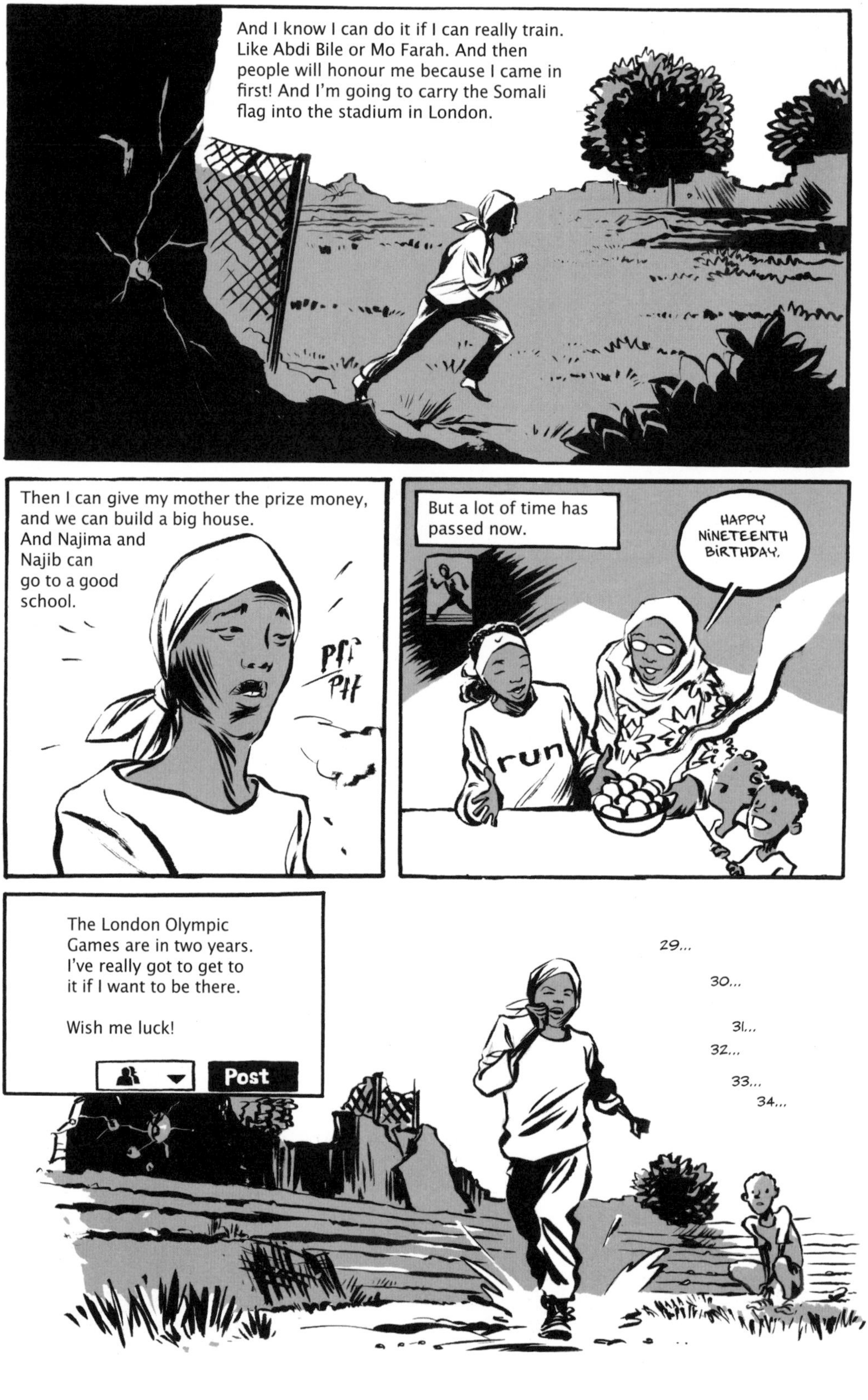

And I know I can do it if I can really train. Like Abdi Bile or Mo Farah. And then people will honour me because I came in first! And I'm going to carry the Somali flag into the stadium in London.
Then I can give my mother the prize money, and we can build a big house. And Najima and Najib can go to a good school.
Pff Pff
But a lot of time has passed now.
HAPPY NINETEENTH BIRTHDAY.
run
The London Olympic Games are in two years. I've really got to get to it if I want to be there.
Wish me luck!
Post
29...
30...
31...
32...
33...
34...

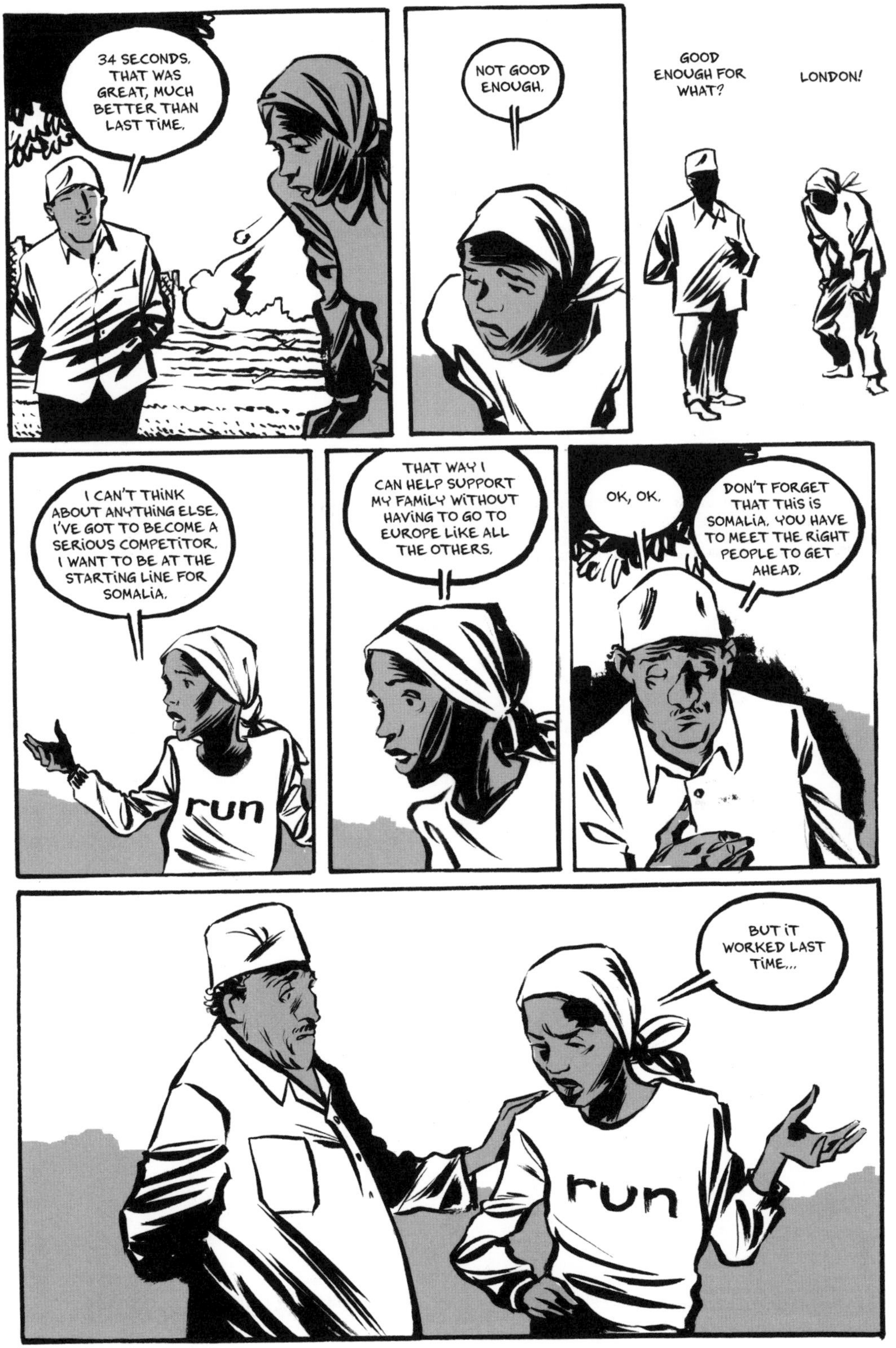
34 SECONDS, THAT WAS GREAT, MUCH BETTER THAN LAST TIME.
NOT GOOD ENOUGH.
GOOD ENOUGH FOR WHAT?
LONDON!
I CAN'T THINK ABOUT ANYTHING ELSE. I'VE GOT TO BECOME A SERIOUS COMPETITOR. I WANT TO BE AT THE STARTING LINE FOR SOMALIA.
THAT WAY I CAN HELP SUPPORT MY FAMILY WITHOUT HAVING TO GO TO EUROPE LIKE ALL THE OTHERS.
OK, OK.
DON'T FORGET THAT THIS IS SOMALIA. YOU HAVE TO MEET THE RIGHT PEOPLE TO GET AHEAD.
run
BUT IT WORKED LAST TIME...
run

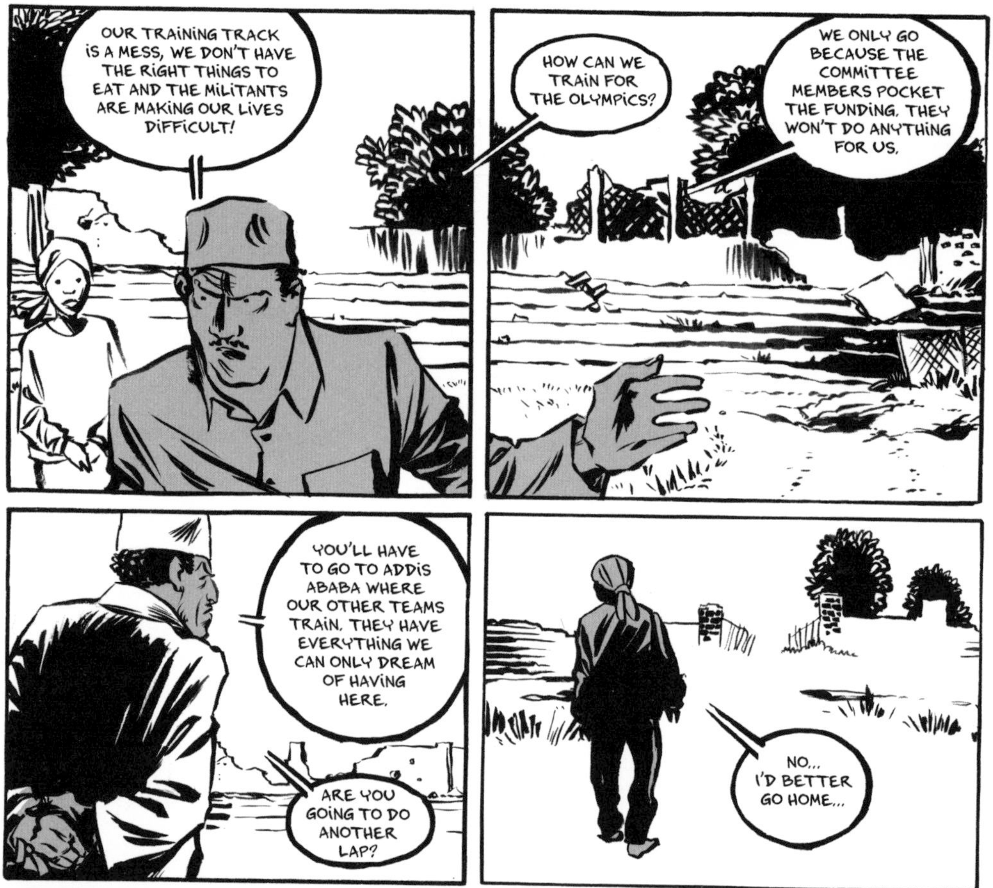
OUR TRAINING TRACK IS A MESS, WE DON'T HAVE THE RIGHT THINGS TO EAT AND THE MILITANTS ARE MAKING OUR LIVES DIFFICULT!
HOW CAN WE TRAIN FOR THE OLYMPICS?
WE ONLY GO BECAUSE THE COMMITTEE MEMBERS POCKET THE FUNDING. THEY WON'T DO ANYTHING FOR US.
YOU'LL HAVE TO GO TO ADDIS ABABA WHERE OUR OTHER TEAMS TRAIN. THEY HAVE EVERYTHING WE CAN ONLY DREAM OF HAVING HERE.
ARE YOU GOING TO DO ANOTHER LAP?
NO... I'D BETTER GO HOME...

facebook

Dear Friends,

Do you know what it's like to realise that your dreams can't ever come true? I have come to the realisation that I can't possibly train properly here in Mogadishu. It's driving me up the wall!

If I could only train with the team in Addis, then I could get a chance to go to Europe, where I could really train and then stand at the starting line for Somalia in London in 2012.

Then I would be a great athlete and could get expensive running gear, especially good running shoes like all the others have.

And I could do all those things we see people do on TV or online: visit other countries, go to the movies or a concert.

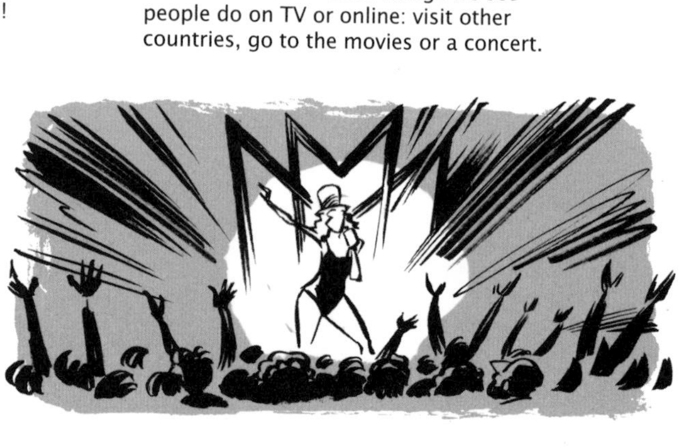

Madonna, for example. I've always wanted to see one of hers. She'll probably never come to Mogadishu!

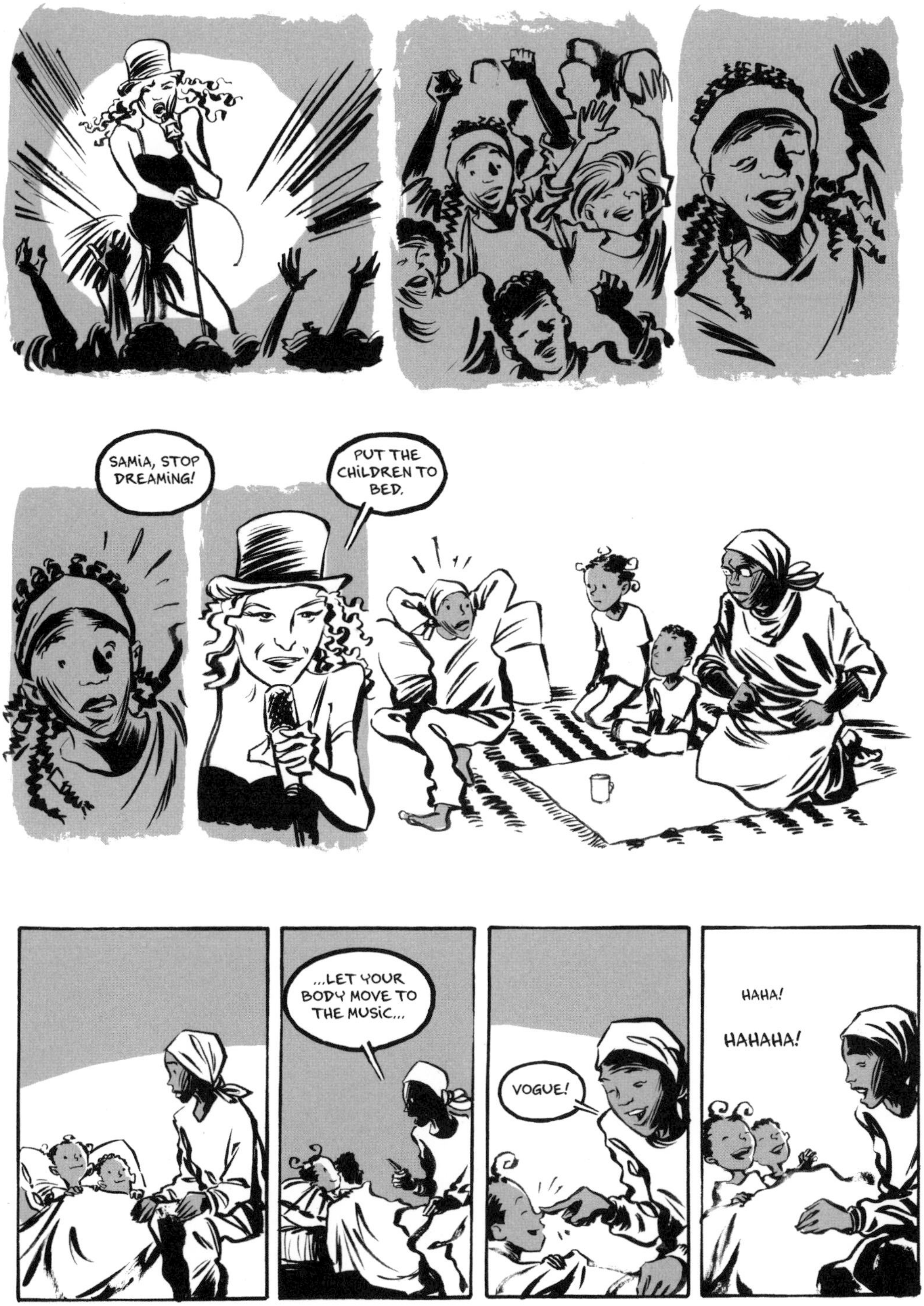
SAMIA, STOP DREAMING!
PUT THE CHILDREN TO BED.
...LET YOUR BODY MOVE TO THE MUSIC...
VOGUE!
HAHA!
HAHAHA!

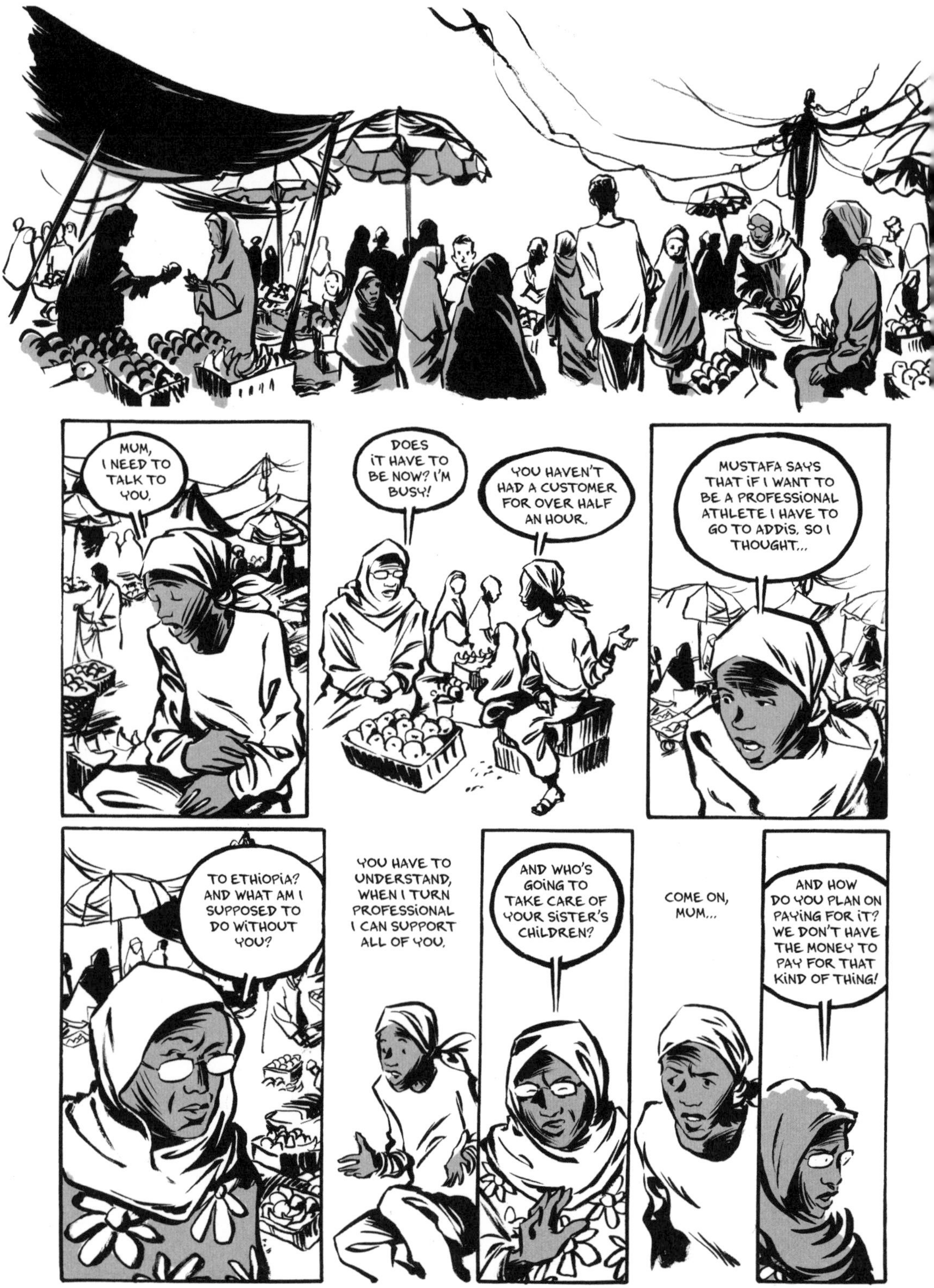
MUM, I NEED TO TALK TO YOU.
DOES IT HAVE TO BE NOW? I'M BUSY!
YOU HAVEN'T HAD A CUSTOMER FOR OVER HALF AN HOUR.
MUSTAFA SAYS THAT IF I WANT TO BE A PROFESSIONAL ATHLETE I HAVE TO GO TO ADDIS. SO I THOUGHT...
TO ETHIOPIA? AND WHAT AM I SUPPOSED TO DO WITHOUT YOU?
YOU HAVE TO UNDERSTAND, WHEN I TURN PROFESSIONAL I CAN SUPPORT ALL OF YOU.
AND WHO'S GOING TO TAKE CARE OF YOUR SISTER'S CHILDREN?
COME ON, MUM...
AND HOW DO YOU PLAN ON PAYING FOR IT? WE DON'T HAVE THE MONEY TO PAY FOR THAT KIND OF THING!

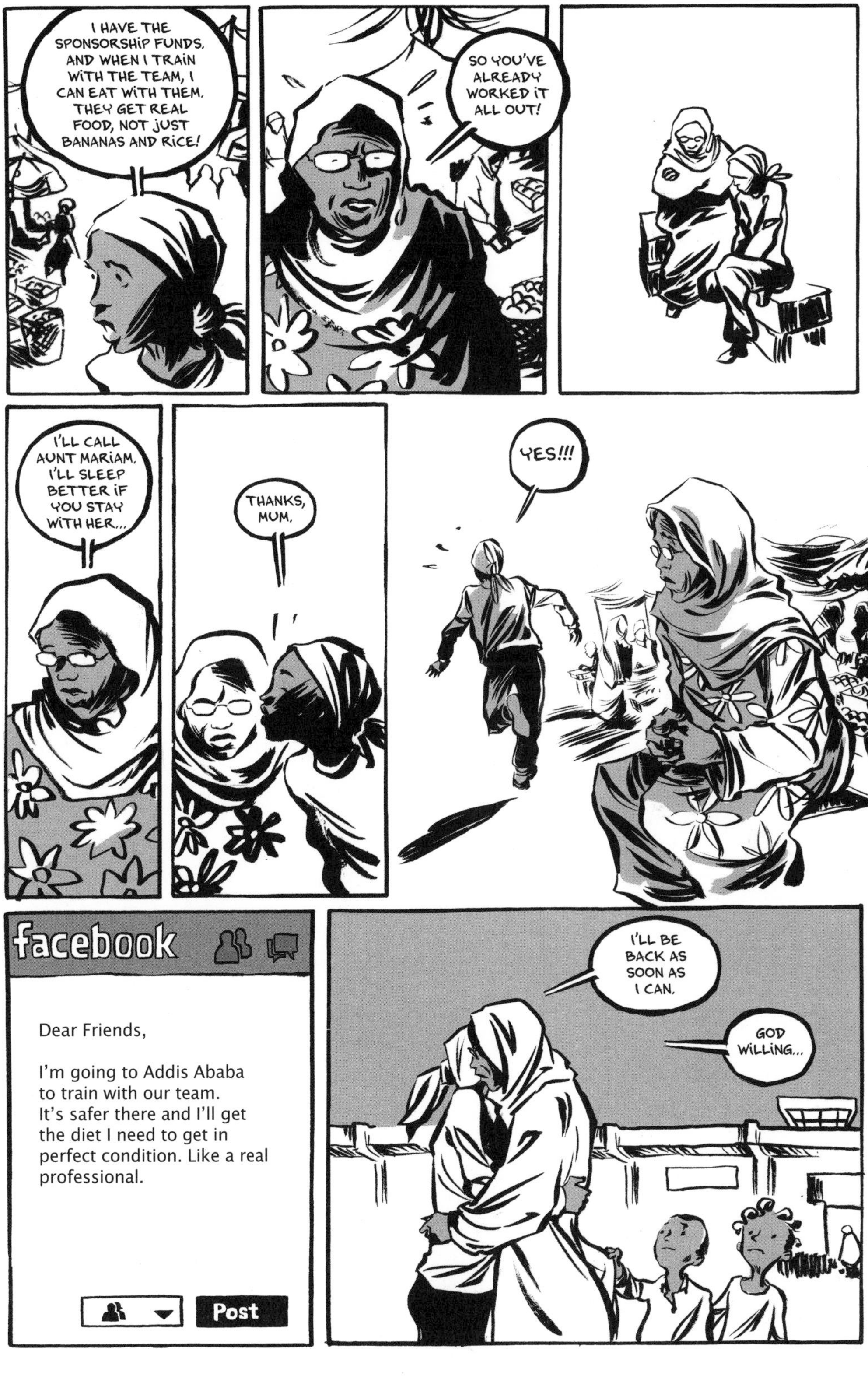
I HAVE THE SPONSORSHIP FUNDS, AND WHEN I TRAIN WITH THE TEAM, I CAN EAT WITH THEM. THEY GET REAL FOOD, NOT JUST BANANAS AND RICE!
SO YOU'VE ALREADY WORKED IT ALL OUT!
I'LL CALL AUNT MARIAM. I'LL SLEEP BETTER IF YOU STAY WITH HER...
THANKS, MUM.
YES!!!
facebook
Dear Friends,
I'm going to Addis Ababa to train with our team. It's safer there and I'll get the diet I need to get in perfect condition. Like a real professional.
Post
I'LL BE BACK AS SOON AS I CAN.
GOD WILLING...

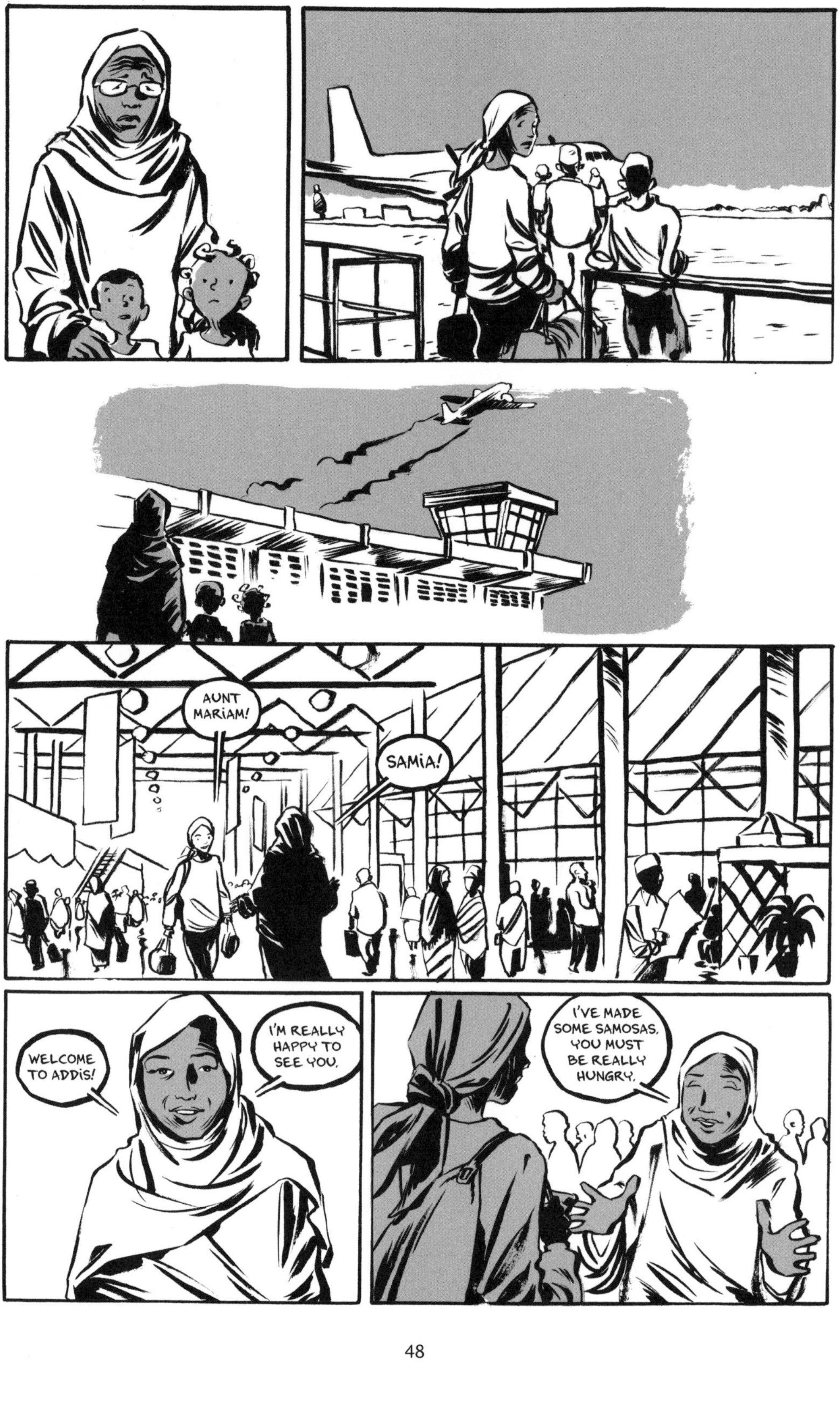
AUNT MARIAM!
SAMIA!
WELCOME TO ADDIS!
I'M REALLY HAPPY TO SEE YOU.
I'VE MADE SOME SAMOSAS. YOU MUST BE REALLY HUNGRY.

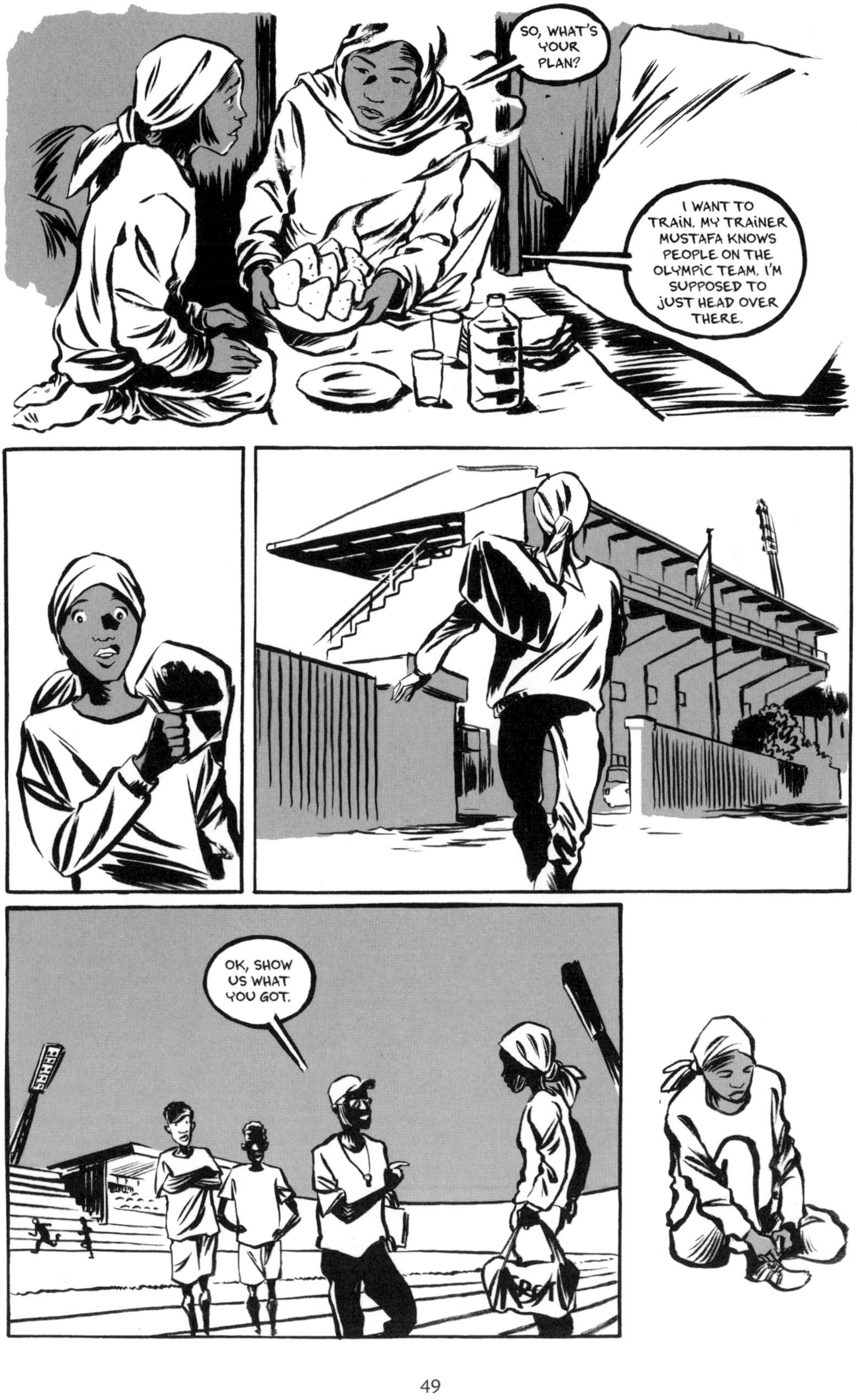
SO, WHAT'S YOUR PLAN?
I WANT TO TRAIN. MY TRAINER MUSTAFA KNOWS PEOPLE ON THE OLYMPIC TEAM. I'M SUPPOSED TO JUST HEAD OVER THERE.
OK, SHOW US WHAT YOU GOT.

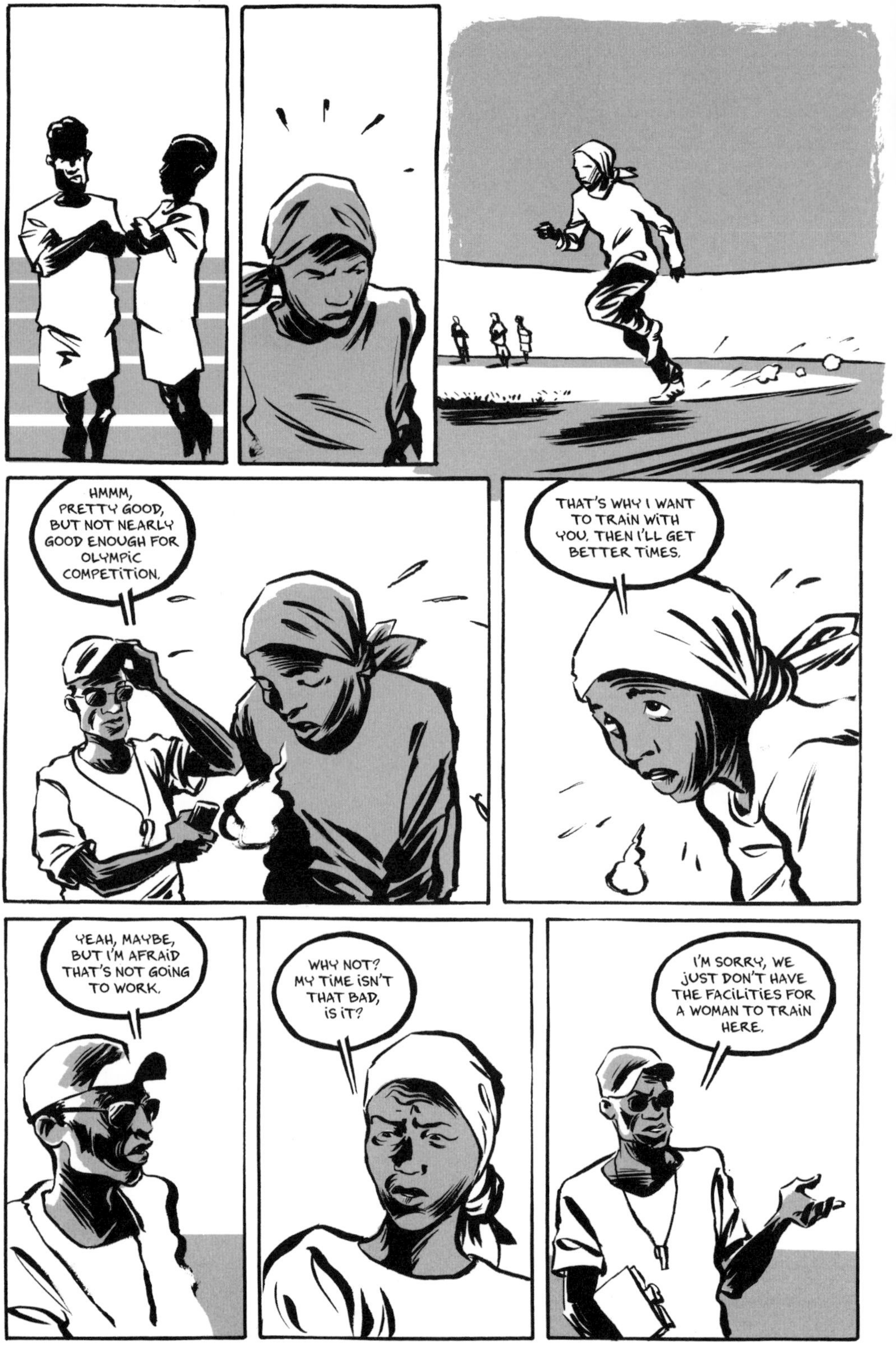
HMMM, PRETTY GOOD, BUT NOT NEARLY GOOD ENOUGH FOR OLYMPIC COMPETITION.
THAT'S WHY I WANT TO TRAIN WITH YOU. THEN I'LL GET BETTER TIMES.
YEAH, MAYBE, BUT I'M AFRAID THAT'S NOT GOING TO WORK.
WHY NOT? MY TIME ISN'T THAT BAD, IS IT?
I'M SORRY, WE JUST DON'T HAVE THE FACILITIES FOR A WOMAN TO TRAIN HERE.

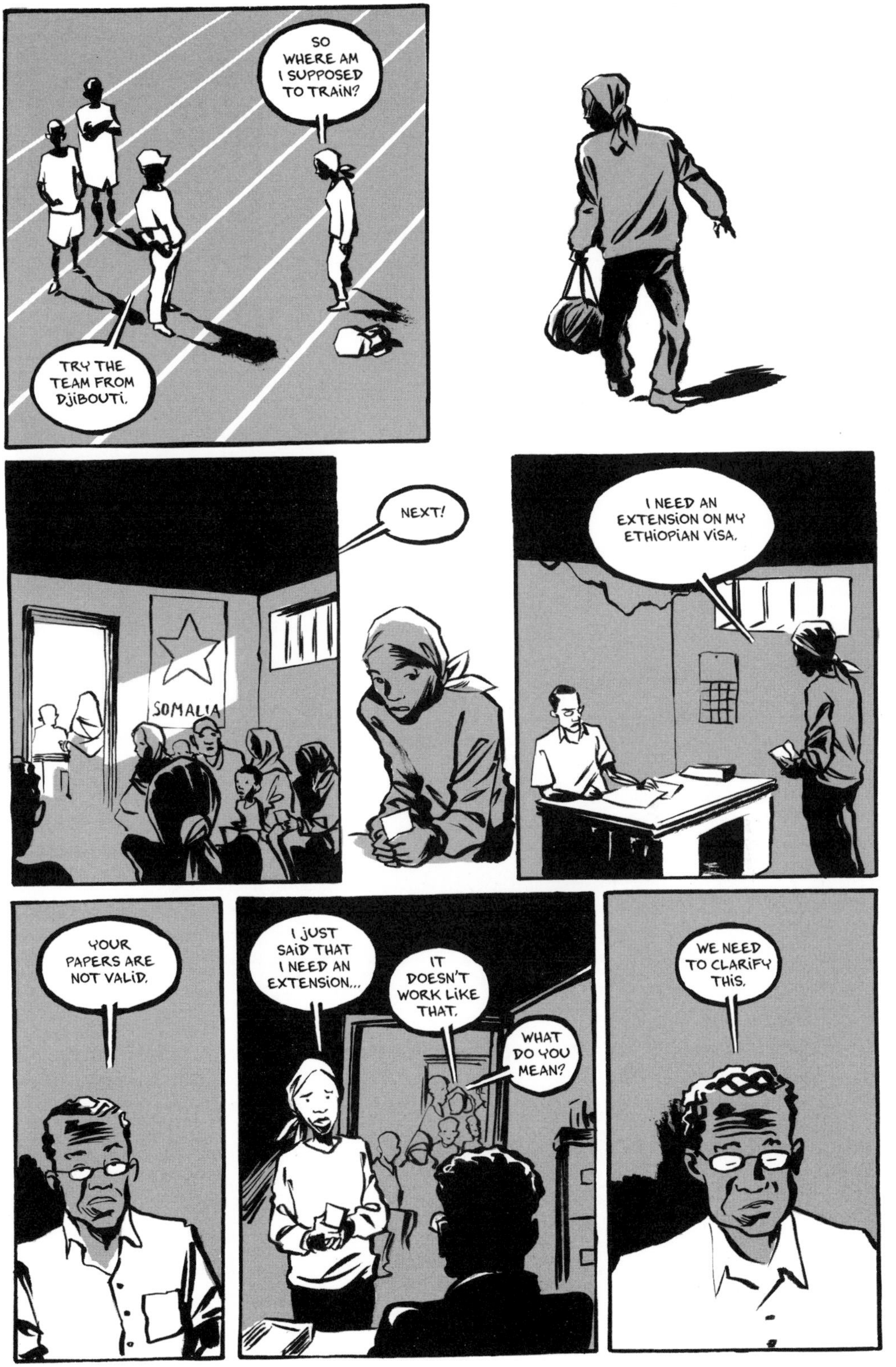
SO WHERE AM I SUPPOSED TO TRAIN?
TRY THE TEAM FROM DJIBOUTI.
NEXT!
I NEED AN EXTENSION ON MY ETHIOPIAN VISA.
SOMALIA
YOUR PAPERS ARE NOT VALID.
I JUST SAID THAT I NEED AN EXTENSION...
IT DOESN'T WORK LIKE THAT.
WHAT DO YOU MEAN?
WE NEED TO CLARIFY THIS.

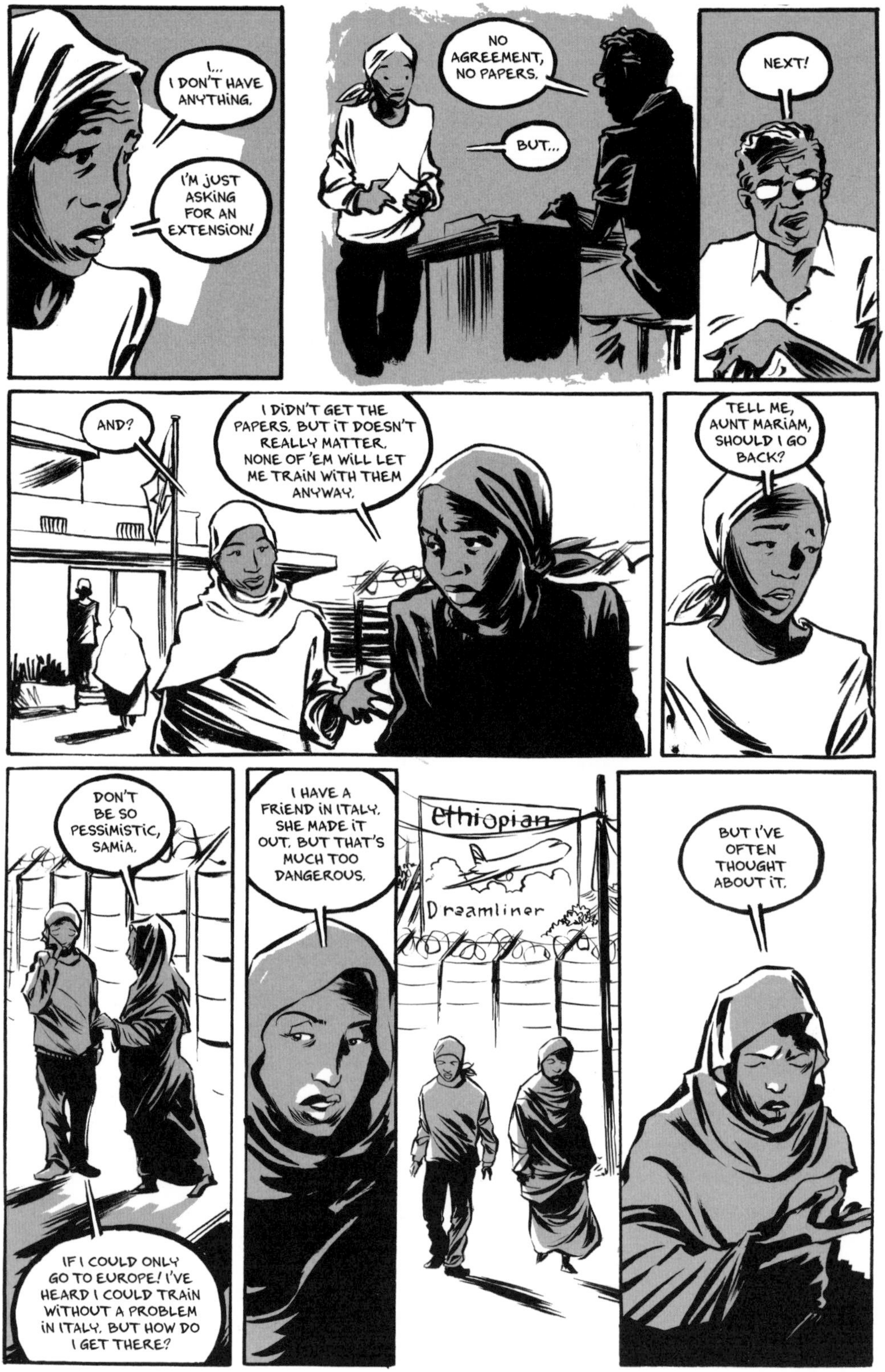
I...
I DON'T HAVE ANYTHING.
I'M JUST ASKING FOR AN EXTENSION!
NO AGREEMENT, NO PAPERS.
BUT...
NEXT!
AND?
I DIDN'T GET THE PAPERS. BUT IT DOESN'T REALLY MATTER. NONE OF 'EM WILL LET ME TRAIN WITH THEM ANYWAY.
TELL ME, AUNT MARIAM, SHOULD I GO BACK?
DON'T BE SO PESSIMISTIC, SAMIA.
IF I COULD ONLY GO TO EUROPE! I'VE HEARD I COULD TRAIN WITHOUT A PROBLEM IN ITALY. BUT HOW DO I GET THERE?
I HAVE A FRIEND IN ITALY. SHE MADE IT OUT. BUT THAT'S MUCH TOO DANGEROUS.
ethiopian
Dreamliner
BUT I'VE OFTEN THOUGHT ABOUT IT.

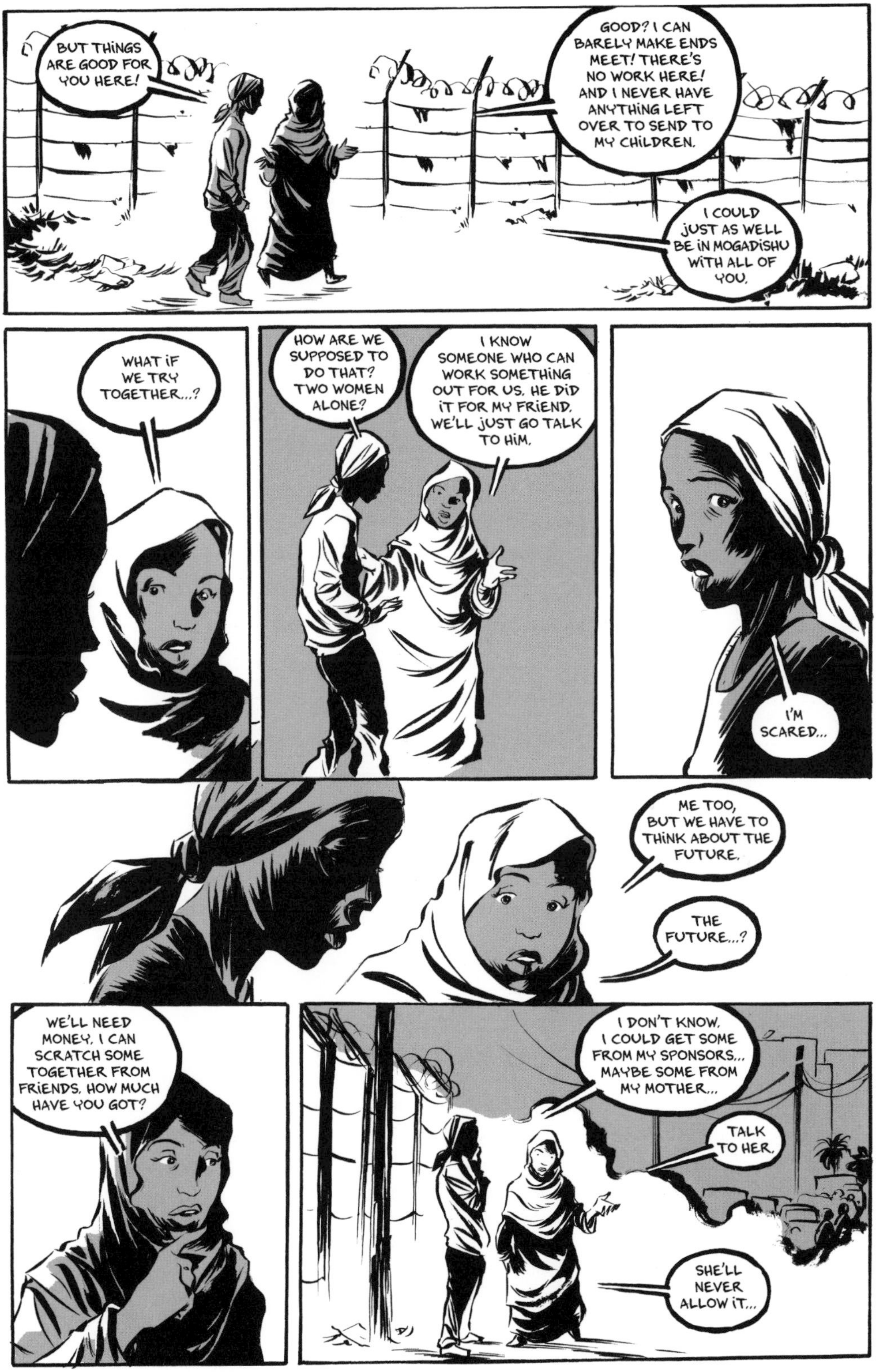

BUT THINGS ARE GOOD FOR YOU HERE!
GOOD? I CAN BARELY MAKE ENDS MEET! THERE'S NO WORK HERE! AND I NEVER HAVE ANYTHING LEFT OVER TO SEND TO MY CHILDREN.
I COULD JUST AS WELL BE IN MOGADISHU WITH ALL OF YOU.
WHAT IF WE TRY TOGETHER...?
HOW ARE WE SUPPOSED TO DO THAT? TWO WOMEN ALONE?
I KNOW SOMEONE WHO CAN WORK SOMETHING OUT FOR US. HE DID IT FOR MY FRIEND. WE'LL JUST GO TALK TO HIM.
I'M SCARED...
ME TOO, BUT WE HAVE TO THINK ABOUT THE FUTURE.
THE FUTURE...?
WE'LL NEED MONEY. I CAN SCRATCH SOME TOGETHER FROM FRIENDS. HOW MUCH HAVE YOU GOT?
I DON'T KNOW. I COULD GET SOME FROM MY SPONSORS... MAYBE SOME FROM MY MOTHER...
TALK TO HER.
SHE'LL NEVER ALLOW IT...

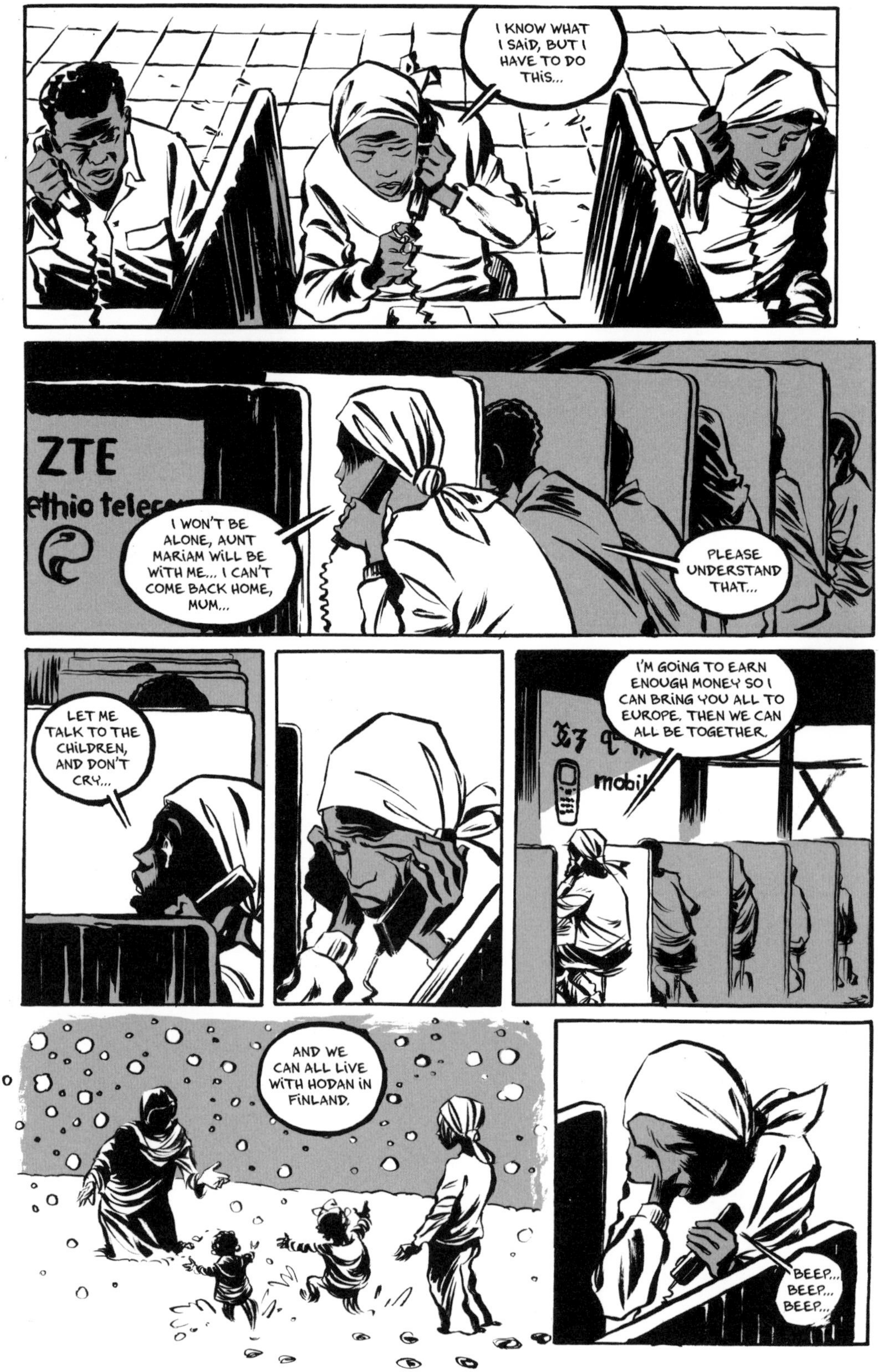
I KNOW WHAT I SAID, BUT I HAVE TO DO THIS...
ZTE
ethio telecom
I WON'T BE ALONE, AUNT MARIAM WILL BE WITH ME... I CAN'T COME BACK HOME, MUM...
PLEASE UNDERSTAND THAT...
LET ME TALK TO THE CHILDREN, AND DON'T CRY...
I'M GOING TO EARN ENOUGH MONEY SO I CAN BRING YOU ALL TO EUROPE. THEN WE CAN ALL BE TOGETHER.
AND WE CAN ALL LIVE WITH HODAN IN FINLAND.
BEEP... BEEP... BEEP...

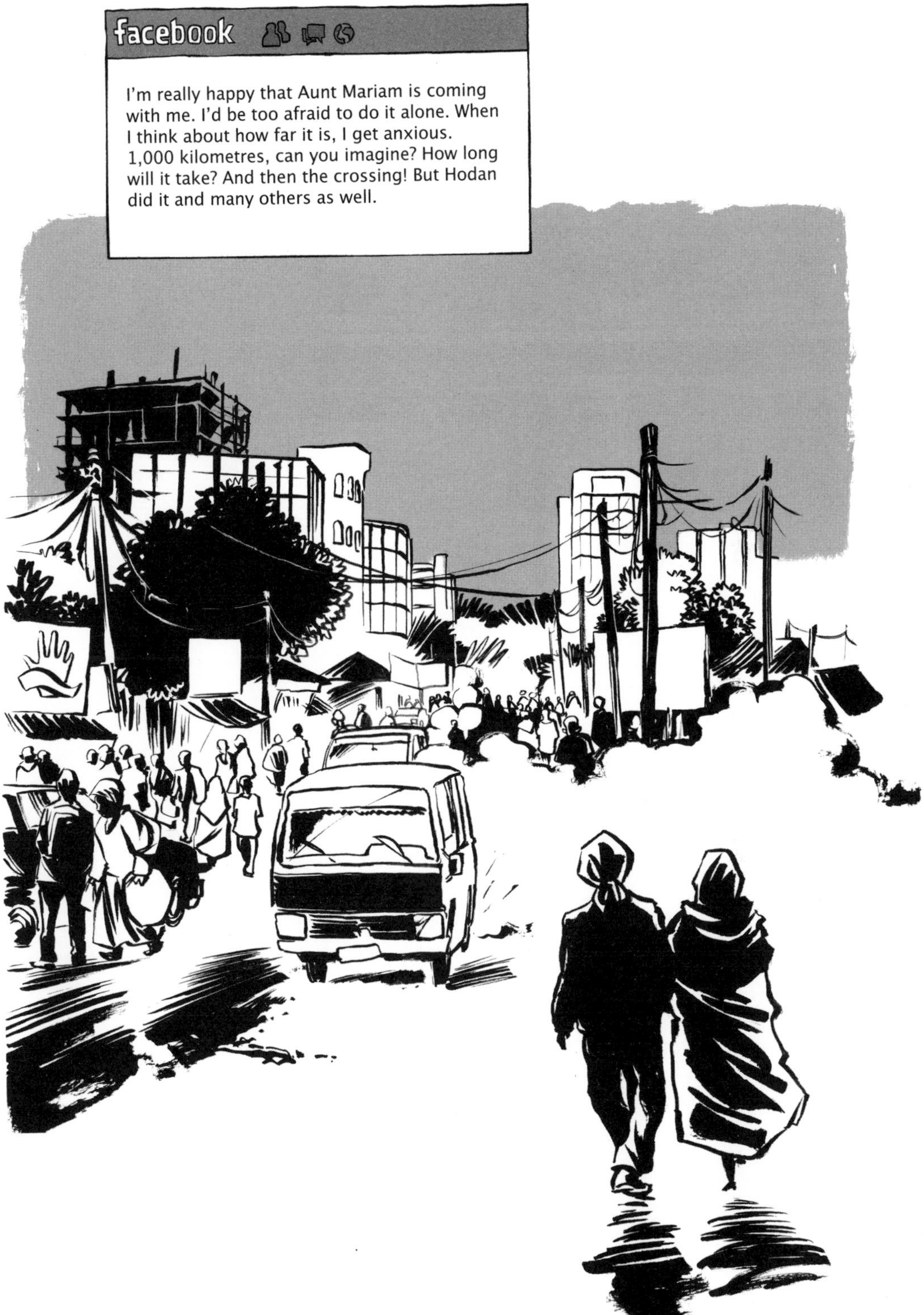
facebook
I'm really happy that Aunt Mariam is coming with me. I'd be too afraid to do it alone. When I think about how far it is, I get anxious. 1,000 kilometres, can you imagine? How long will it take? And then the crossing! But Hodan did it and many others as well.

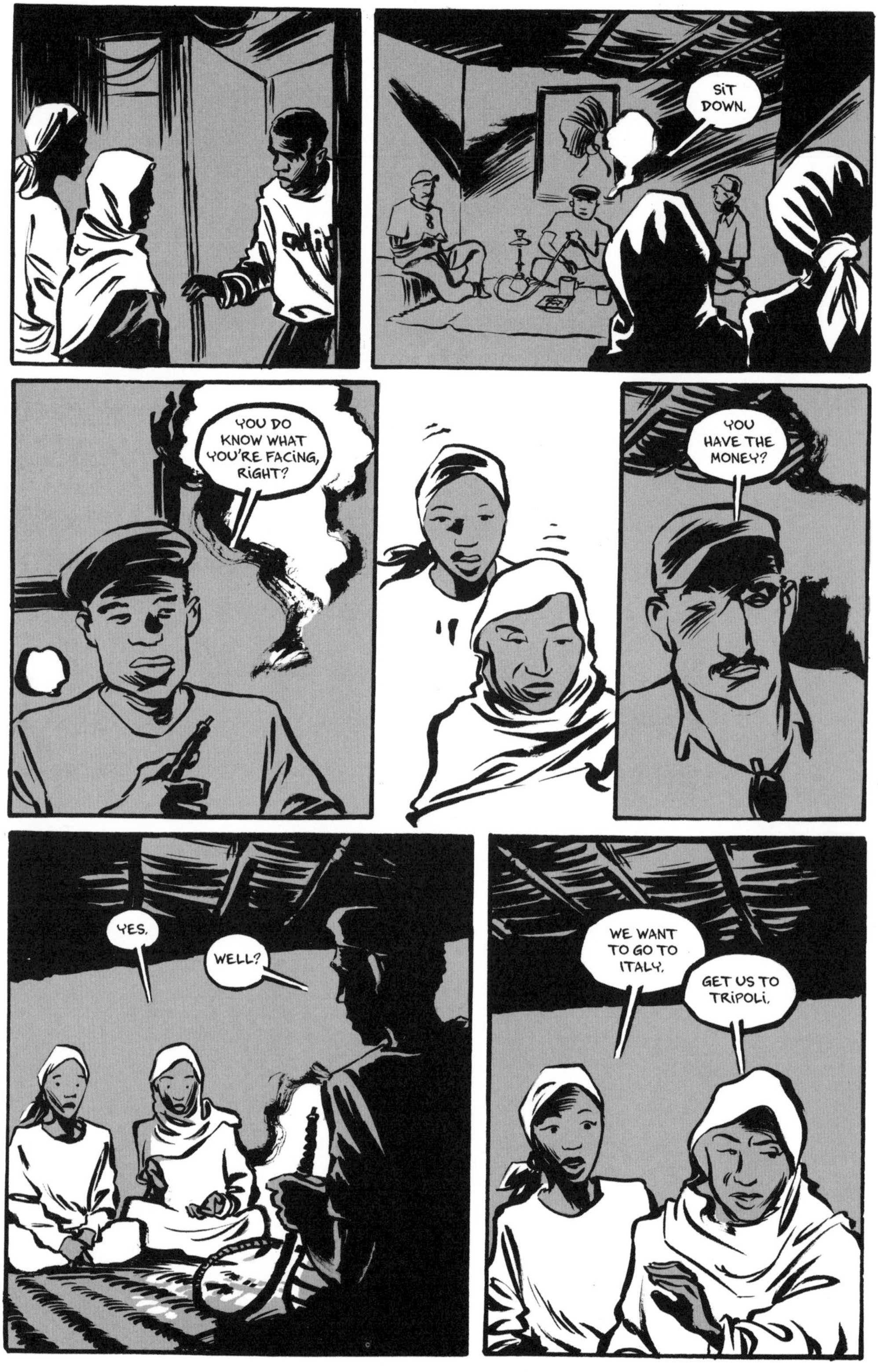
SIT DOWN.
YOU DO KNOW WHAT YOU'RE FACING, RIGHT?
YOU HAVE THE MONEY?
YES.
WELL?
WE WANT TO GO TO ITALY.
GET US TO TRIPOLI.

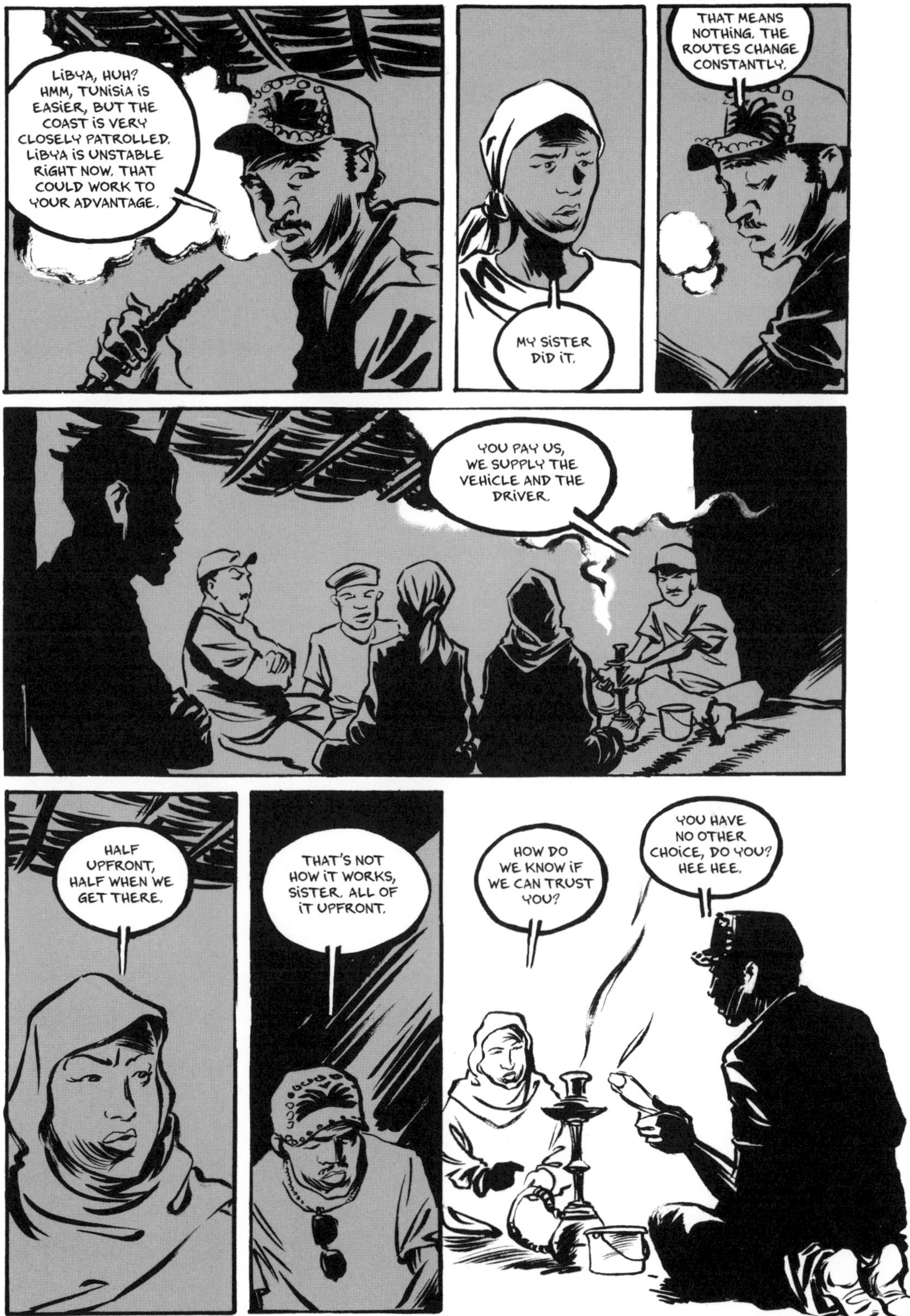
LiBYA, HUH? HMM, TUNiSiA iS EASiER, BUT THE COAST iS VERY CLOSELY PATROLLED. LiBYA iS UNSTABLE RiGHT NOW. THAT COULD WORK TO YOUR ADVANTAGE.
MY SiSTER DiD iT.
THAT MEANS NOTHiNG. THE ROUTES CHANGE CONSTANTLY.
YOU PAY US, WE SUPPLY THE VEHiCLE AND THE DRiVER.
HALF UPFRONT, HALF WHEN WE GET THERE.
THAT'S NOT HOW iT WORKS, SiSTER. ALL OF iT UPFRONT.
HOW DO WE KNOW iF WE CAN TRUST YOU?
YOU HAVE NO OTHER CHOiCE, DO YOU? HEE HEE.

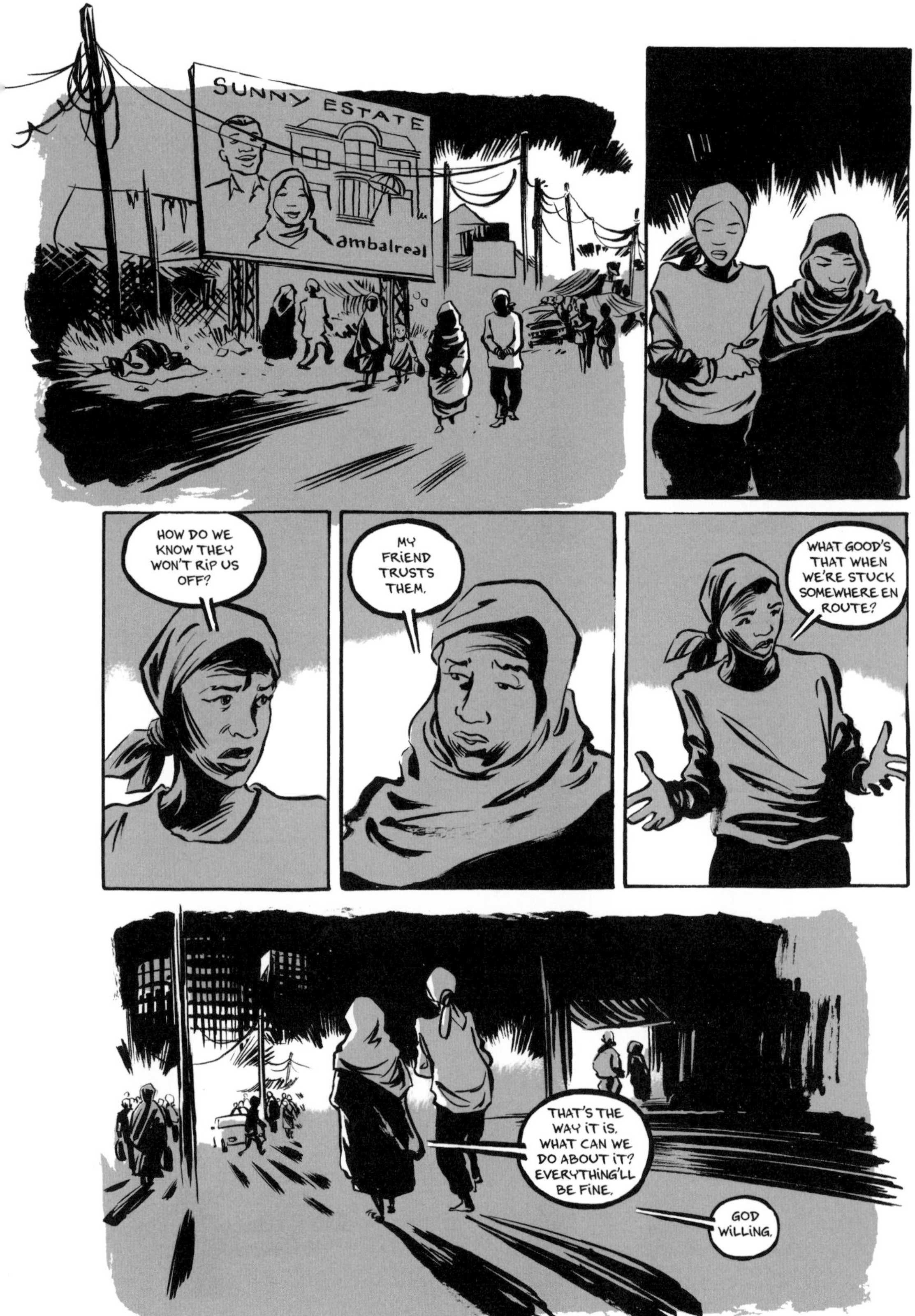
SUNNY ESTATE
ambalreal
HOW DO WE KNOW THEY WON'T RIP US OFF?
MY FRIEND TRUSTS THEM.
WHAT GOOD'S THAT WHEN WE'RE STUCK SOMEWHERE EN ROUTE?
THAT'S THE WAY IT IS. WHAT CAN WE DO ABOUT IT? EVERYTHING'LL BE FINE.
GOD WILLING.

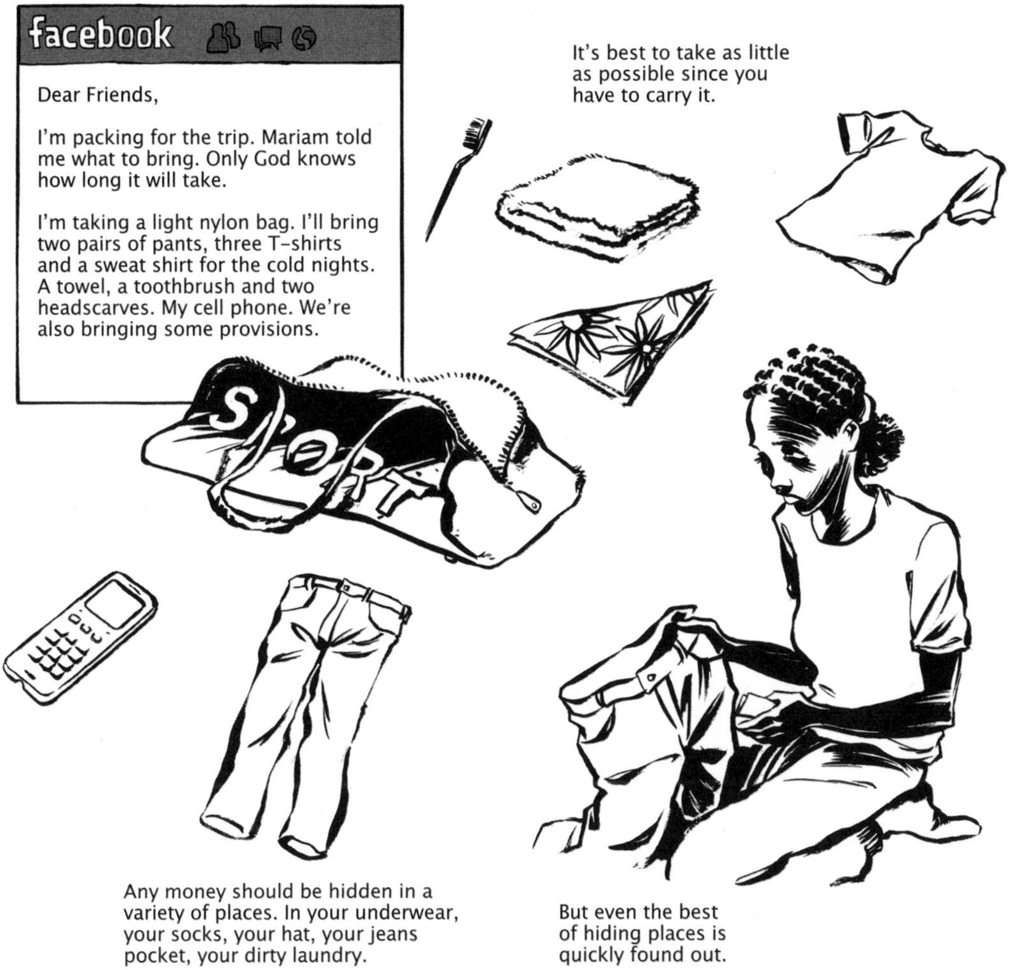
facebook
Dear Friends,
I'm packing for the trip. Mariam told me what to bring. Only God knows how long it will take.
I'm taking a light nylon bag. I'll bring two pairs of pants, three T-shirts and a sweat shirt for the cold nights. A towel, a toothbrush and two headscarves. My cell phone. We're also bringing some provisions.
It's best to take as little as possible since you have to carry it.
SPORT
Any money should be hidden in a variety of places. In your underwear, your socks, your hat, your jeans pocket, your dirty laundry.
But even the best of hiding places is quickly found out.

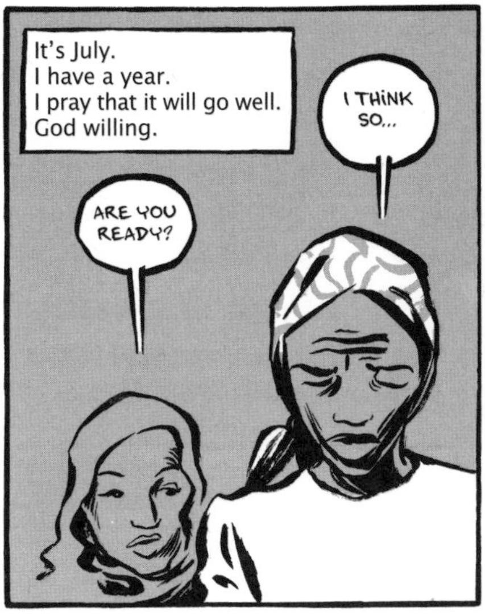
It's July.
I have a year.
I pray that it will go well.
God willing.
ARE YOU READY?
I THINK SO...

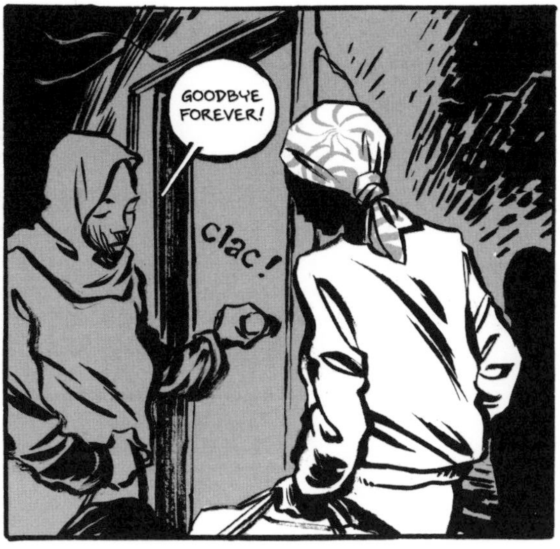
GOODBYE FOREVER!
CLAC!

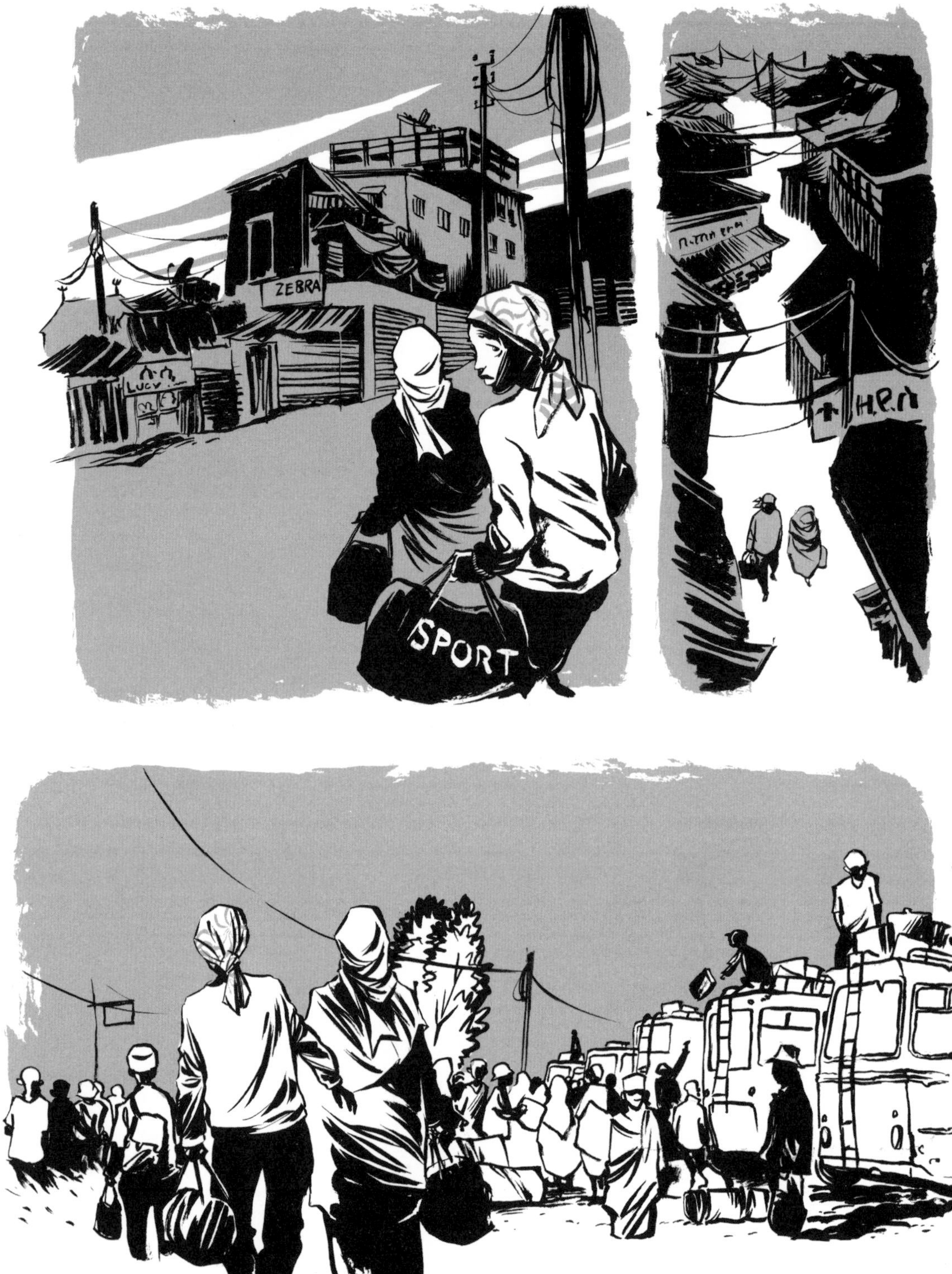

ZEBRA
LUCY
SPORT

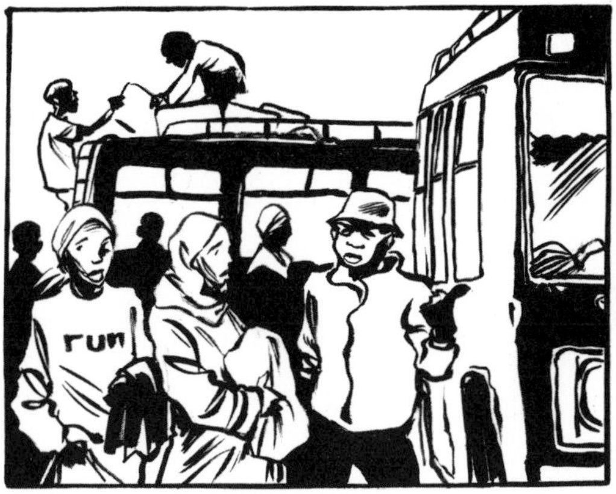
run

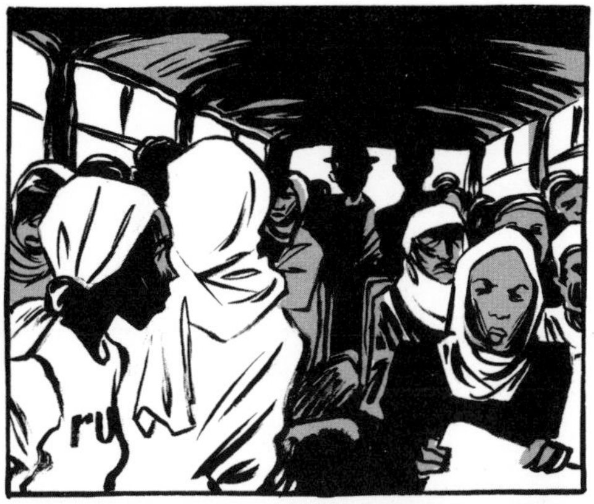

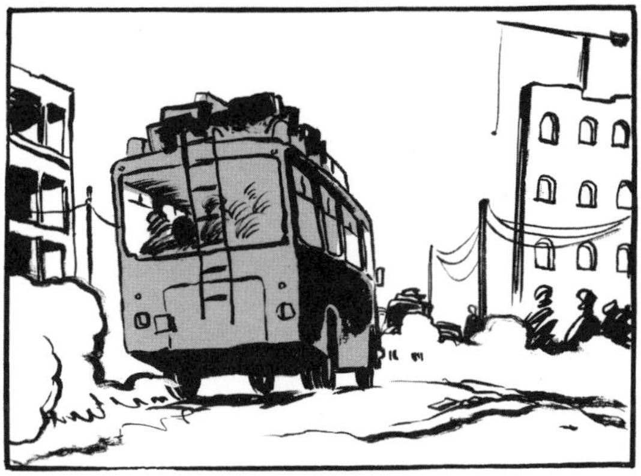

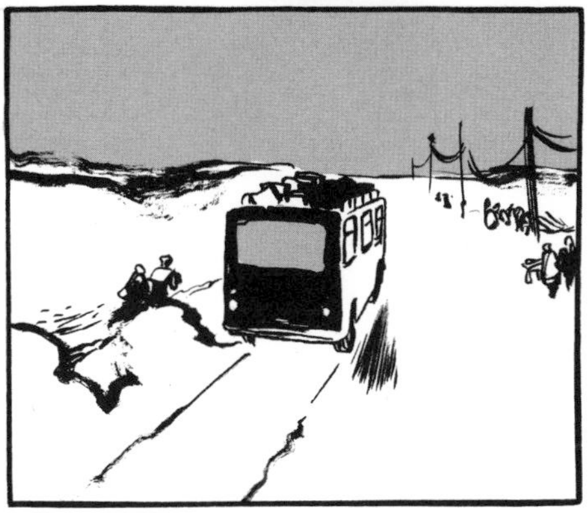

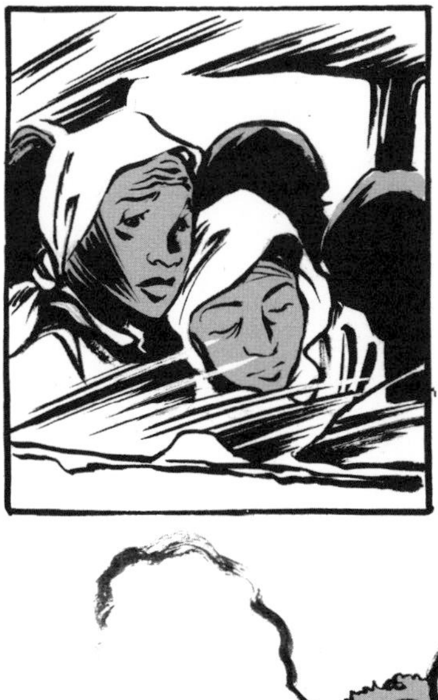

It's the first time I've ever been so far from home, except for Beijing. But I wasn't alone there and everything was organised for me — all I had to do was follow someone around. This is different. I have no idea when we will get to eat again. We're going to be in this smelly bus for days. And this is only the beginning of our trip. I'm so glad that Aunt Mariam is with me.

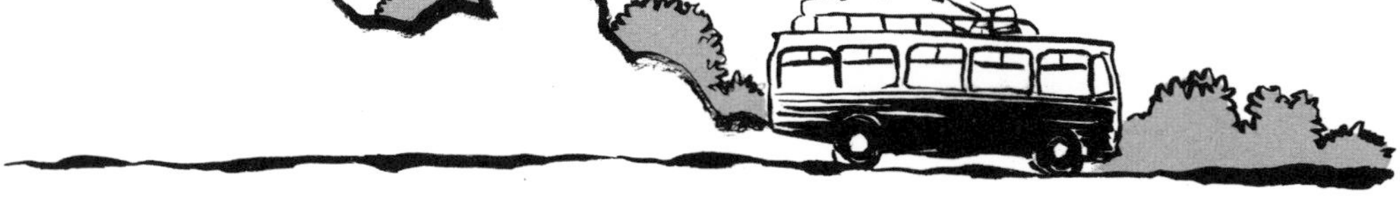

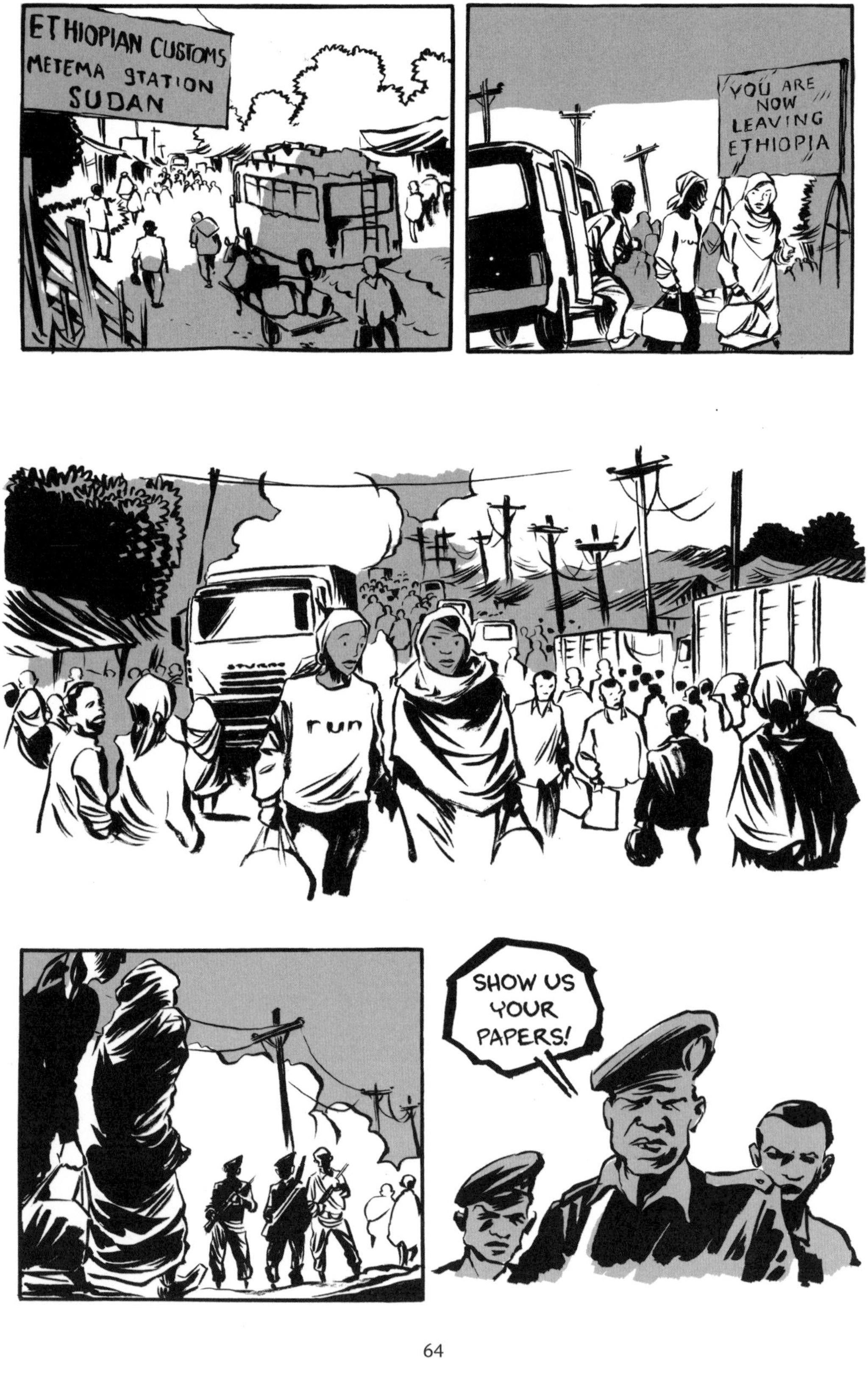
ETHIOPIAN CUSTOMS
METEMA STATION
SUDAN
YOU ARE NOW LEAVING ETHIOPIA
run
SHOW US YOUR PAPERS!

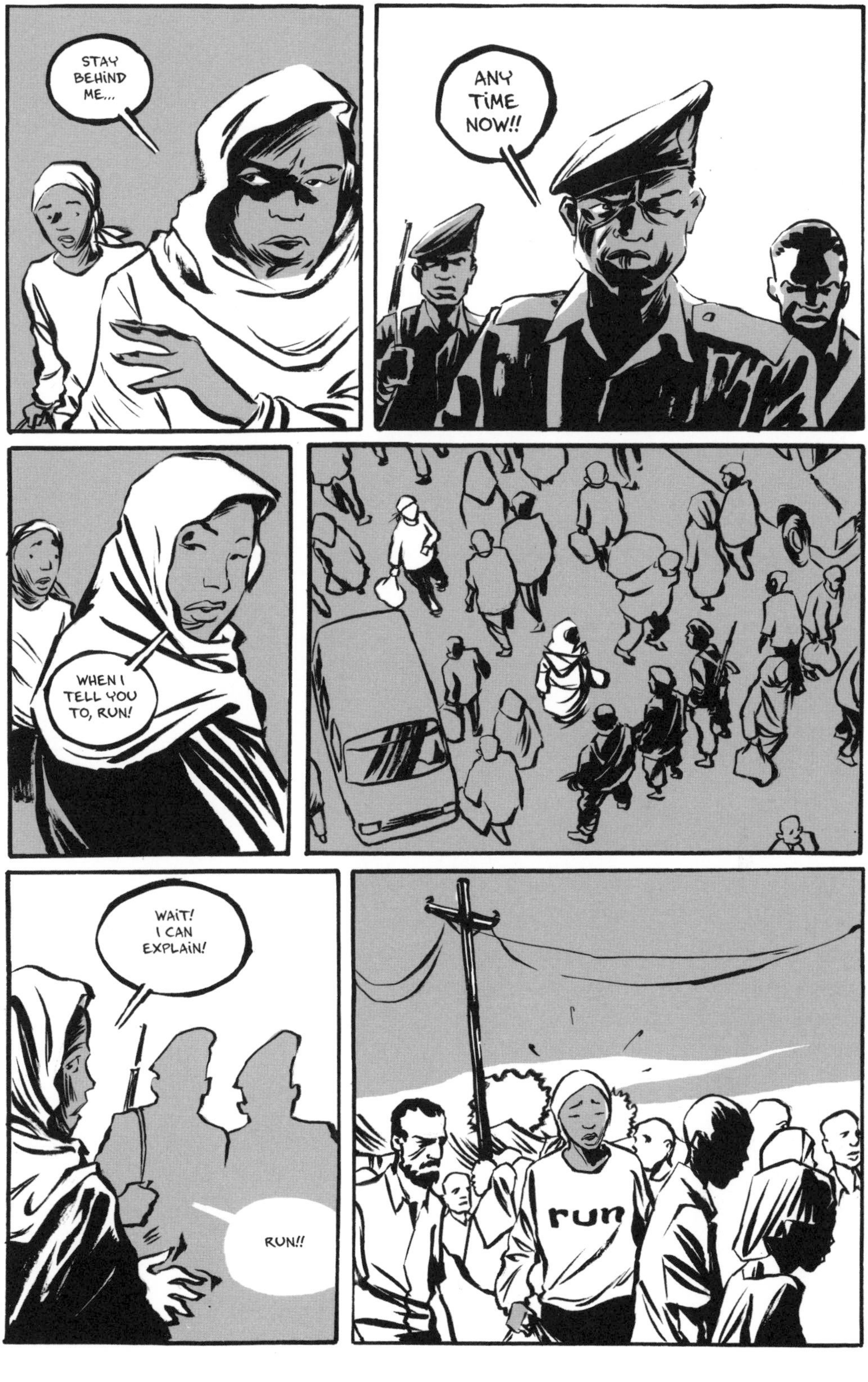
STAY BEHIND ME...
ANY TIME NOW!!
WHEN I TELL YOU TO, RUN!
WAIT! I CAN EXPLAIN!
RUN!!
run

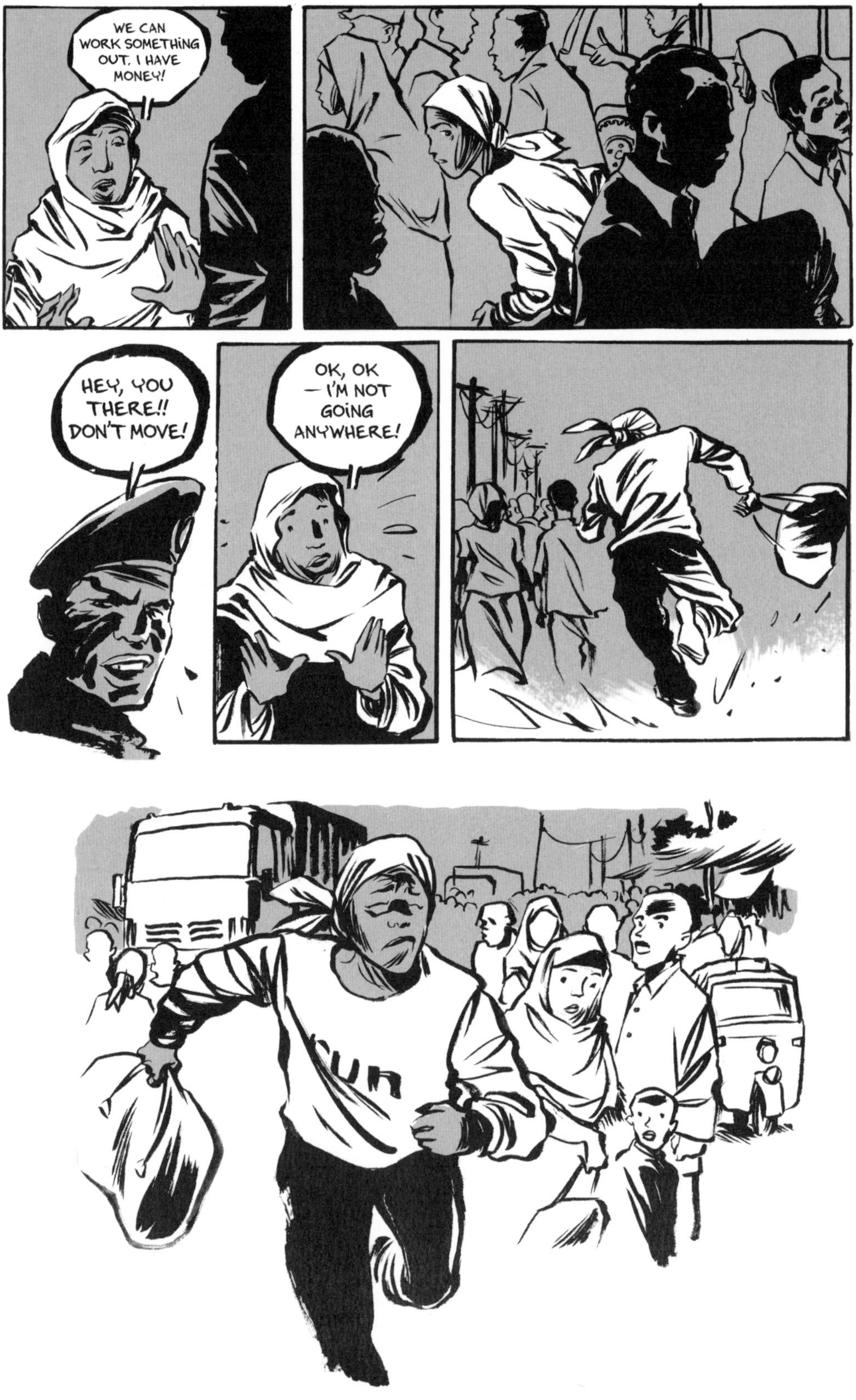
WE CAN WORK SOMETHING OUT. I HAVE MONEY!
HEY, YOU THERE!! DON'T MOVE!
OK, OK — I'M NOT GOING ANYWHERE!
CUR

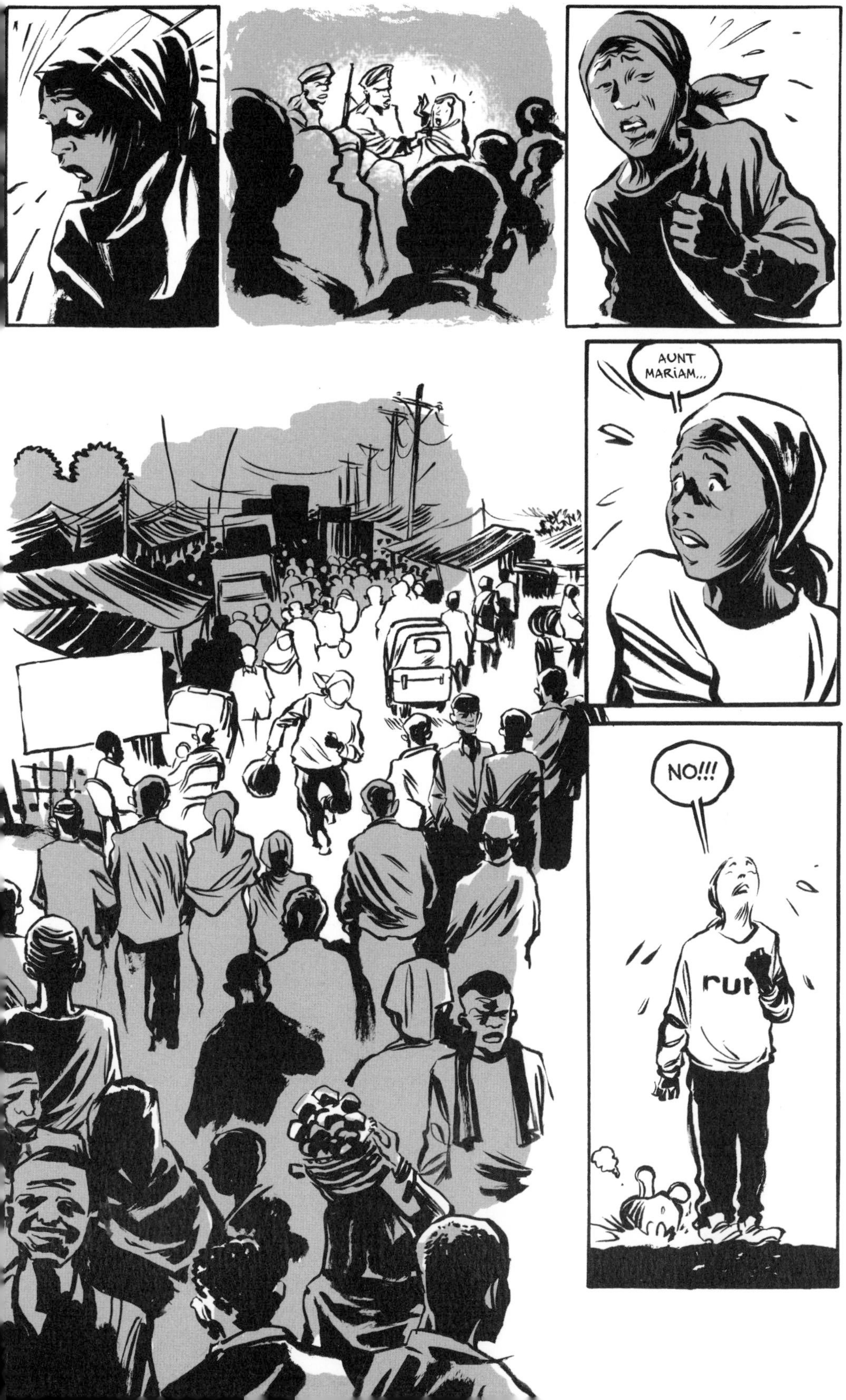
AUNT MARIAM...
NO!!!
run

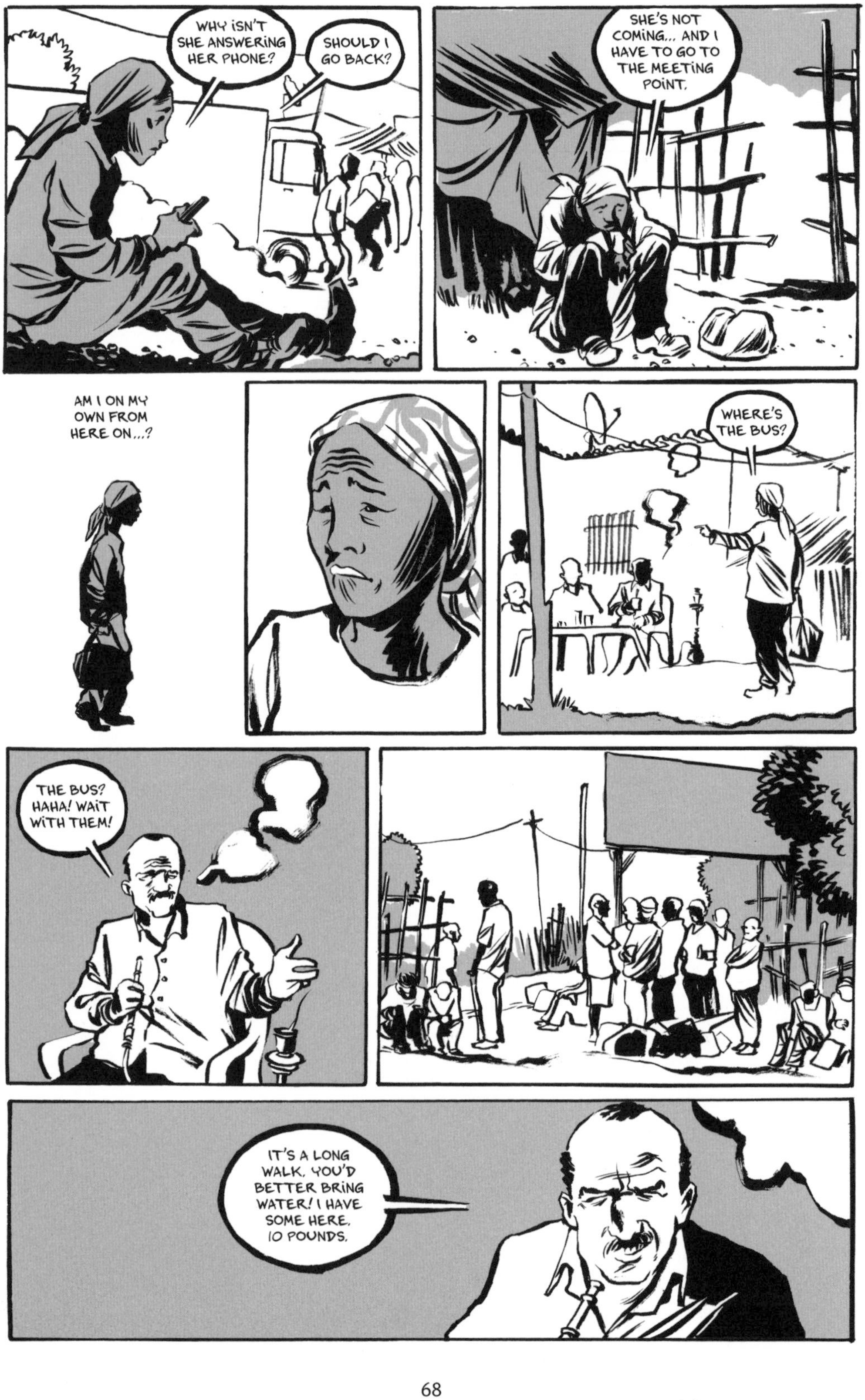

WHY iSN'T SHE ANSWERiNG HER PHONE?
SHOULD I GO BACK?
SHE'S NOT COMiNG... AND I HAVE TO GO TO THE MEETiNG POiNT.
AM I ON MY OWN FROM HERE ON...?
WHERE'S THE BUS?
THE BUS? HAHA! WAiT WiTH THEM!
IT'S A LONG WALK. YOU'D BETTER BRiNG WATER! I HAVE SOME HERE. 10 POUNDS.

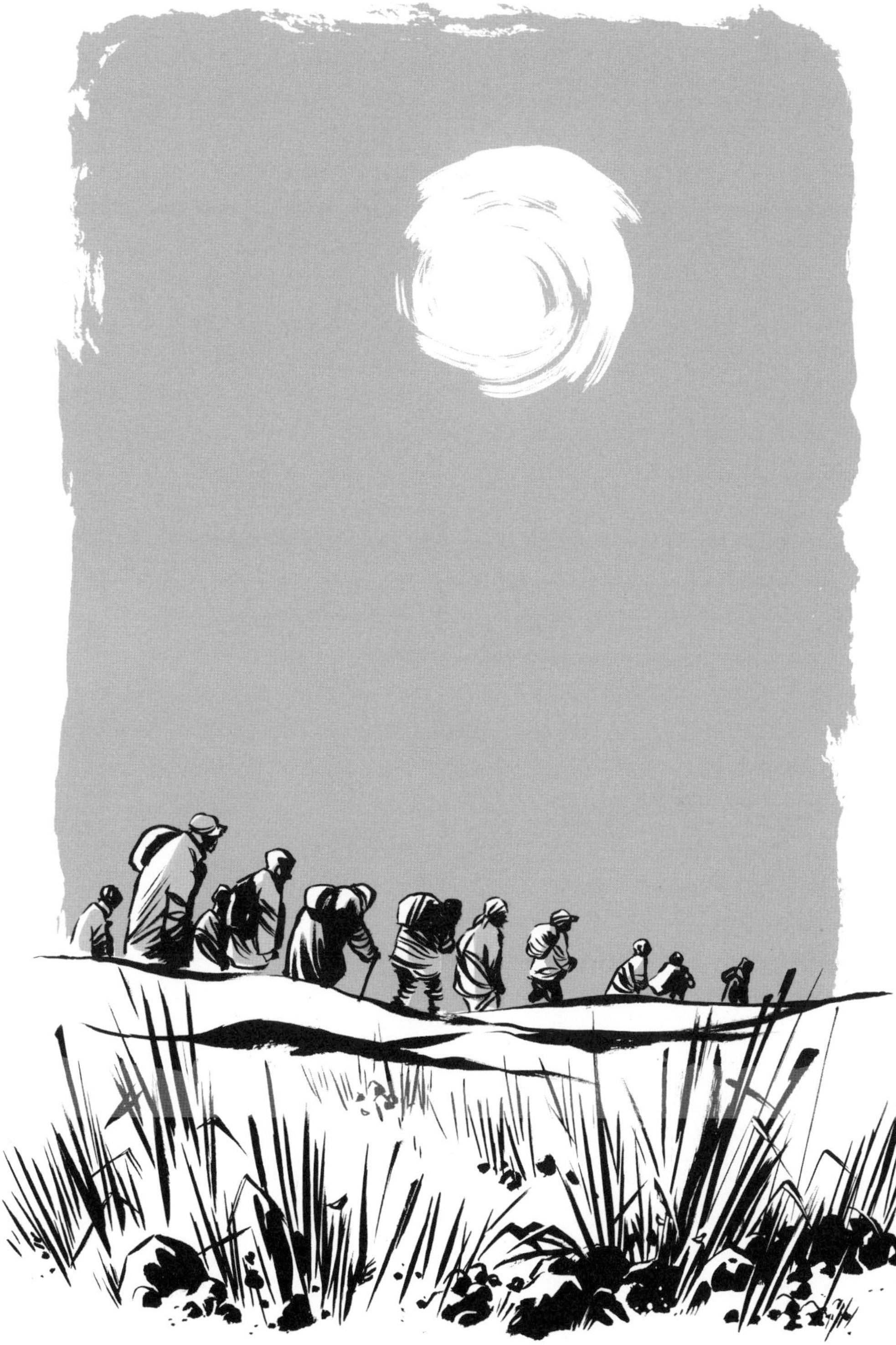

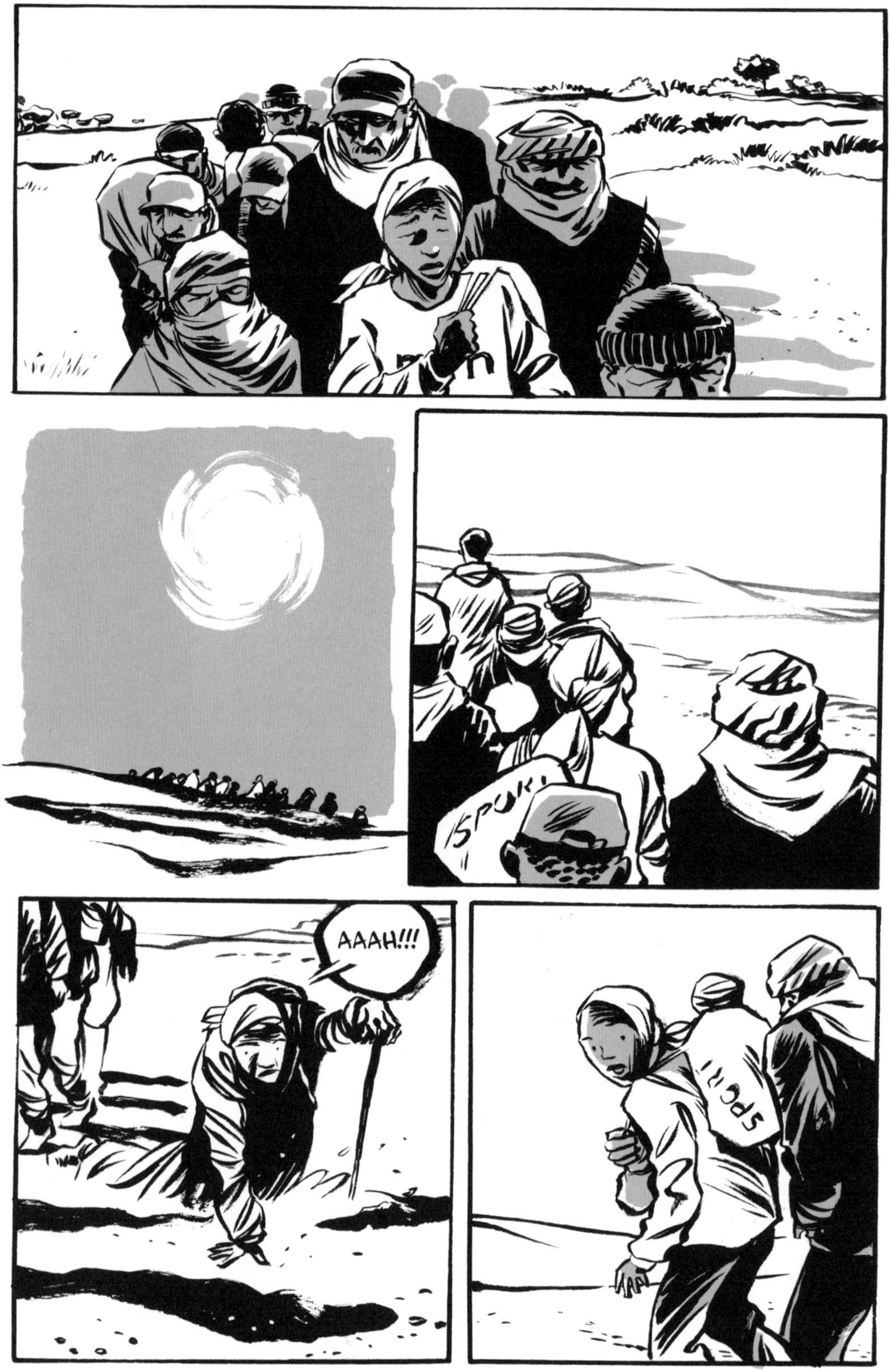
AAAH!!!

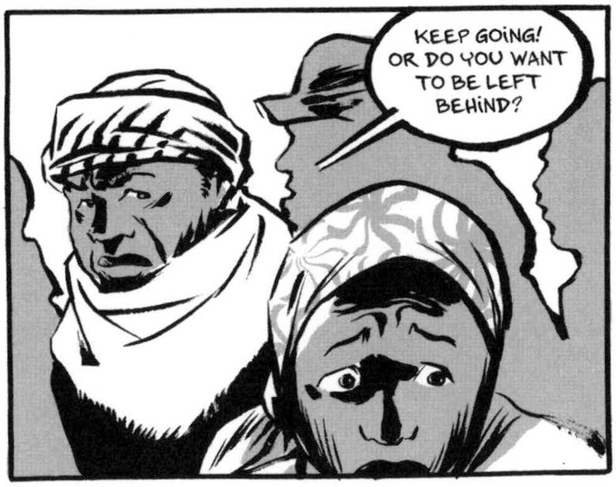
KEEP GOiNG! OR DO YOU WANT TO BE LEFT BEHiND?

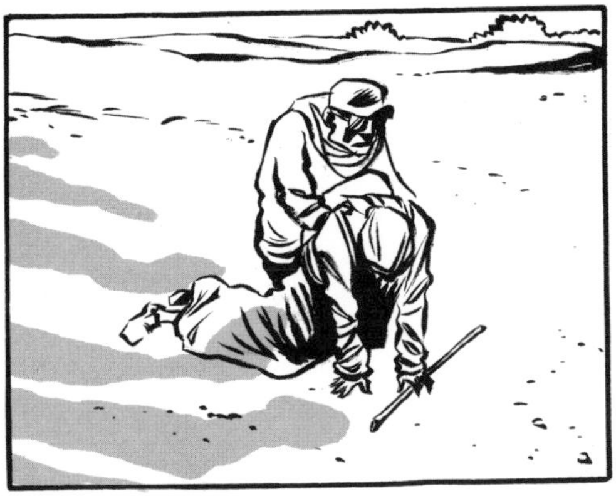

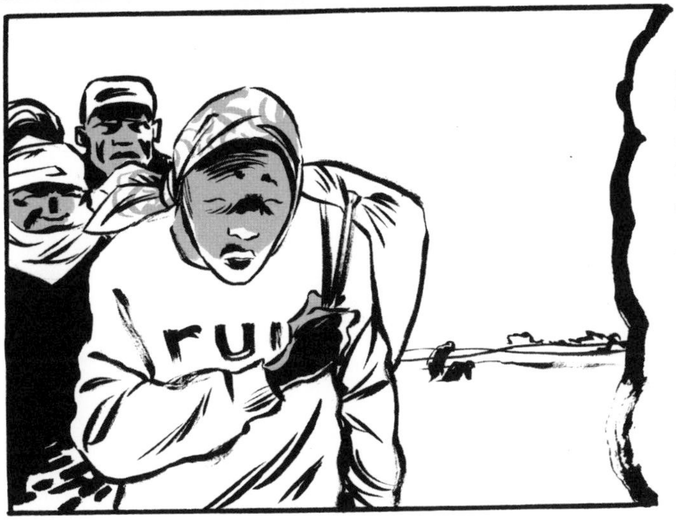

My mother always taught me to help others...

Will I ever see Mariam again? She knows the plan.

We've been walking for hours in this heat. Where's the bus?

Mariam said we shouldn't trust anyone except ourselves. But she's not here any more. Should I have waited? Oh, I just don't know...

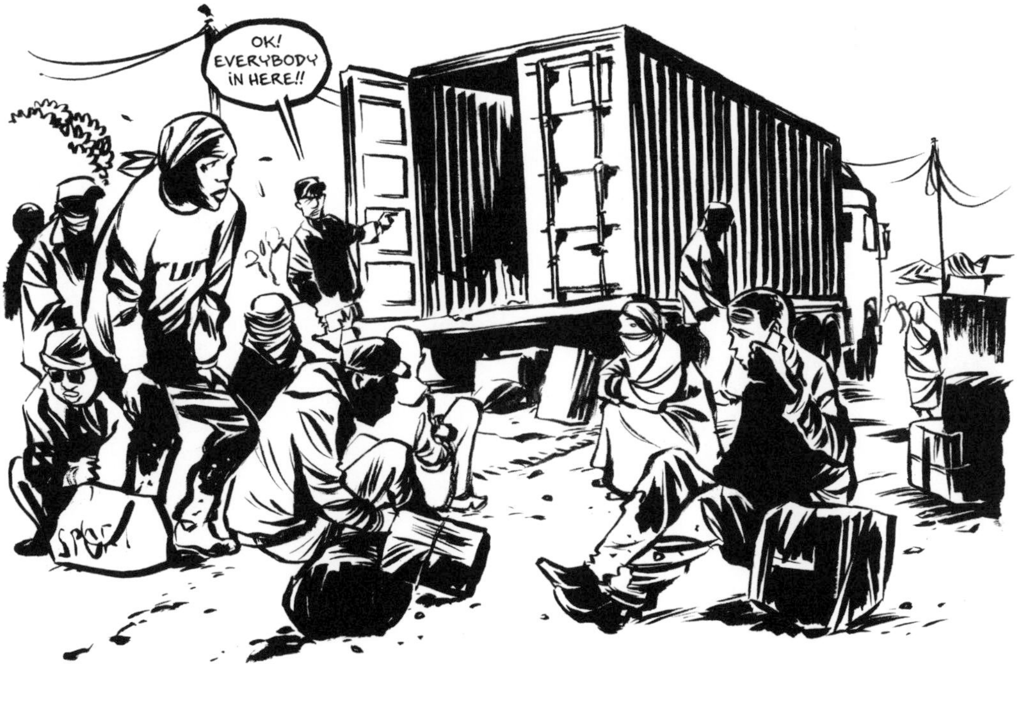
OK! EVERYBODY iN HERE!!

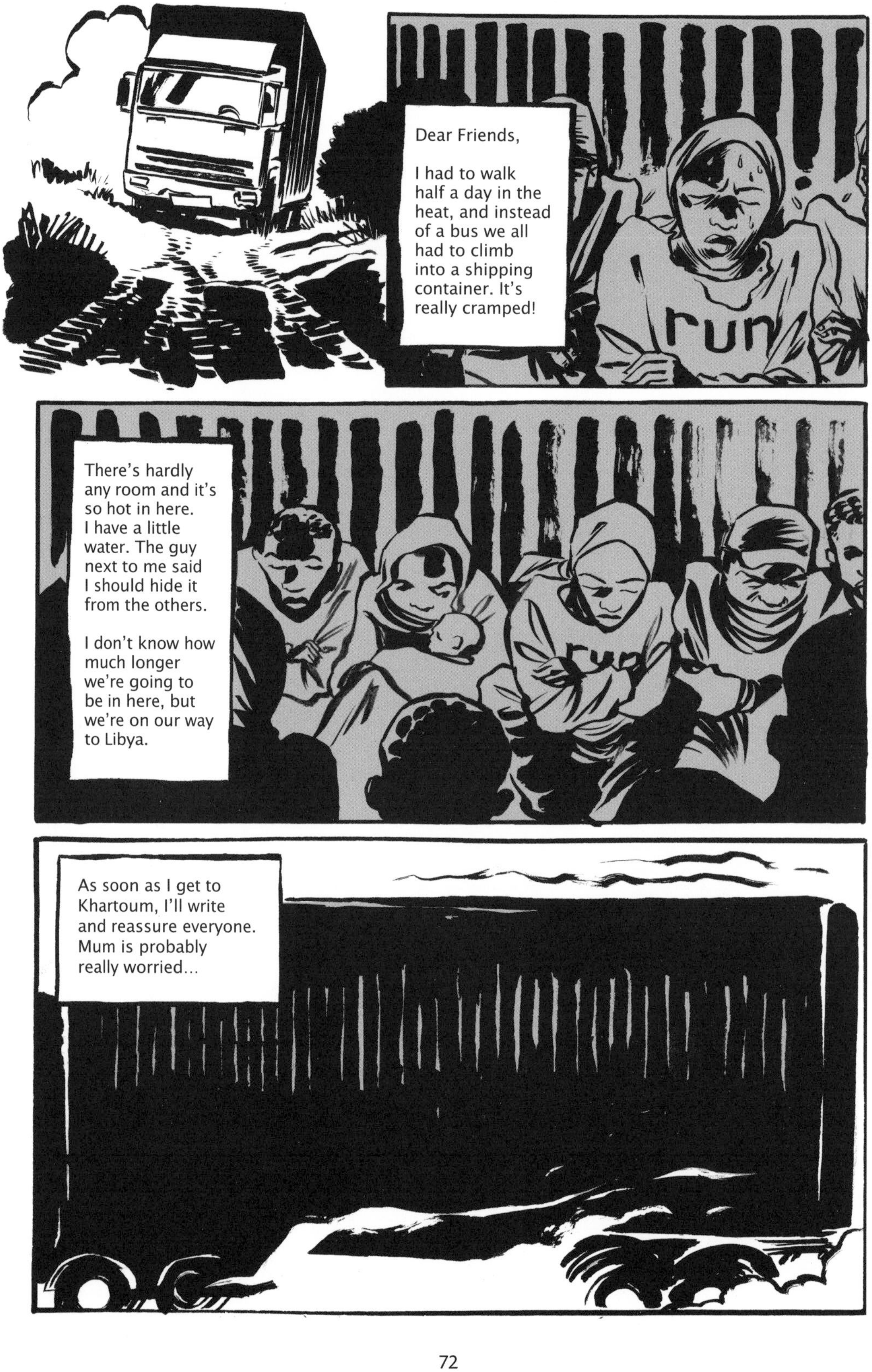
Dear Friends,
I had to walk half a day in the heat, and instead of a bus we all had to climb into a shipping container. It's really cramped!
run
There's hardly any room and it's so hot in here. I have a little water. The guy next to me said I should hide it from the others.
I don't know how much longer we're going to be in here, but we're on our way to Libya.
As soon as I get to Khartoum, I'll write and reassure everyone. Mum is probably really worried...

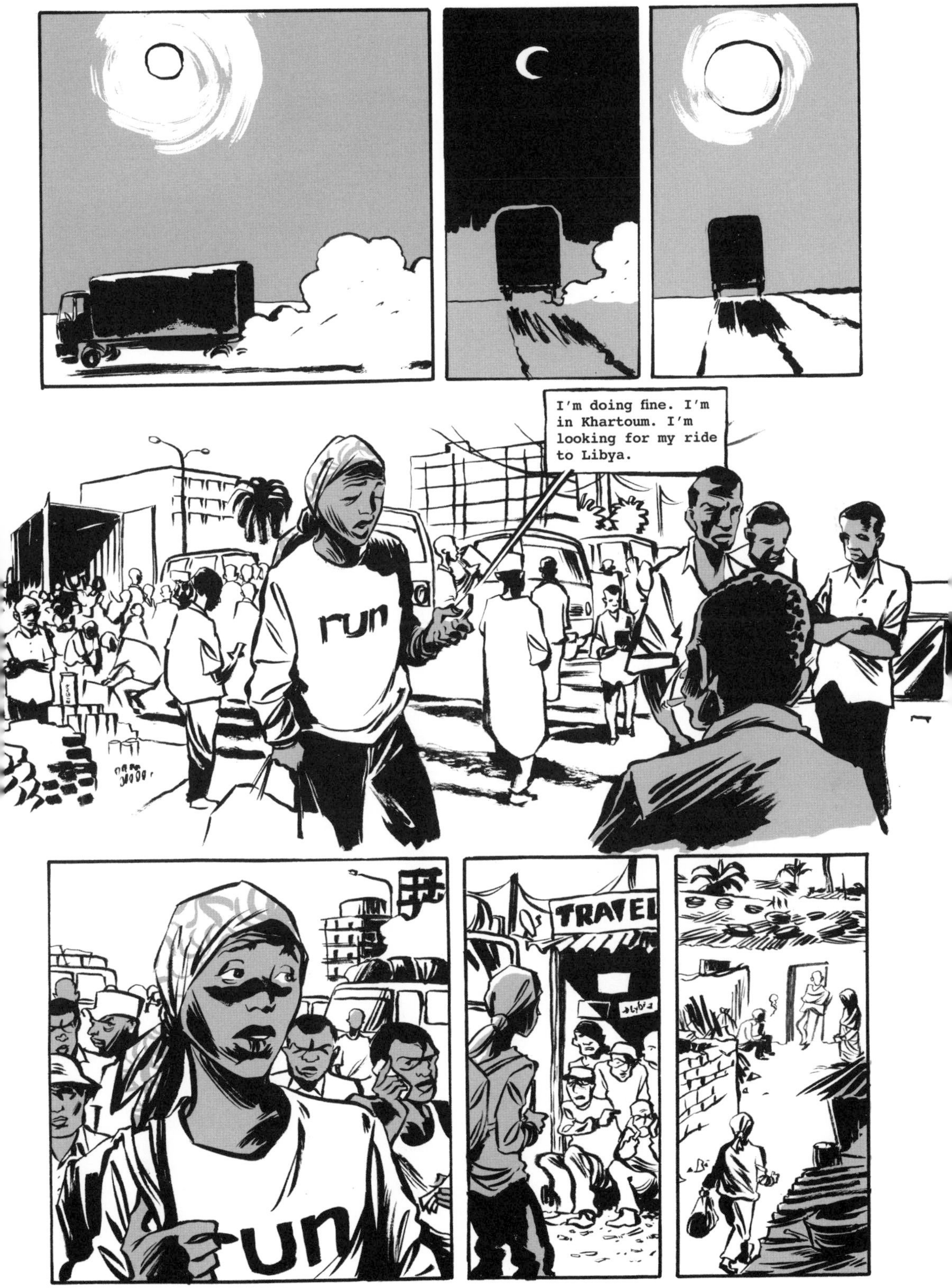
I'm doing fine. I'm in Khartoum. I'm looking for my ride to Libya.
run
TRAVEL

I've been in Khartoum for weeks waiting to go on. I haven't heard anything from the people who were supposed to arrange the ride. Luckily I've been able to sleep with some other Somalis in a hut near the bus station.

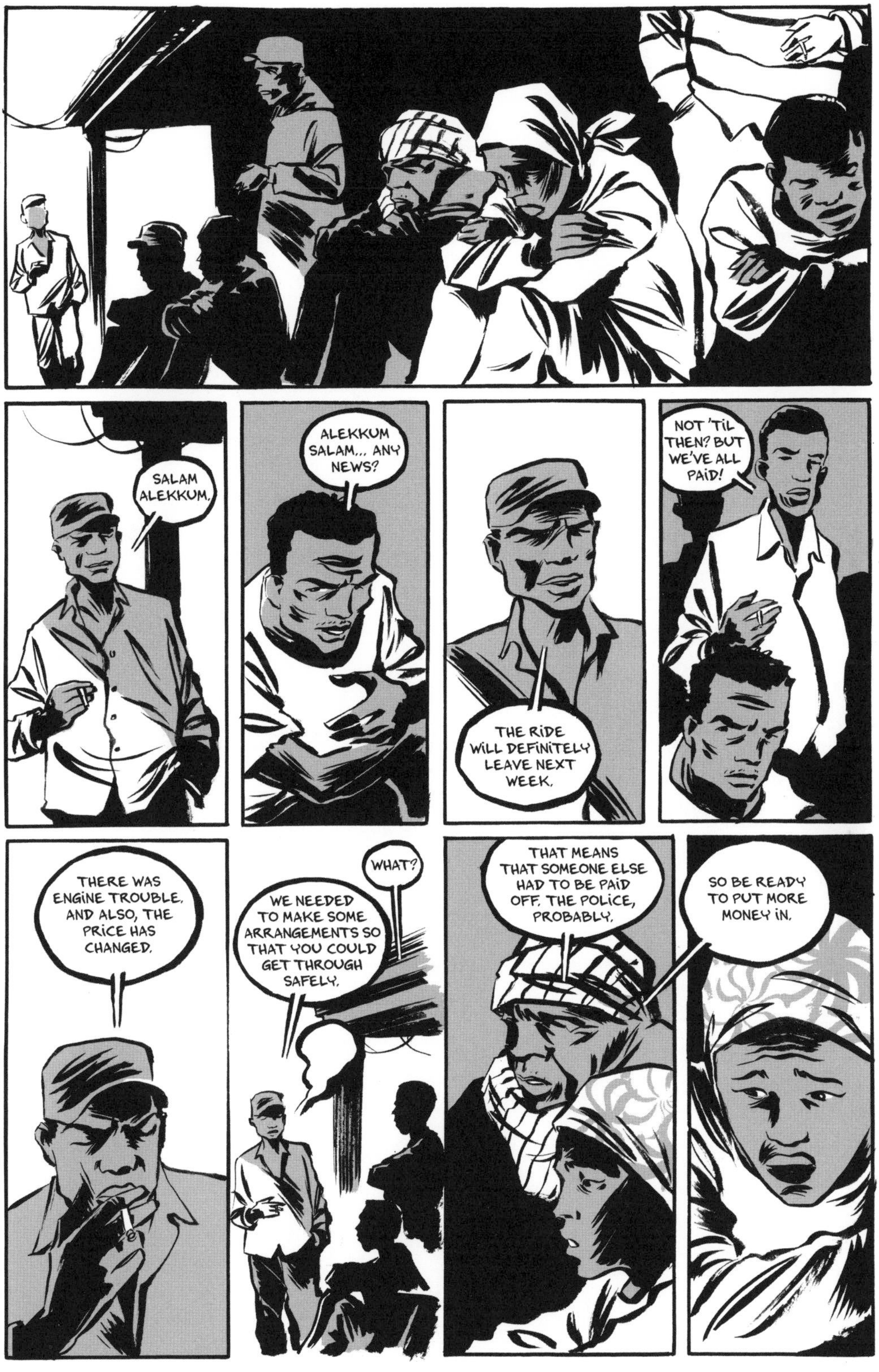
SALAM ALEKKUM.
ALEKKUM SALAM... ANY NEWS?
THE RIDE WILL DEFINITELY LEAVE NEXT WEEK.
NOT 'TIL THEN? BUT WE'VE ALL PAID!
THERE WAS ENGINE TROUBLE, AND ALSO, THE PRICE HAS CHANGED.
WE NEEDED TO MAKE SOME ARRANGEMENTS SO THAT YOU COULD GET THROUGH SAFELY.
WHAT?
THAT MEANS THAT SOMEONE ELSE HAD TO BE PAID OFF. THE POLICE, PROBABLY.
SO BE READY TO PUT MORE MONEY IN.

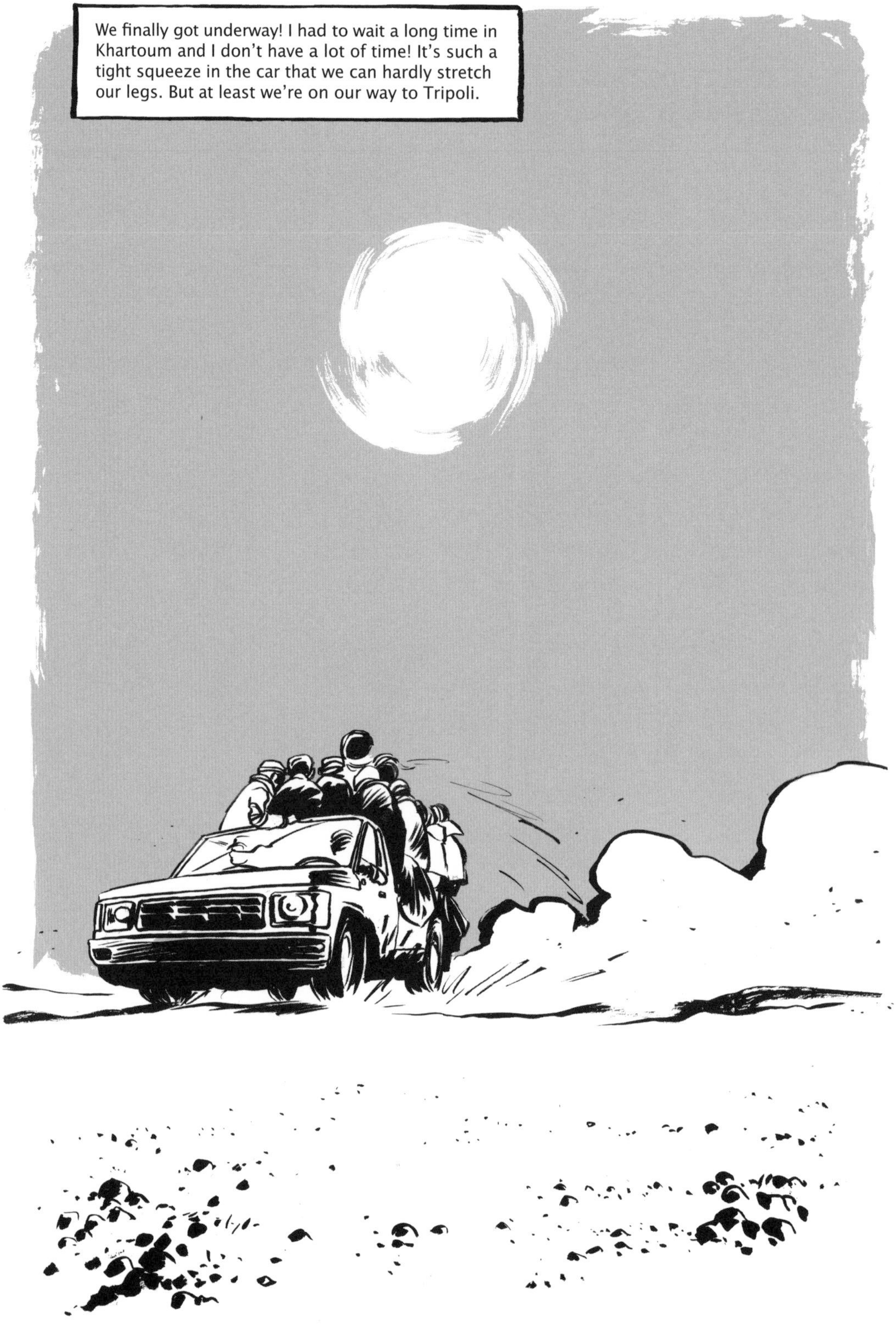
We finally got underway! I had to wait a long time in Khartoum and I don't have a lot of time! It's such a tight squeeze in the car that we can hardly stretch our legs. But at least we're on our way to Tripoli.

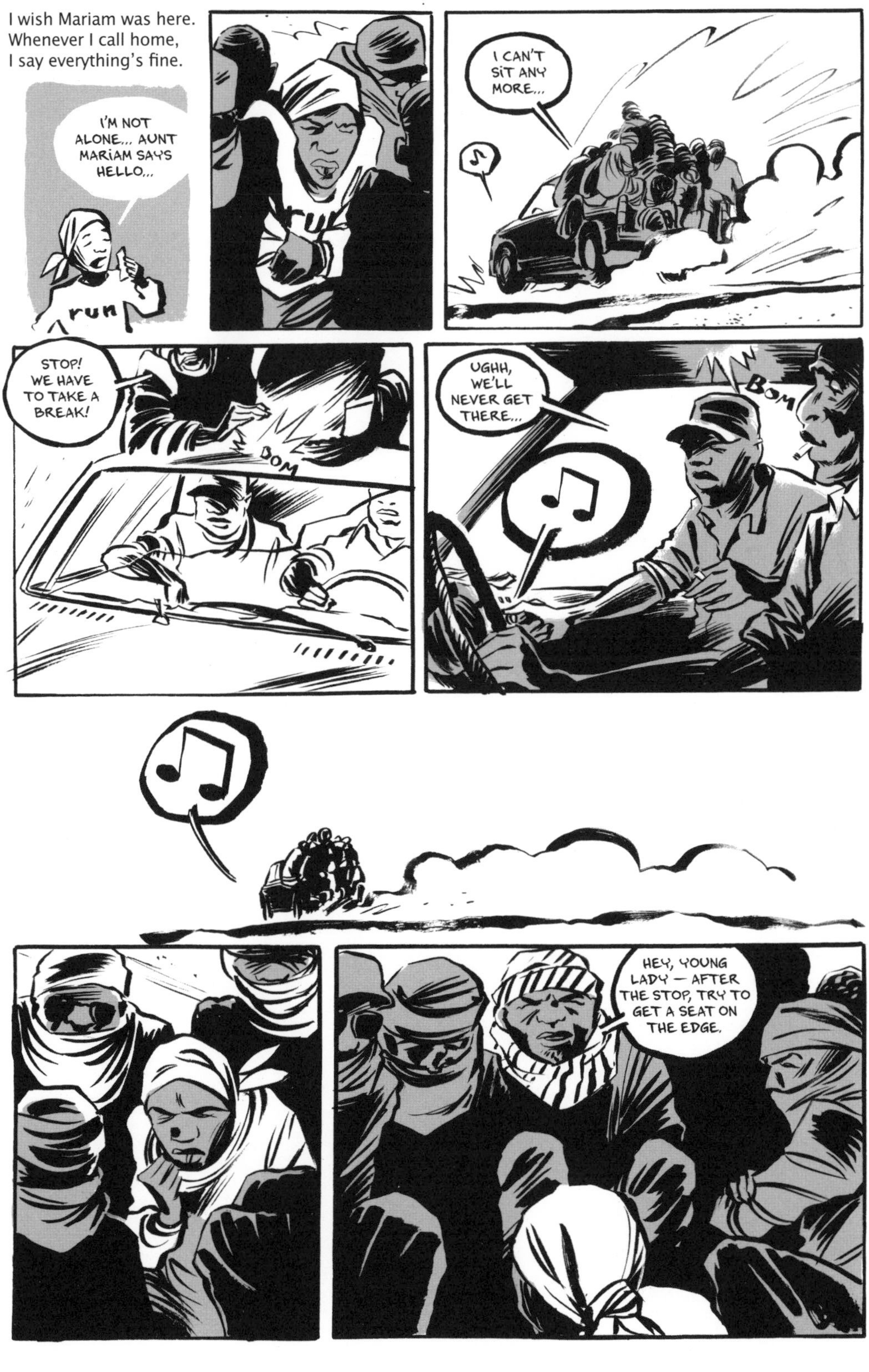
I wish Mariam was here.
Whenever I call home,
I say everything's fine.
I'M NOT ALONE... AUNT MARIAM SAYS HELLO...
run
I CAN'T SIT ANY MORE...
STOP! WE HAVE TO TAKE A BREAK!
BOM
UGHH, WE'LL NEVER GET THERE...
BOM
HEY, YOUNG LADY — AFTER THE STOP, TRY TO GET A SEAT ON THE EDGE.

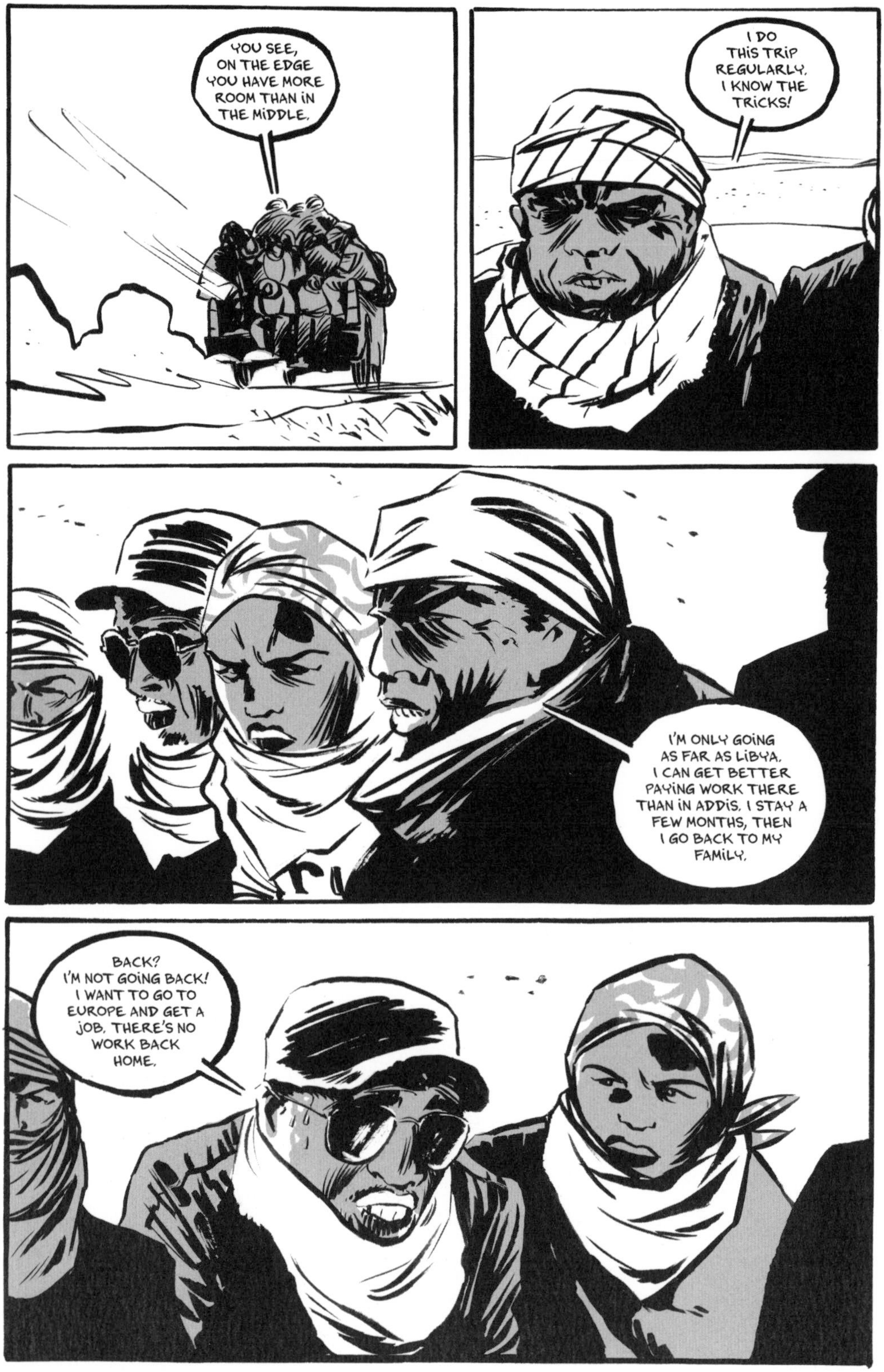
YOU SEE, ON THE EDGE YOU HAVE MORE ROOM THAN IN THE MIDDLE.
I DO THIS TRIP REGULARLY. I KNOW THE TRICKS!
I'M ONLY GOING AS FAR AS LIBYA. I CAN GET BETTER PAYING WORK THERE THAN IN ADDIS. I STAY A FEW MONTHS, THEN I GO BACK TO MY FAMILY.
BACK? I'M NOT GOING BACK! I WANT TO GO TO EUROPE AND GET A JOB. THERE'S NO WORK BACK HOME.

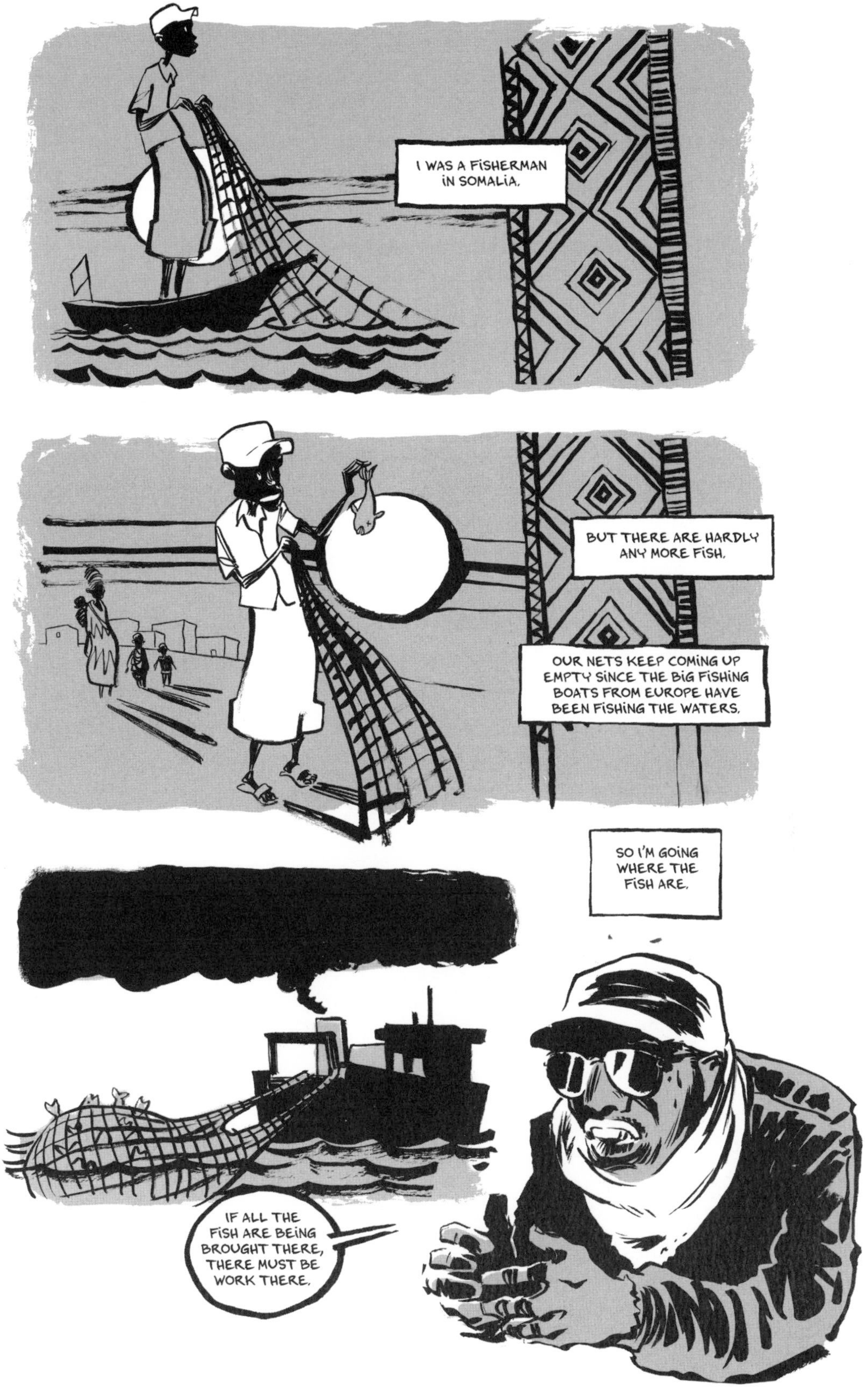
I WAS A FISHERMAN IN SOMALIA.
BUT THERE ARE HARDLY ANY MORE FISH.
OUR NETS KEEP COMING UP EMPTY SINCE THE BIG FISHING BOATS FROM EUROPE HAVE BEEN FISHING THE WATERS.
SO I'M GOING WHERE THE FISH ARE.
IF ALL THE FISH ARE BEING BROUGHT THERE, THERE MUST BE WORK THERE.

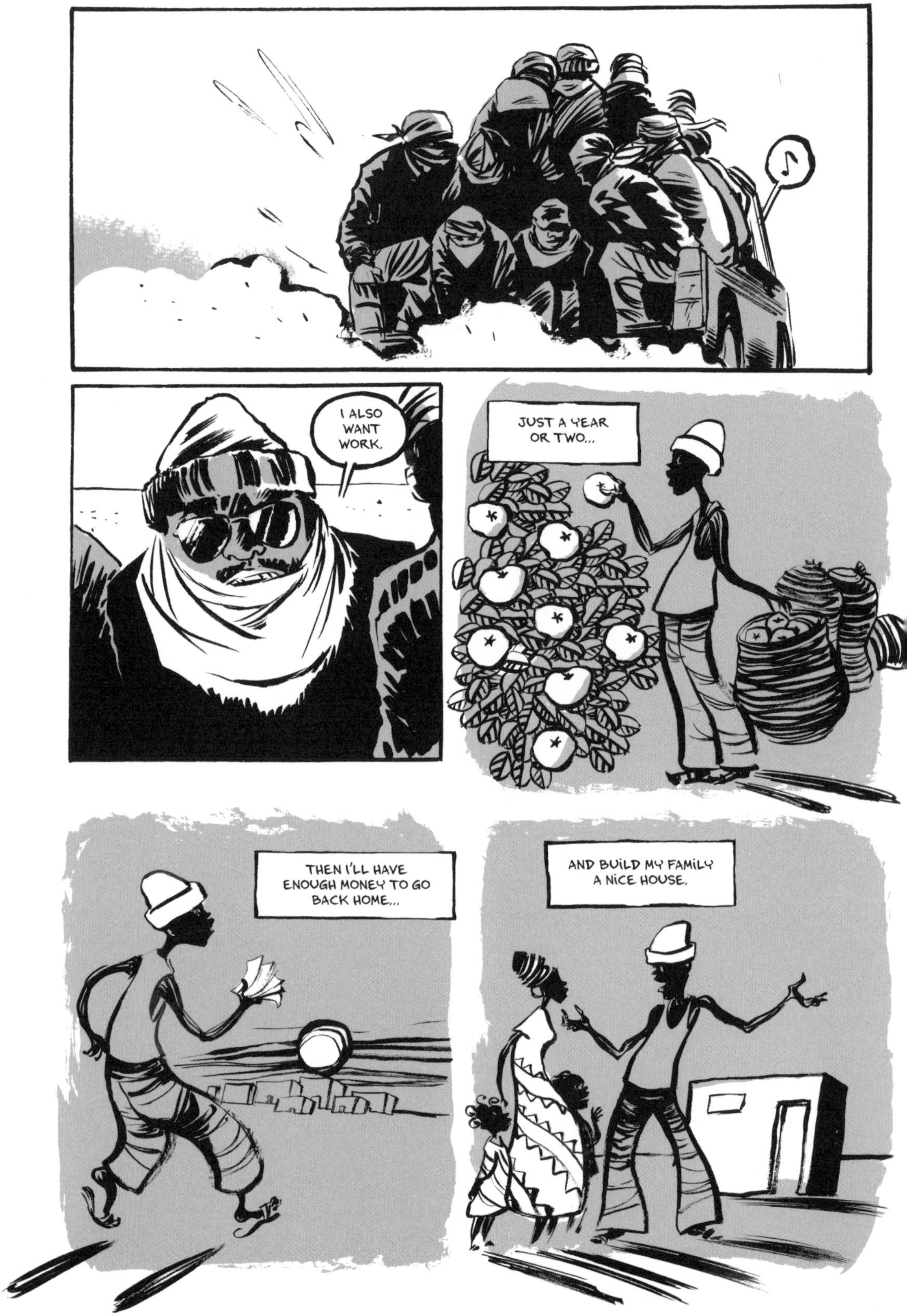

I ALSO WANT WORK.
JUST A YEAR OR TWO...
THEN I'LL HAVE ENOUGH MONEY TO GO BACK HOME...
AND BUILD MY FAMILY A NICE HOUSE.

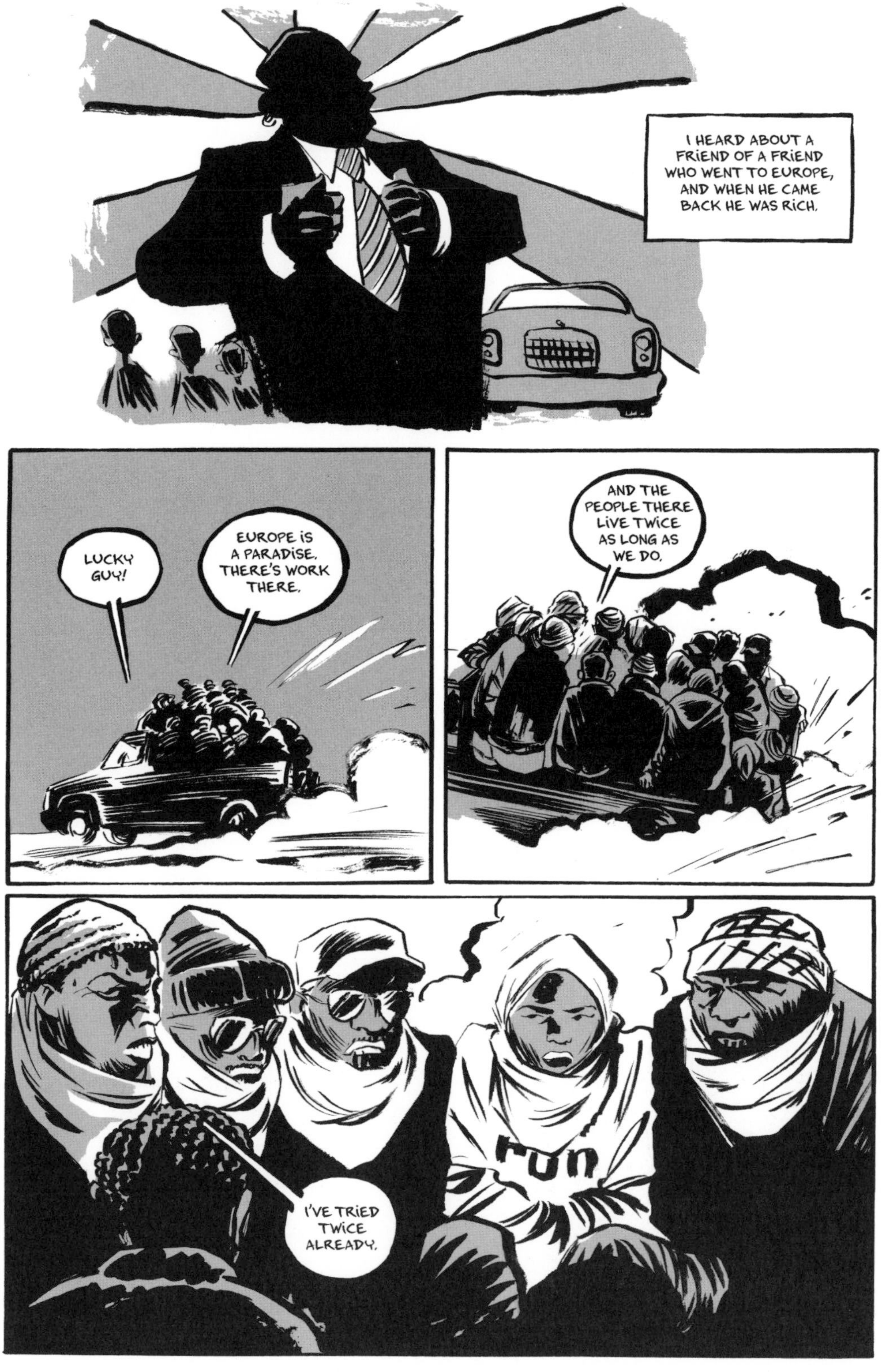
I HEARD ABOUT A FRIEND OF A FRIEND WHO WENT TO EUROPE, AND WHEN HE CAME BACK HE WAS RICH.
LUCKY GUY!
EUROPE IS A PARADISE. THERE'S WORK THERE.
AND THE PEOPLE THERE LIVE TWICE AS LONG AS WE DO.
run
I'VE TRIED TWICE ALREADY.

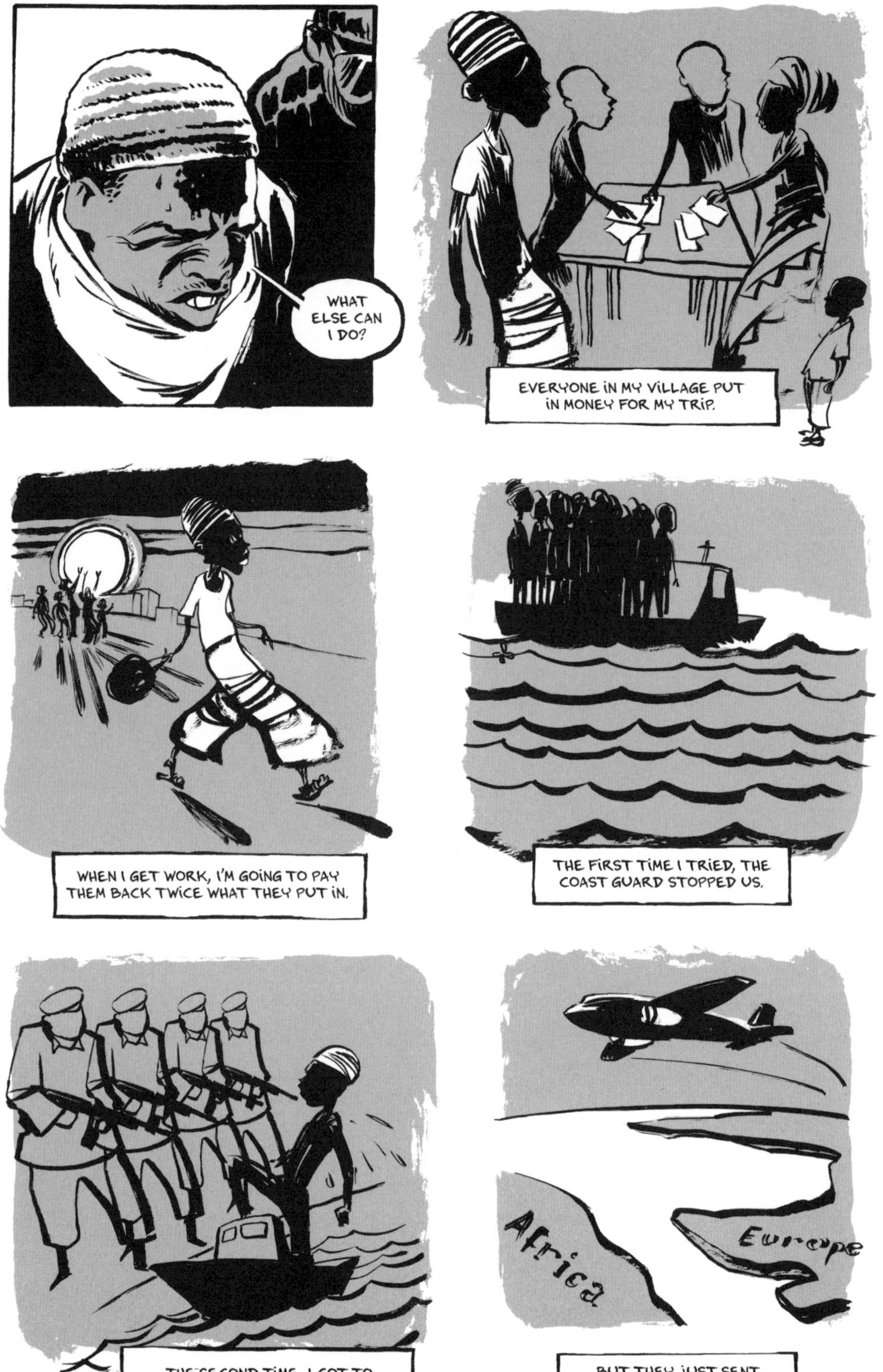
WHAT ELSE CAN I DO?
EVERYONE IN MY VILLAGE PUT IN MONEY FOR MY TRIP.
WHEN I GET WORK, I'M GOING TO PAY THEM BACK TWICE WHAT THEY PUT IN.
THE FIRST TIME I TRIED, THE COAST GUARD STOPPED US.
THE SECOND TIME, I GOT TO ITALY AND WAS SURE I'D DONE IT.
Africa
Europe
BUT THEY JUST SENT ME BACK.

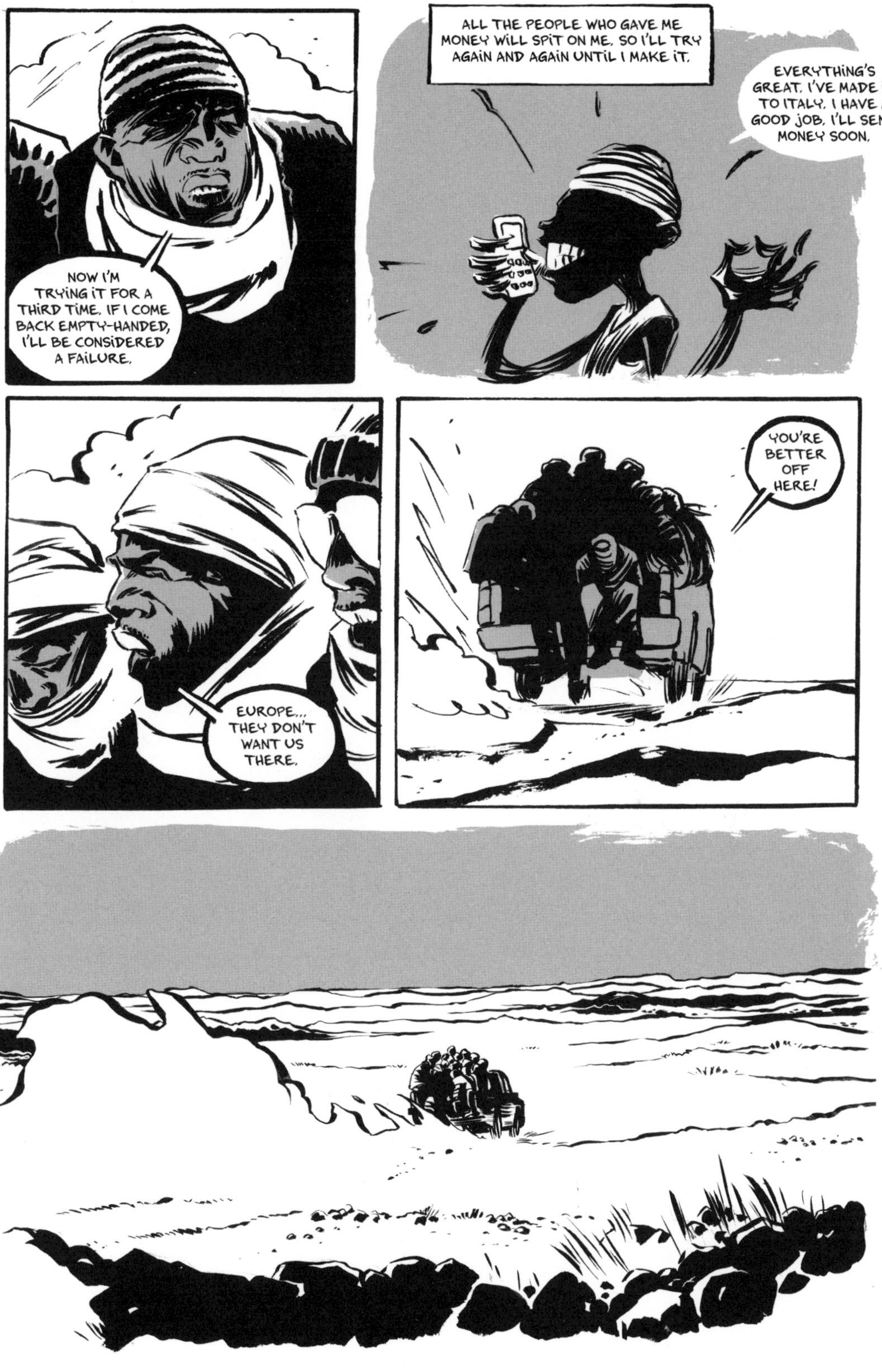
NOW I'M TRYING IT FOR A THIRD TIME. IF I COME BACK EMPTY-HANDED, I'LL BE CONSIDERED A FAILURE.
ALL THE PEOPLE WHO GAVE ME MONEY WILL SPIT ON ME, SO I'LL TRY AGAIN AND AGAIN UNTIL I MAKE IT.
EVERYTHING'S GREAT. I'VE MADE IT TO ITALY. I HAVE A GOOD JOB. I'LL SEND MONEY SOON.
EUROPE... THEY DON'T WANT US THERE.
YOU'RE BETTER OFF HERE!

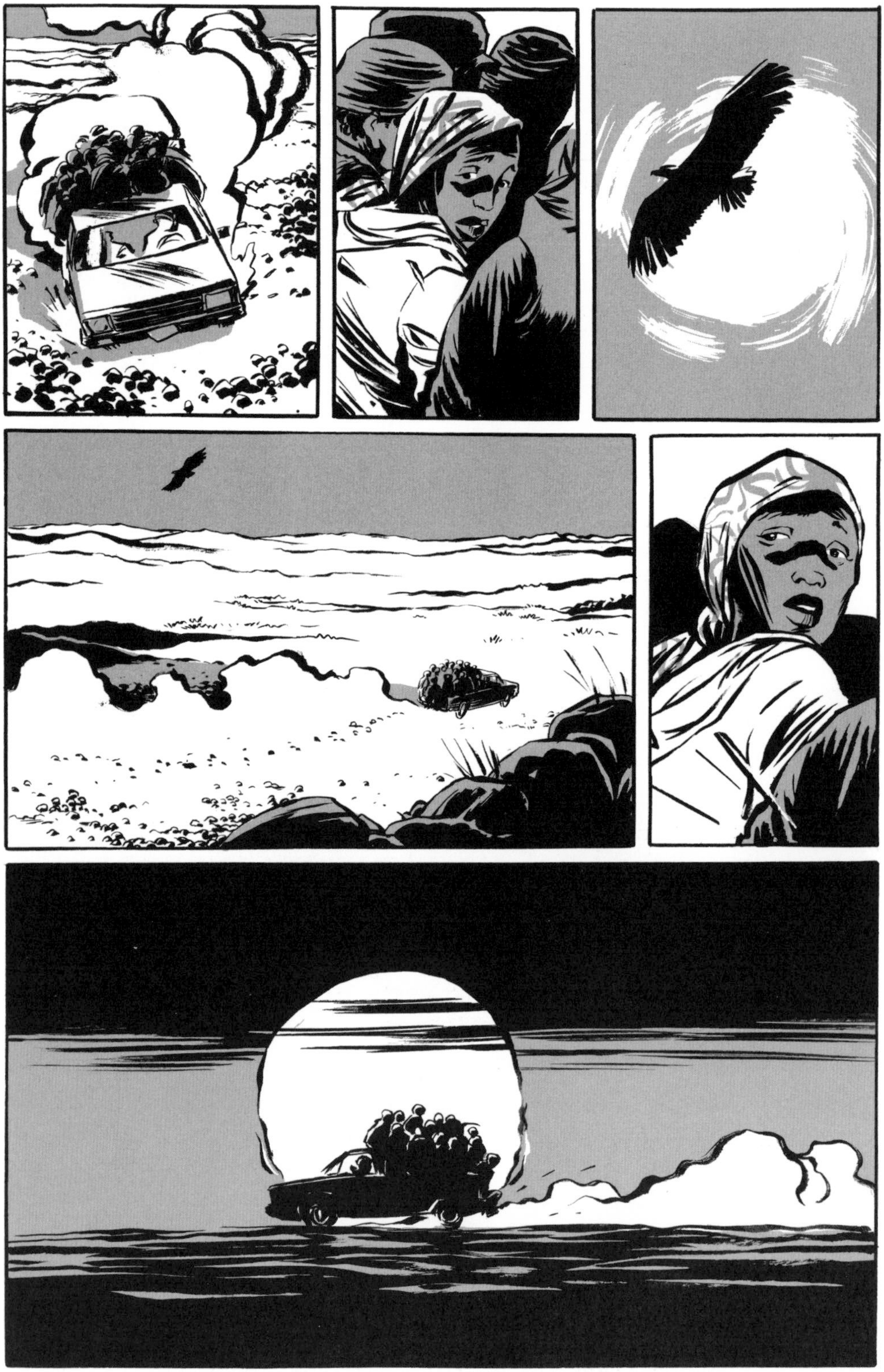

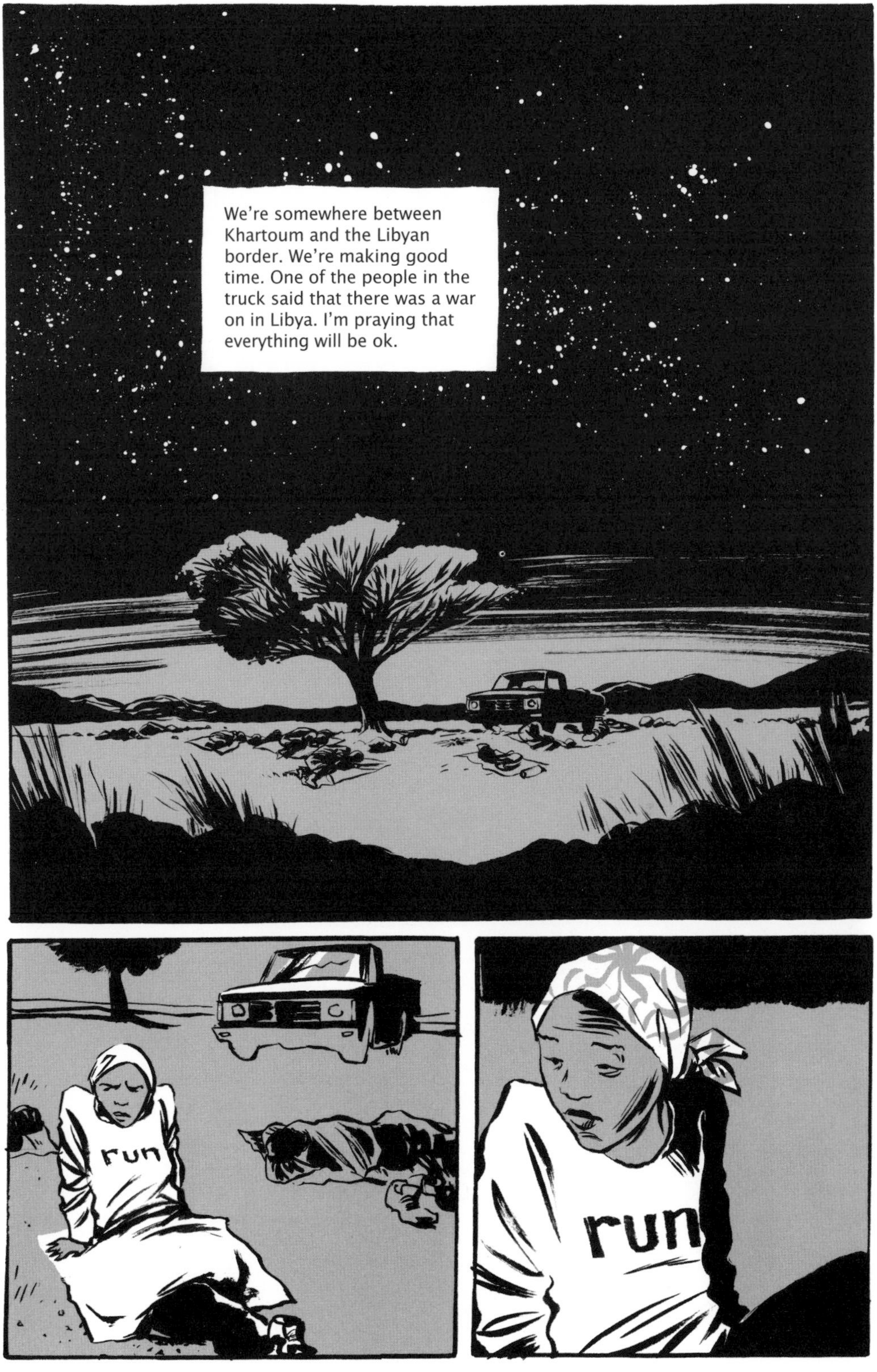
We're somewhere between Khartoum and the Libyan border. We're making good time. One of the people in the truck said that there was a war on in Libya. I'm praying that everything will be ok.
run
run

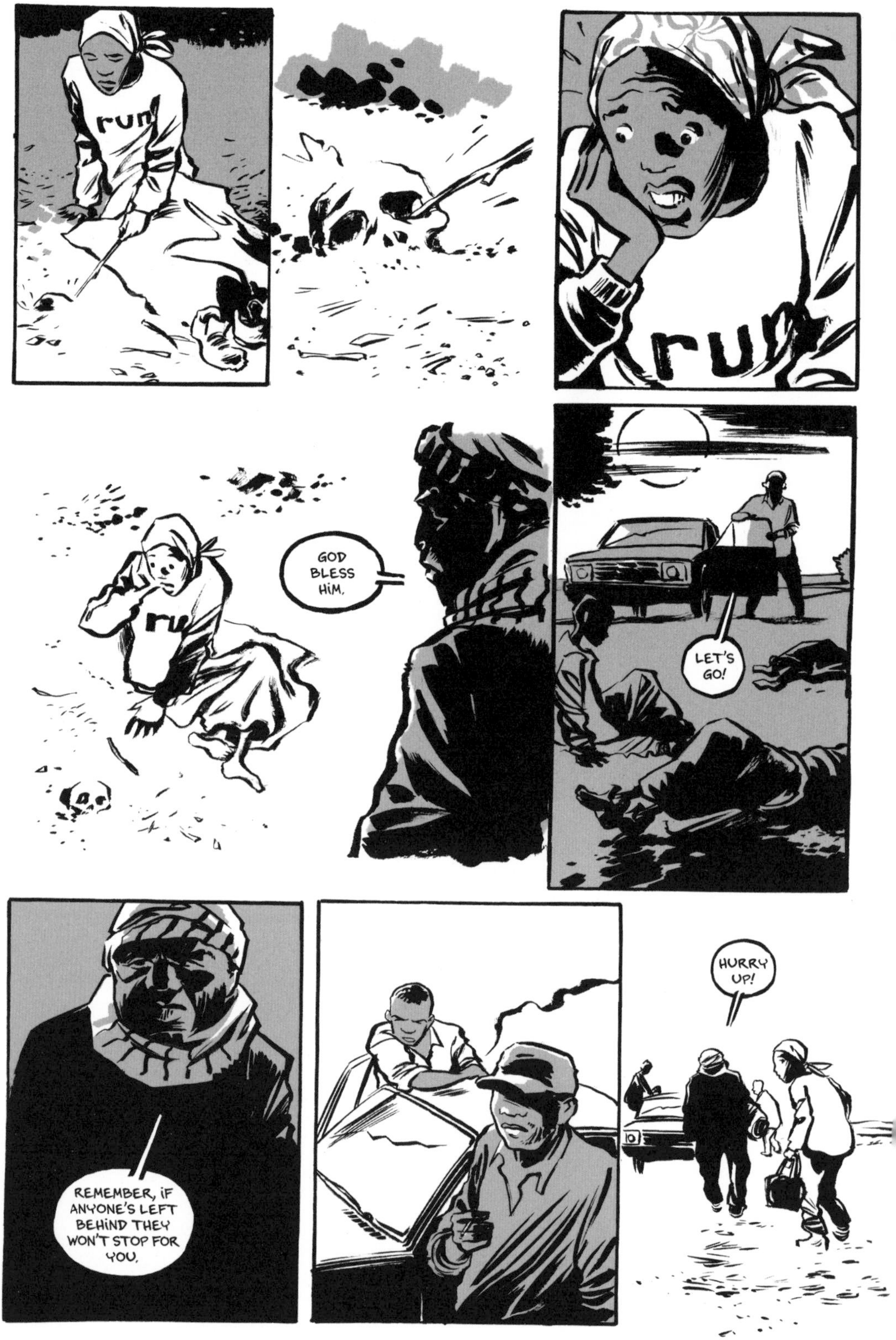
run
run
run
run
GOD BLESS HIM.
LET'S GO!
REMEMBER, IF ANYONE'S LEFT BEHIND THEY WON'T STOP FOR YOU.
HURRY UP!

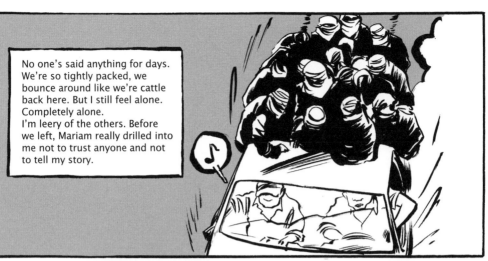

No one's said anything for days. We're so tightly packed, we bounce around like we're cattle back here. But I still feel alone. Completely alone.
I'm leery of the others. Before we left, Mariam really drilled into me not to trust anyone and not to tell my story.

How long has it been since I've heard someone laugh? I miss the children, my mother, my home. Where am I? And when will I have another chance to send a message?

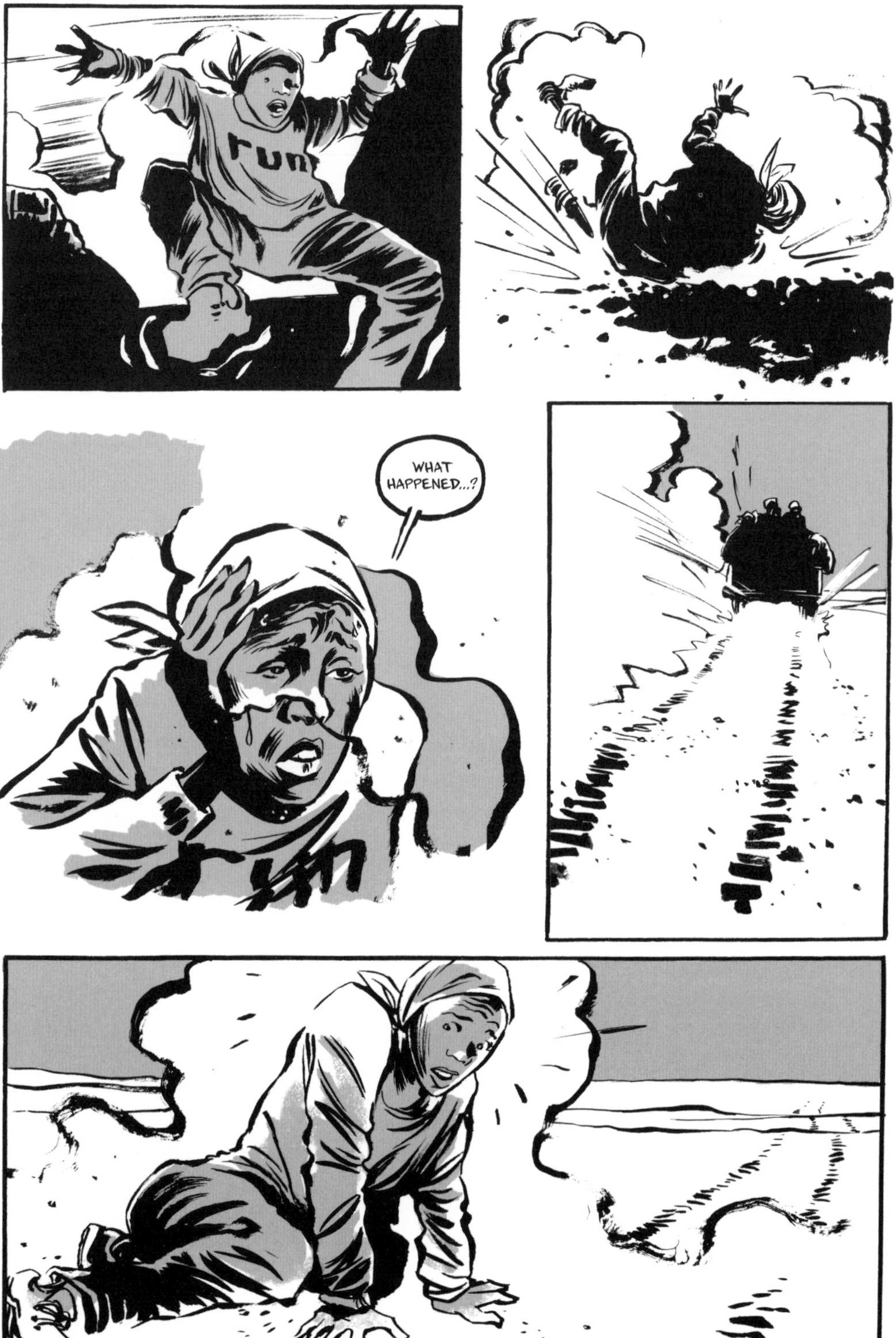
WHAT HAPPENED...?

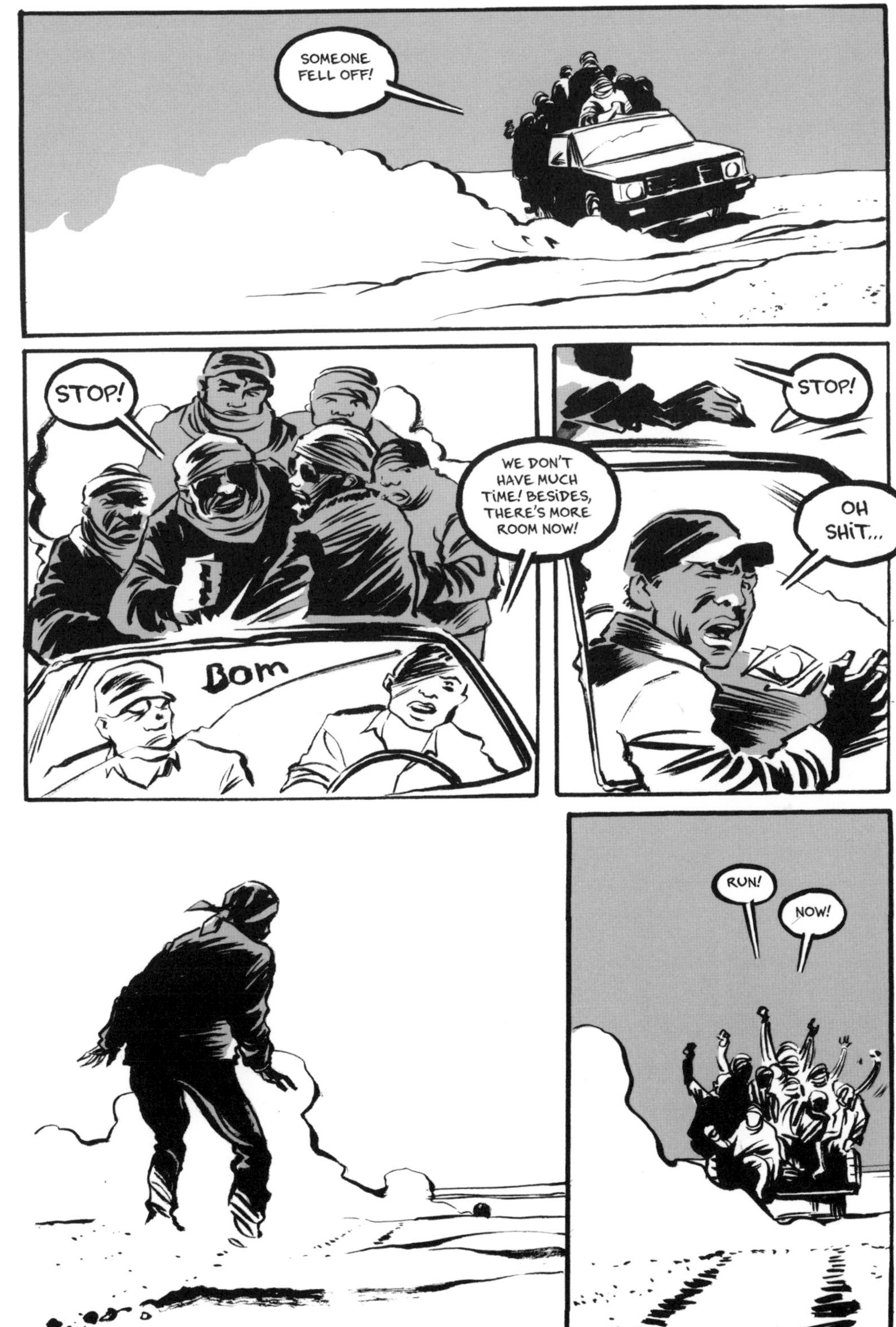
SOMEONE FELL OFF!
STOP!
Bom
WE DON'T HAVE MUCH TIME! BESIDES, THERE'S MORE ROOM NOW!
STOP!
OH SHIT...
RUN!
NOW!

run
H
HH
STAY AWAKE NOW!!

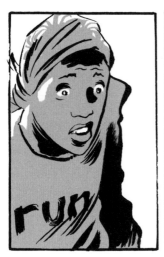

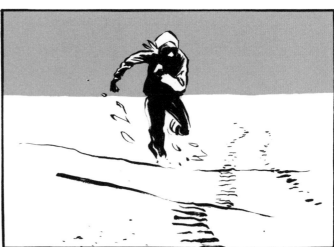

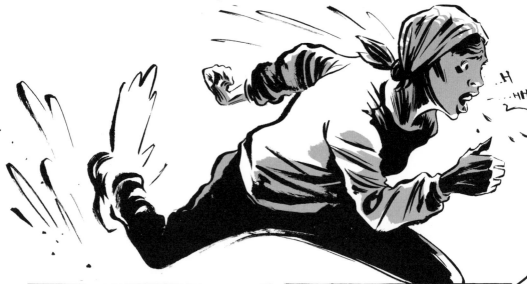

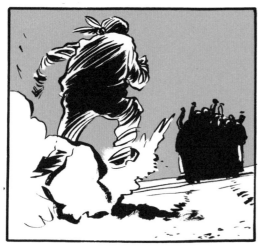

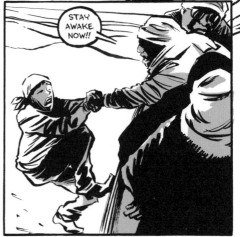

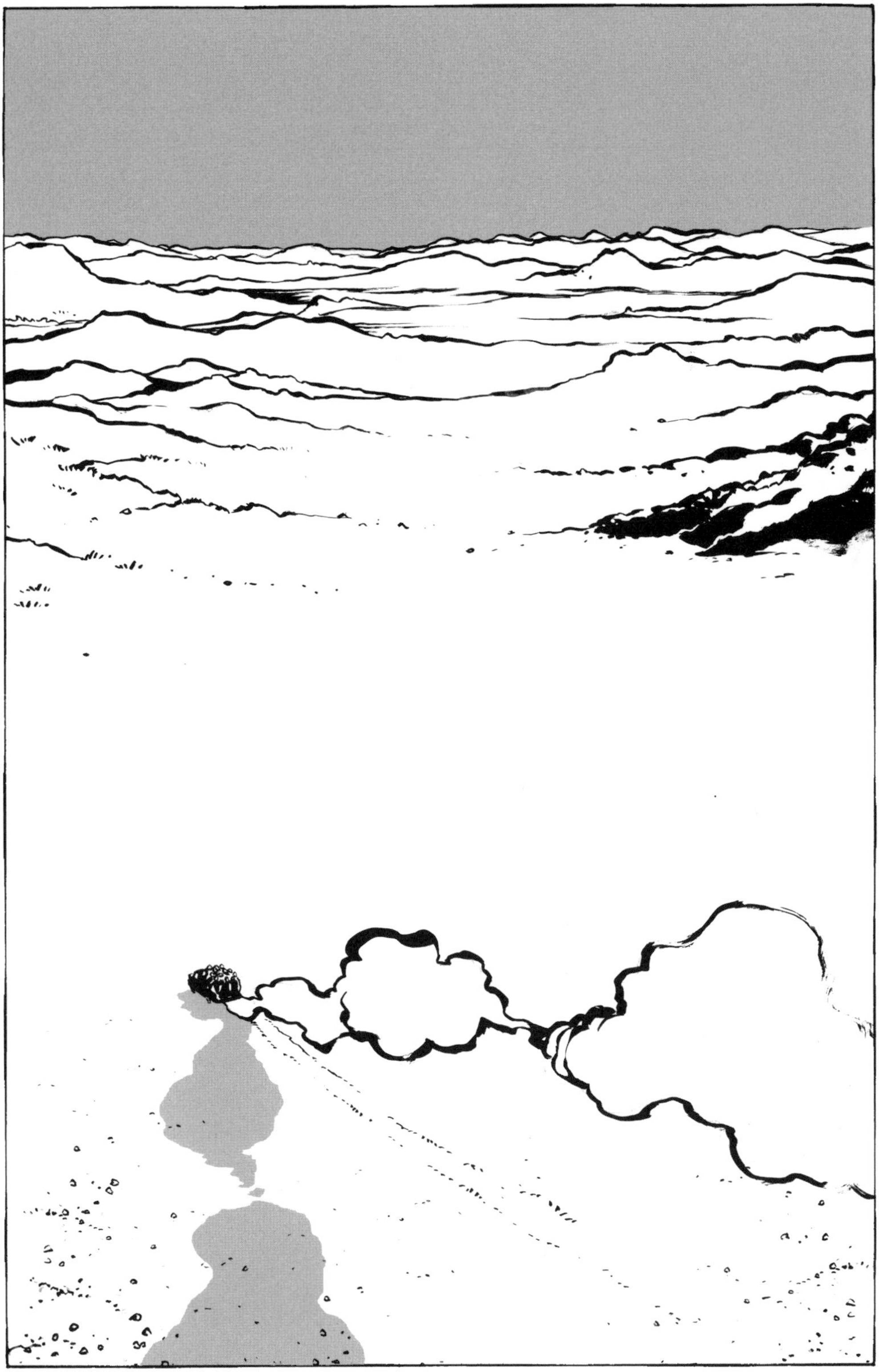

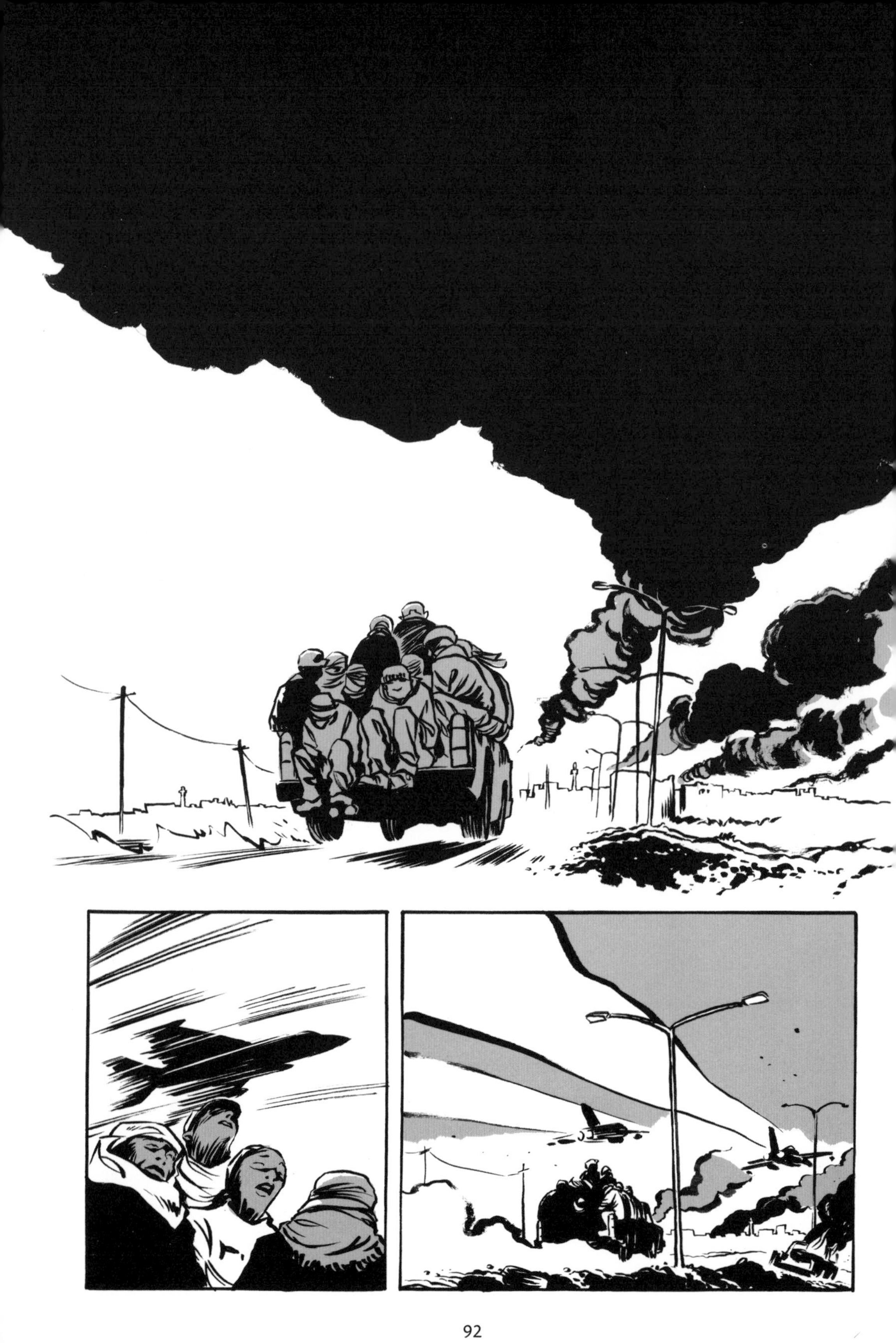

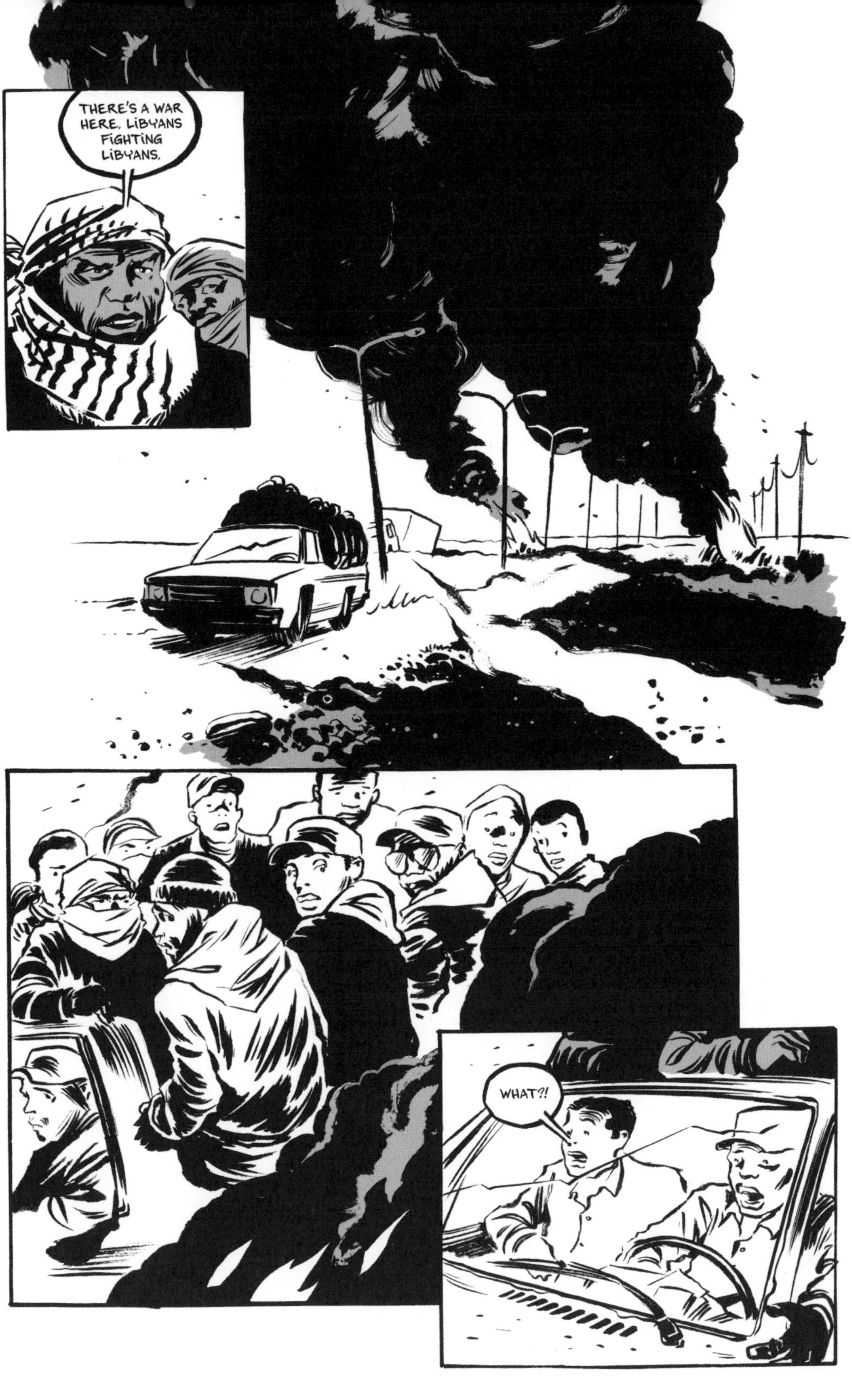
THERE'S A WAR HERE. LIBYANS FIGHTING LIBYANS.
WHAT?!

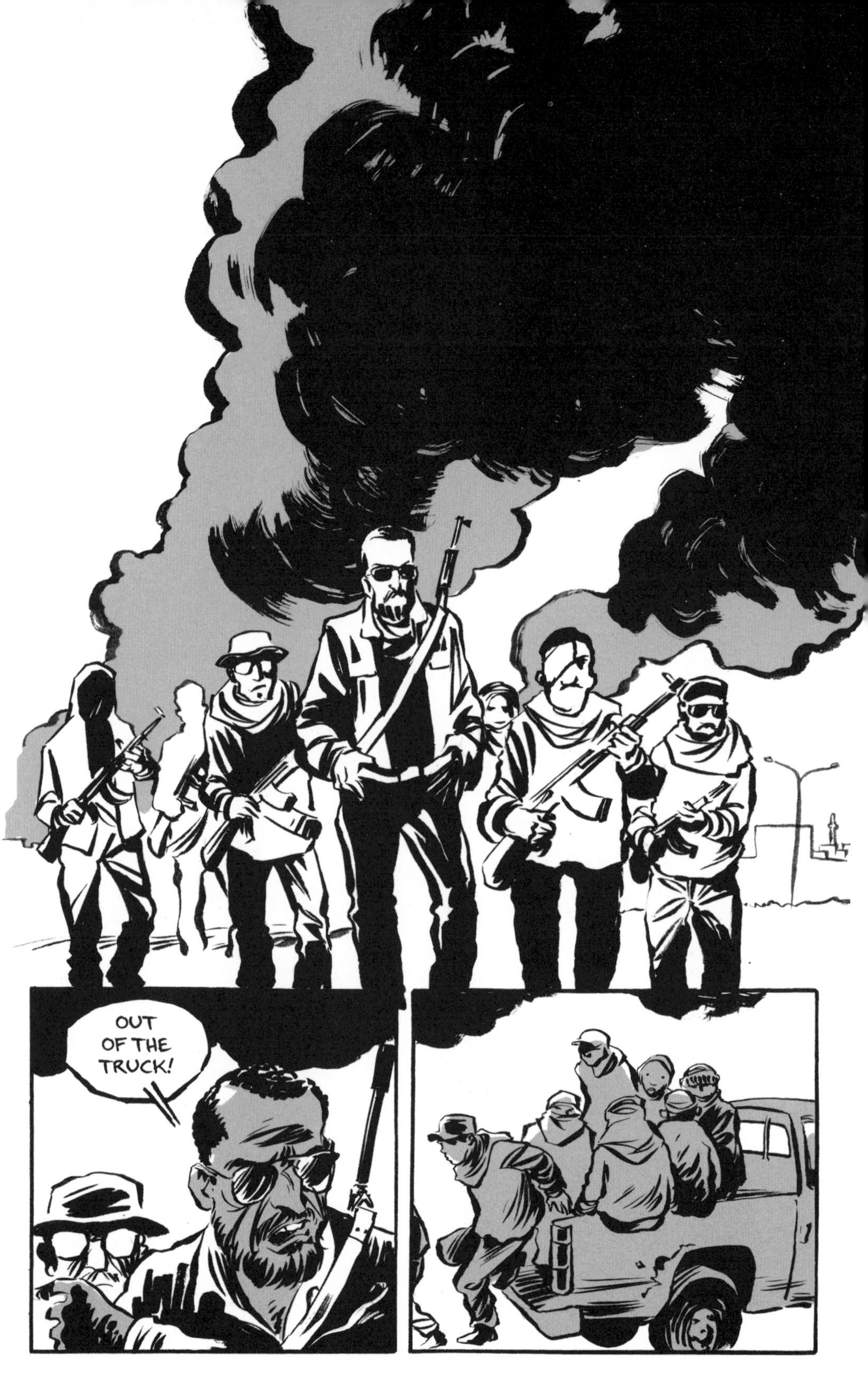
OUT OF THE TRUCK!

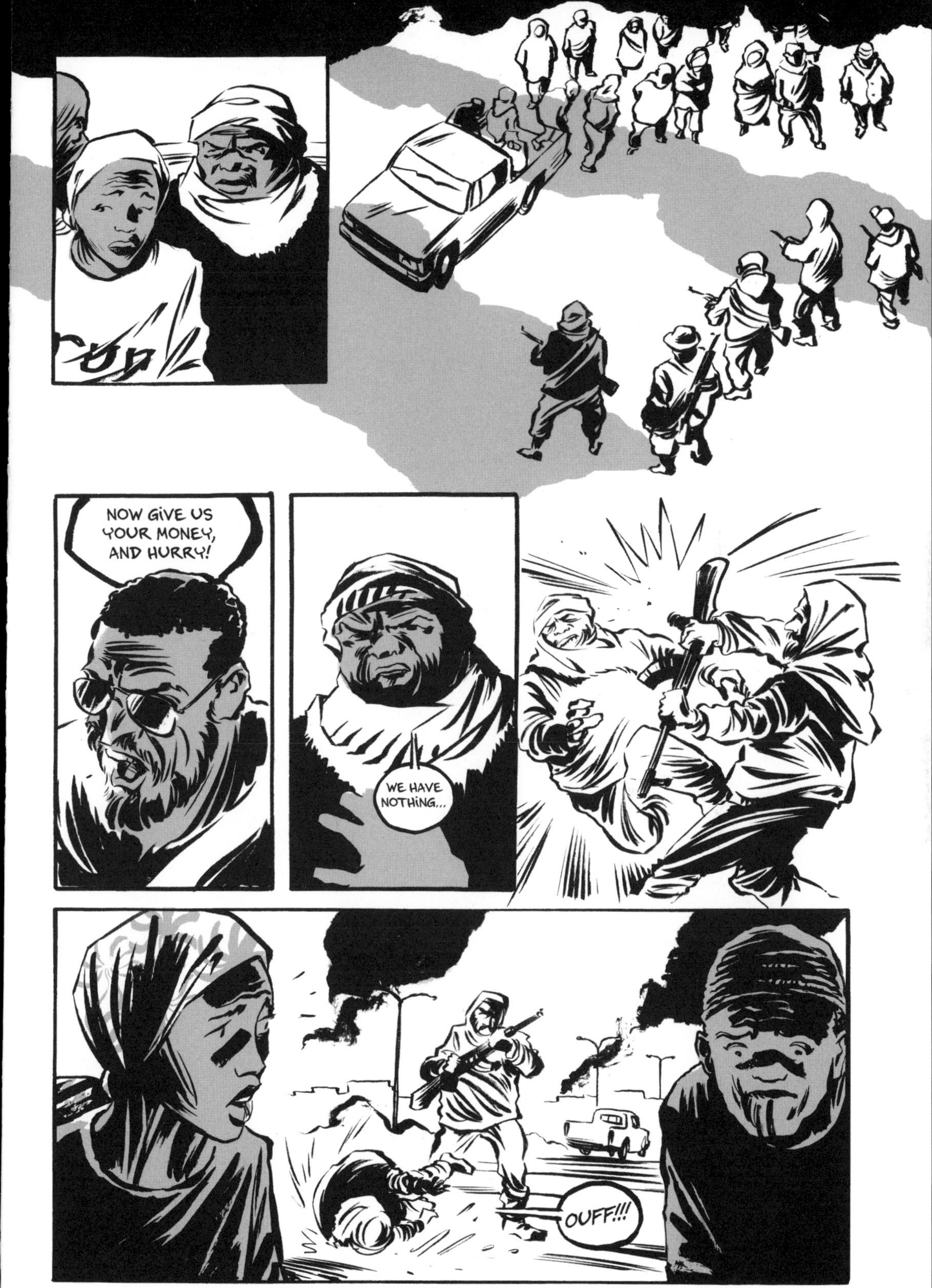
NOW GIVE US YOUR MONEY, AND HURRY!
WE HAVE NOTHING...
OUFF!!!

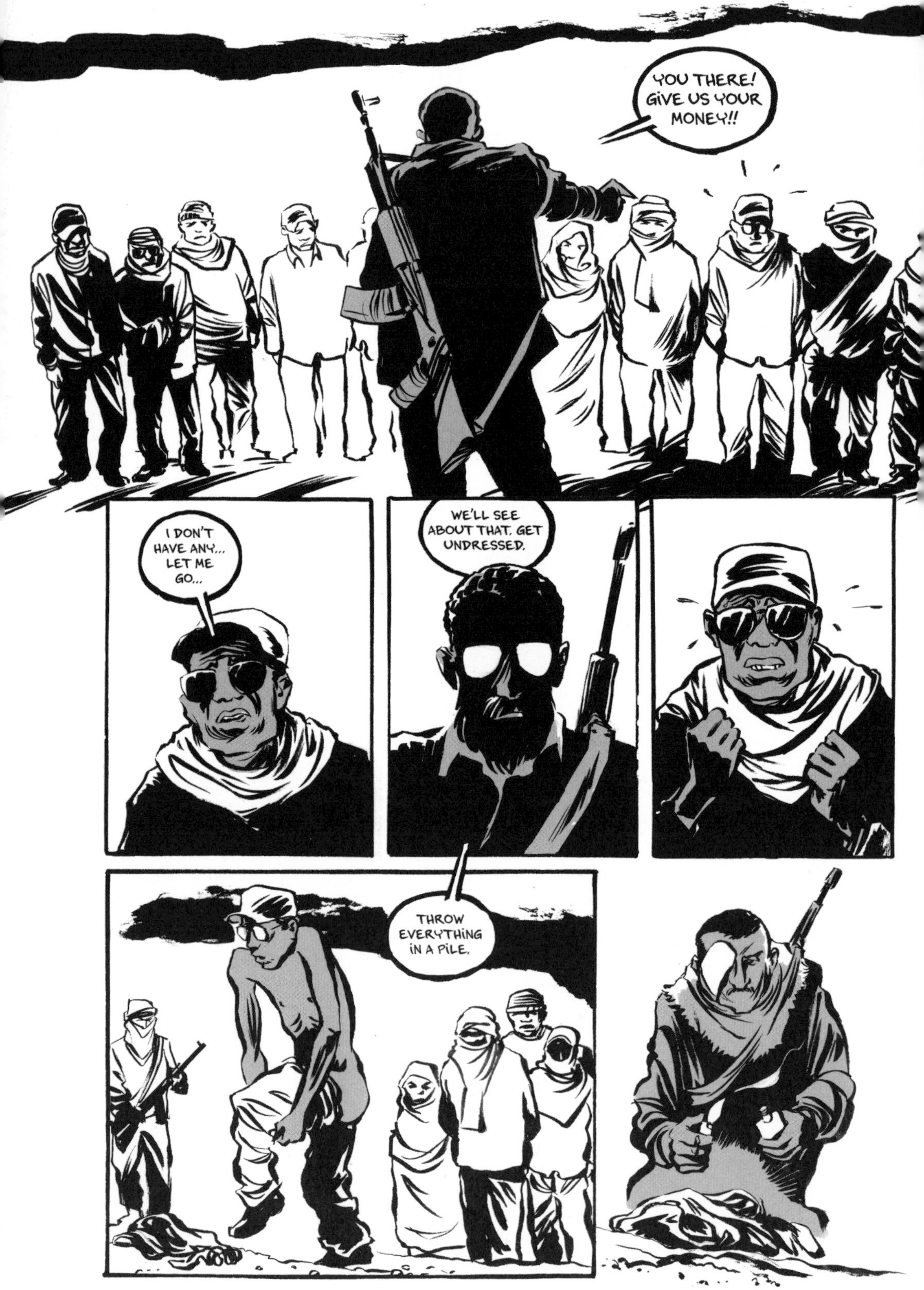
YOU THERE! GIVE US YOUR MONEY!!
I DON'T HAVE ANY... LET ME GO...
WE'LL SEE ABOUT THAT. GET UNDRESSED.
THROW EVERYTHING IN A PILE.

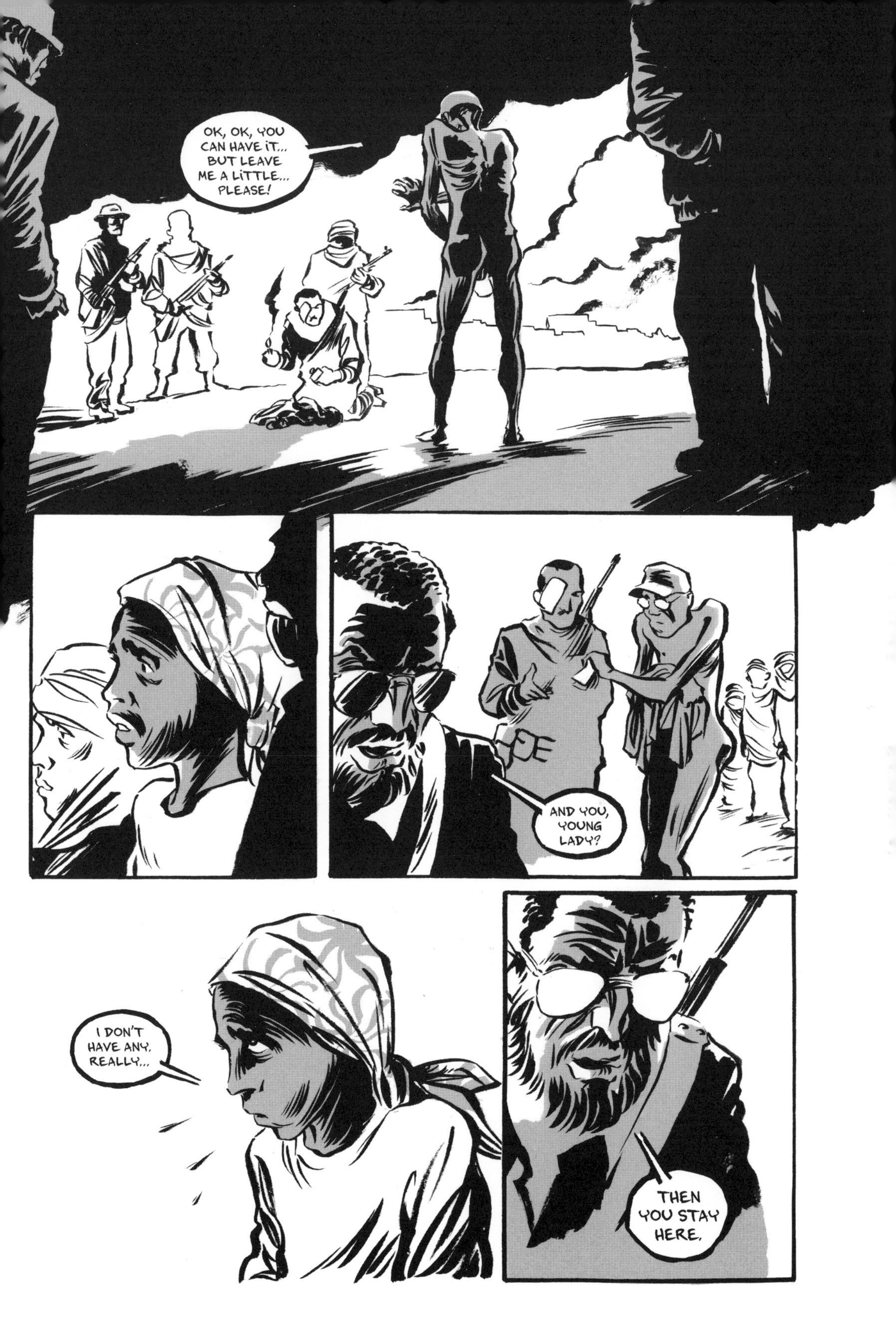
OK, OK, YOU CAN HAVE IT... BUT LEAVE ME A LITTLE... PLEASE!
AND YOU, YOUNG LADY?
I DON'T HAVE ANY, REALLY...
THEN YOU STAY HERE.

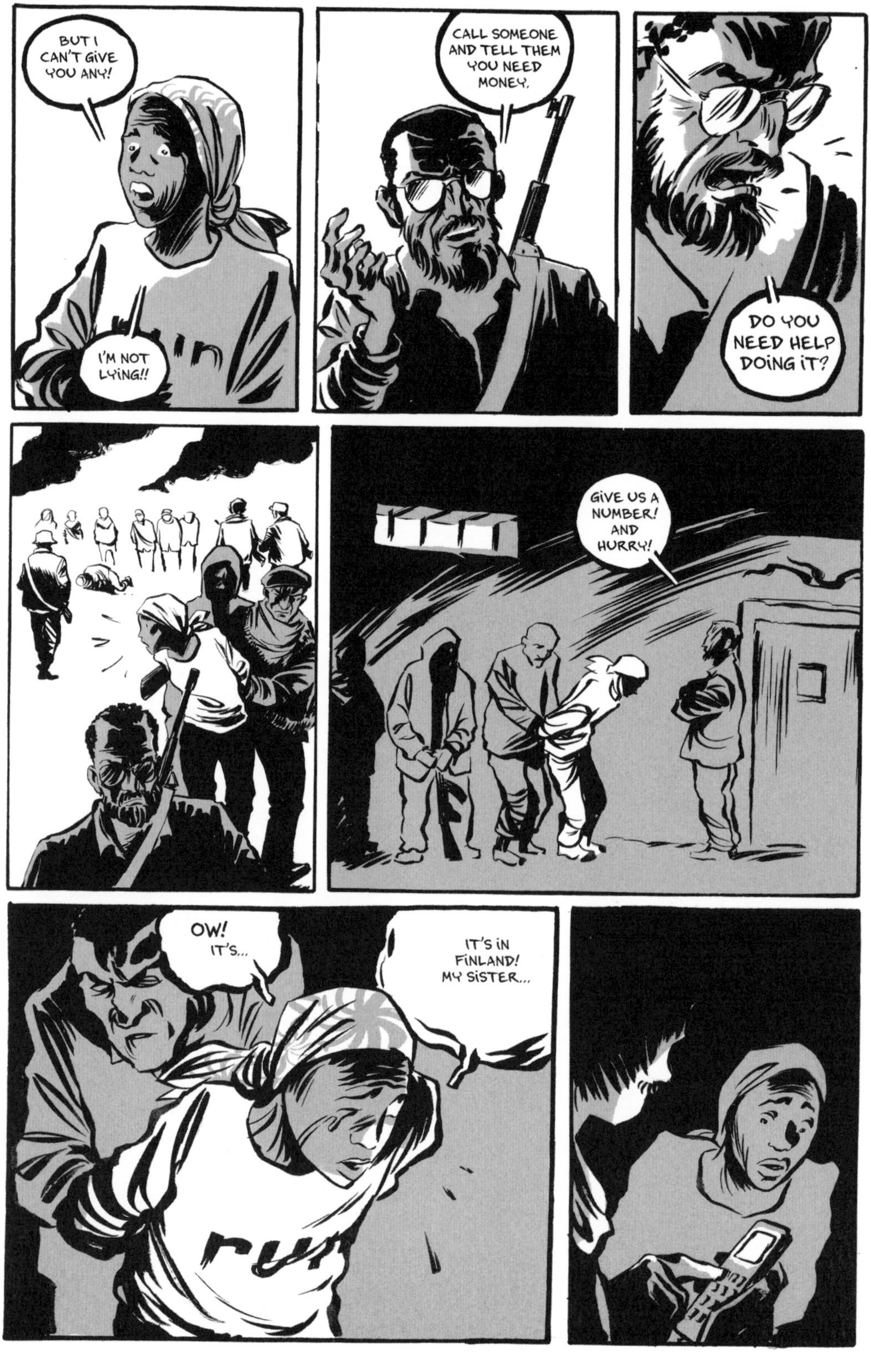
BUT I CAN'T GIVE YOU ANY!
I'M NOT LYING!!
CALL SOMEONE AND TELL THEM YOU NEED MONEY.
DO YOU NEED HELP DOING IT?
GIVE US A NUMBER! AND HURRY!
OW! IT'S...
IT'S IN FINLAND! MY SISTER...

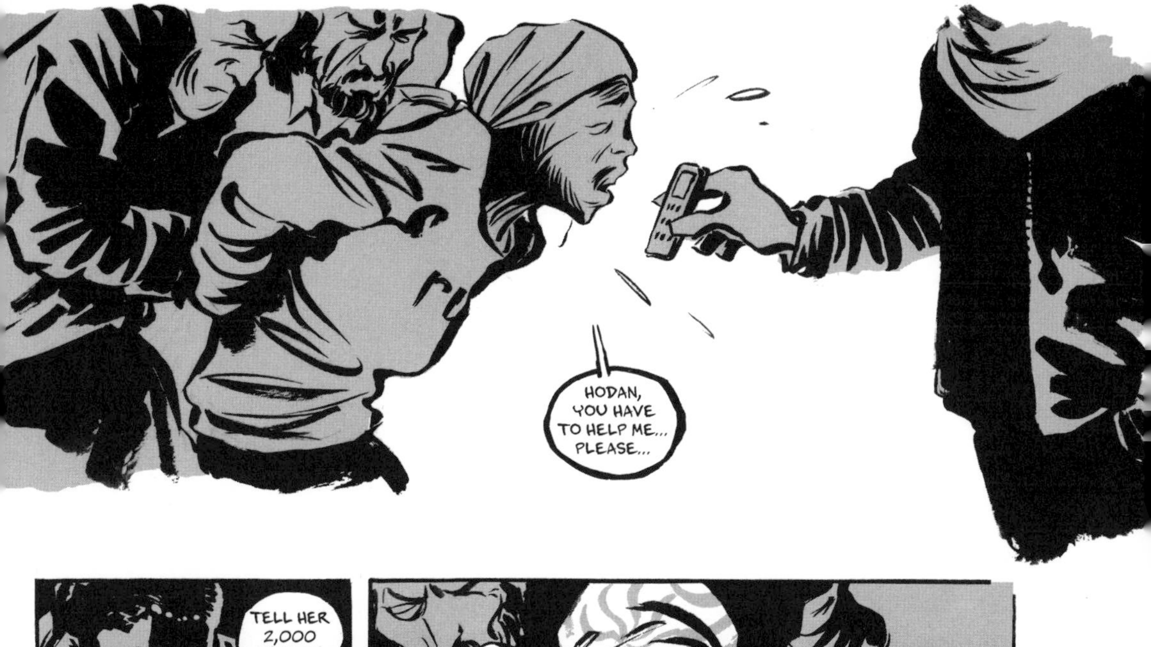
HODAN, YOU HAVE TO HELP ME... PLEASE...

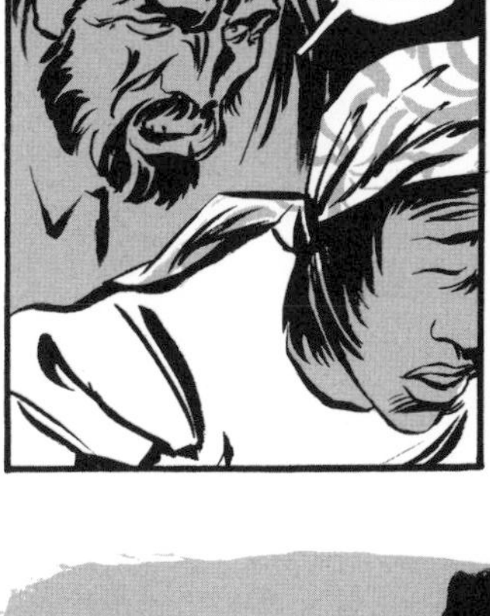
TELL HER 2,000 DINARS!

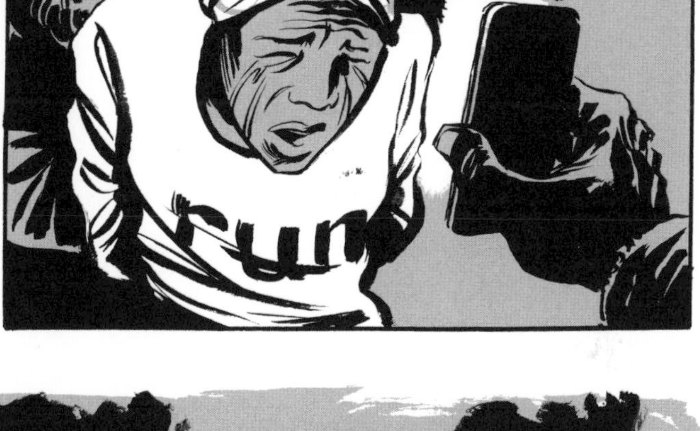

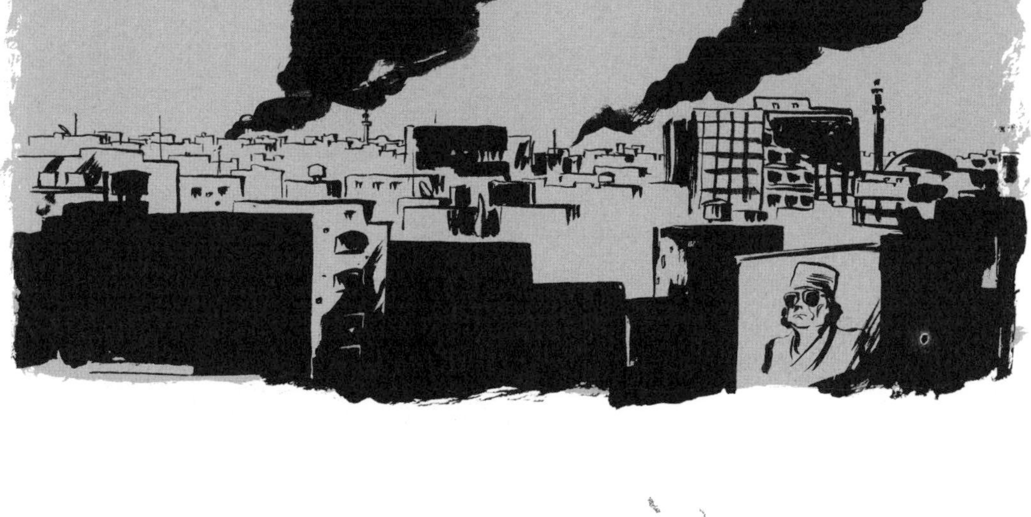

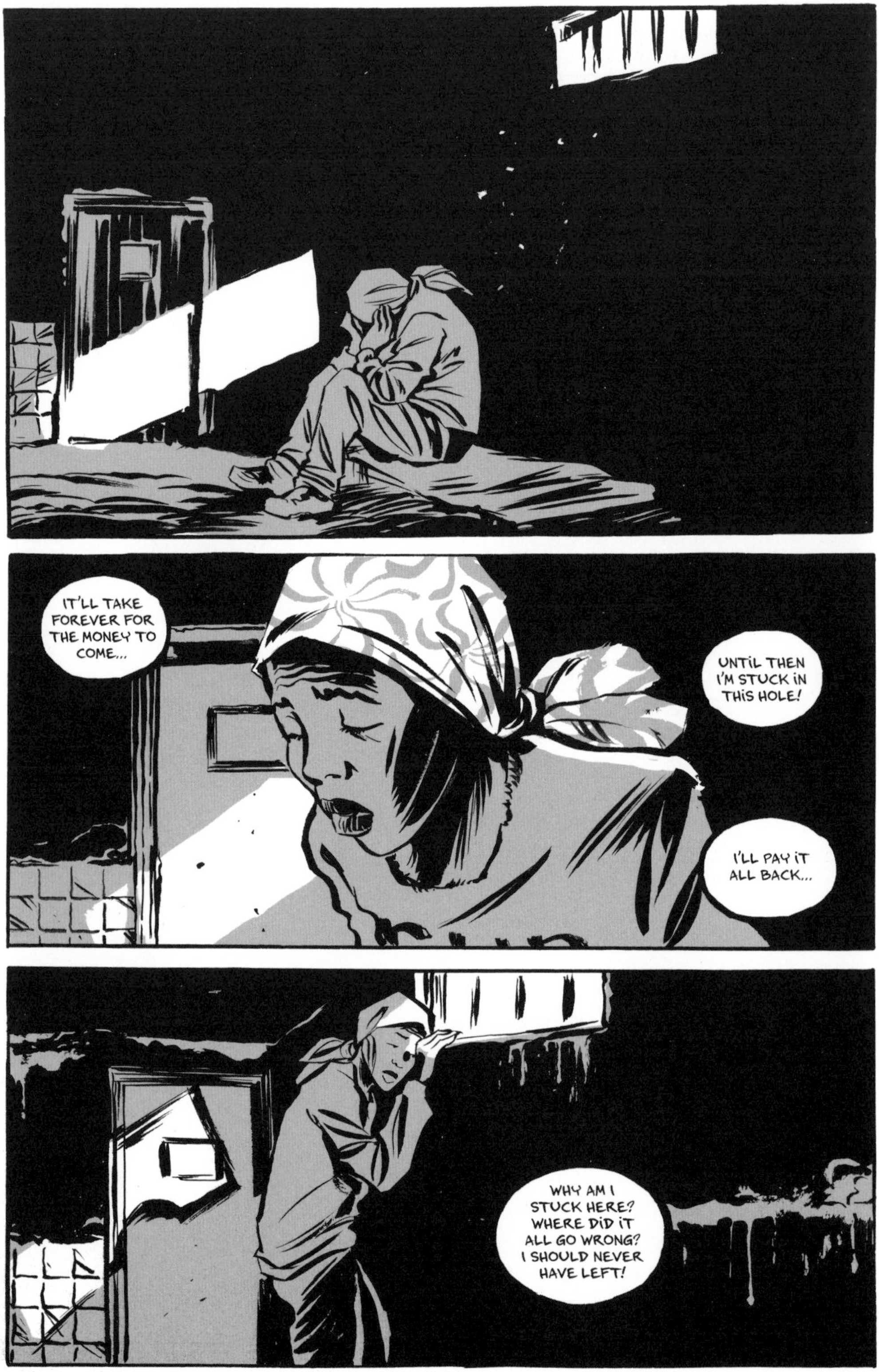
IT'LL TAKE FOREVER FOR THE MONEY TO COME...
UNTIL THEN I'M STUCK IN THIS HOLE!
I'LL PAY IT ALL BACK...
WHY AM I STUCK HERE? WHERE DID IT ALL GO WRONG? I SHOULD NEVER HAVE LEFT!

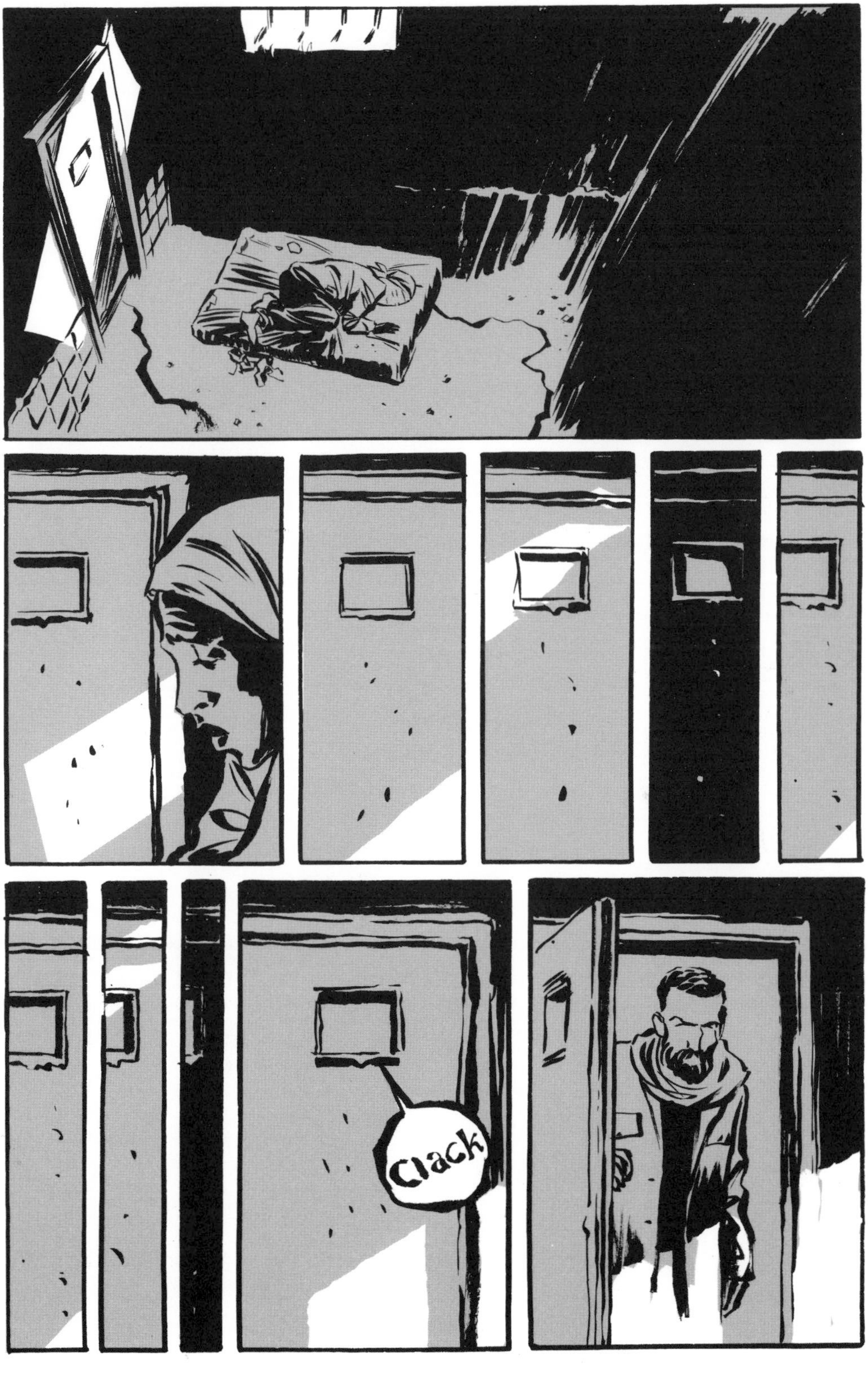
Clack

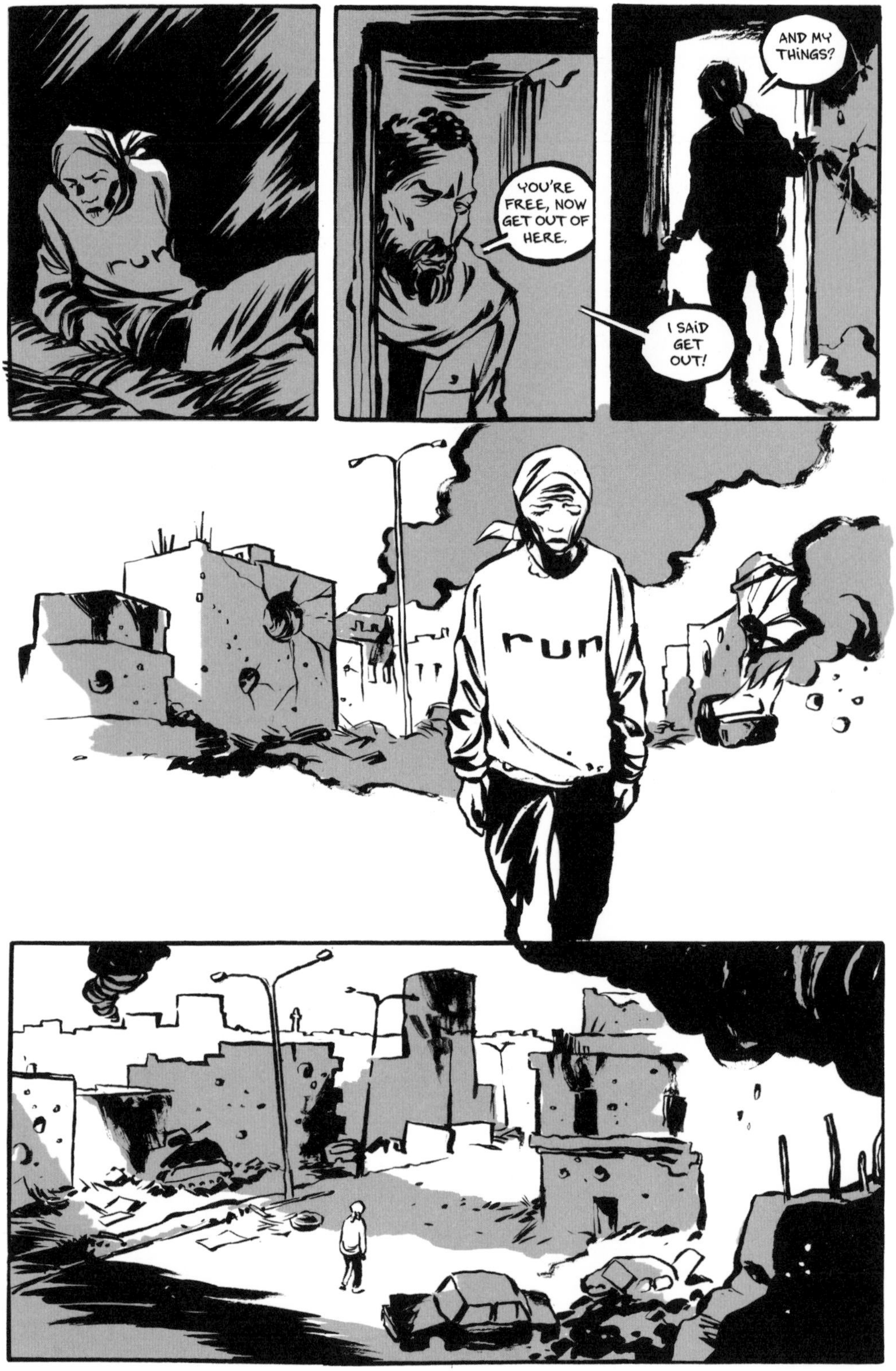
run
YOU'RE FREE, NOW GET OUT OF HERE.
AND MY THINGS?
I SAID GET OUT!
run

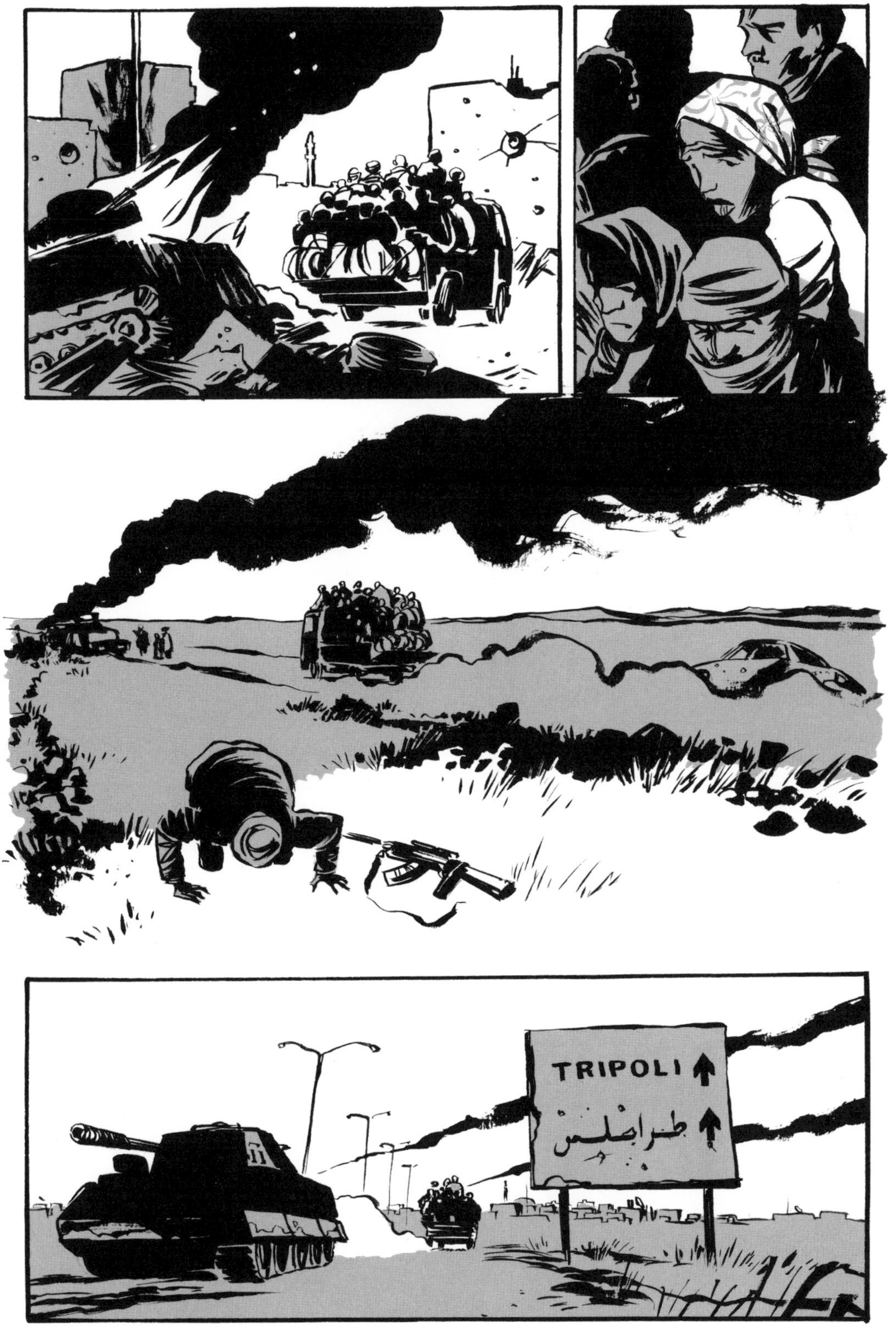

TRIPOLI
طرابلس

facebook

Dear Friends,

It's been three months since I last wrote from Sabha. I couldn't write, but I'm ok. I found some other Somalis who took me with them to Tripoli. I didn't think I'd ever make it. There are only eight more months until the London Olympics. I have to hurry if I want to make it to Italy in time to train.

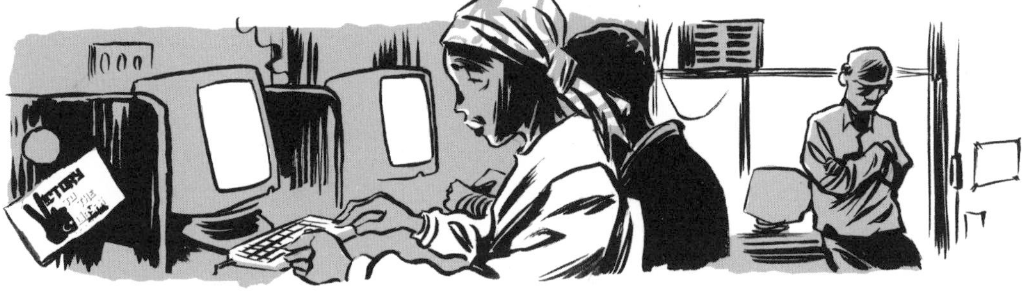

I can't think about anything except the next leg. I don't talk to anyone. I don't dream at night any more. The people in Tripoli are not at all nice to us. They look down on us as though they're better than us. They are at war just like us, just not for as long.

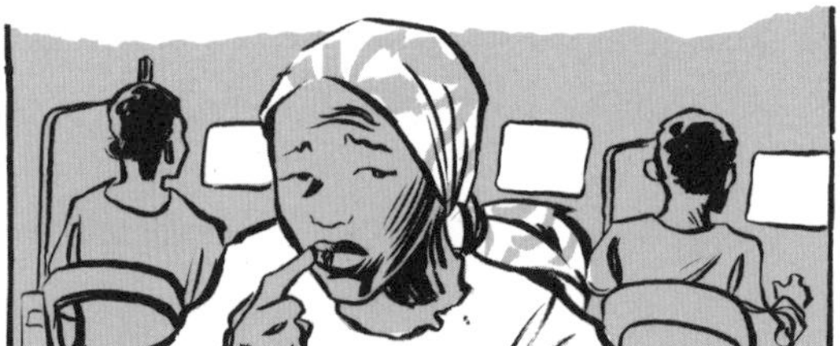

I'm so lonely. I miss my mother and the children. But I can't go back. Italy is closer than home. Than Mogadishu.

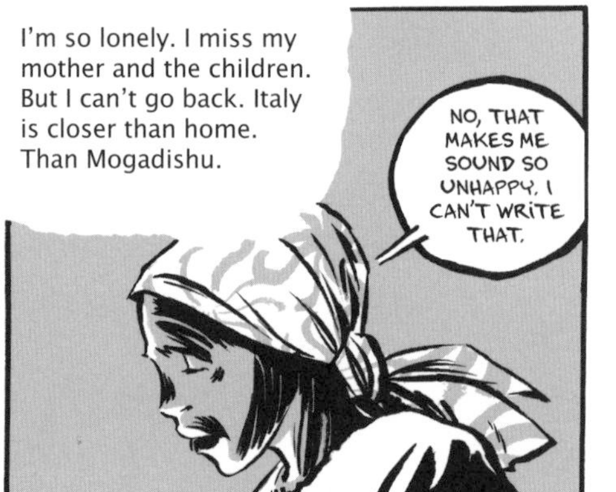
NO, THAT MAKES ME SOUND SO UNHAPPY. I CAN'T WRITE THAT.

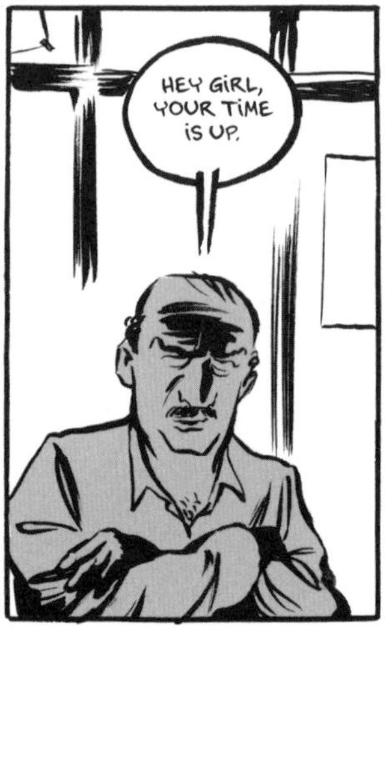
HEY GIRL, YOUR TIME IS UP.

Please send me money. I need to find a boat that will take me to Italy, either through Malta like Hodan or through Lampedusa.

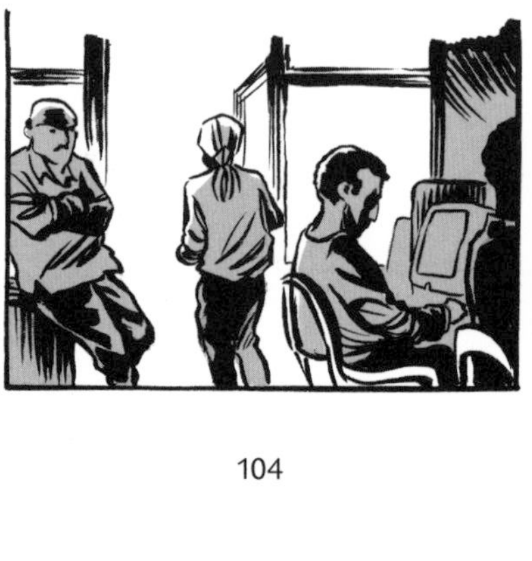

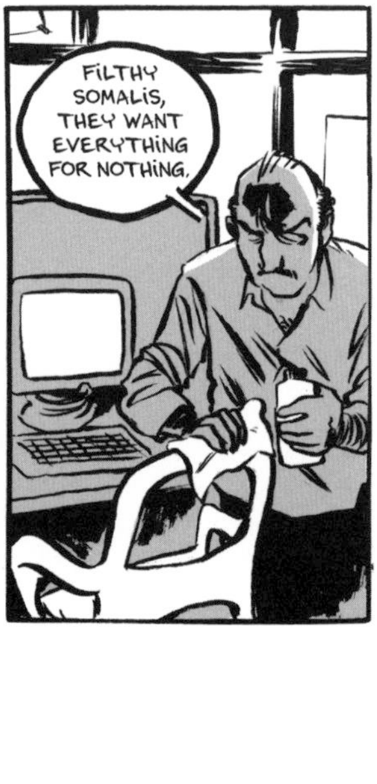
FILTHY SOMALIS, THEY WANT EVERYTHING FOR NOTHING.

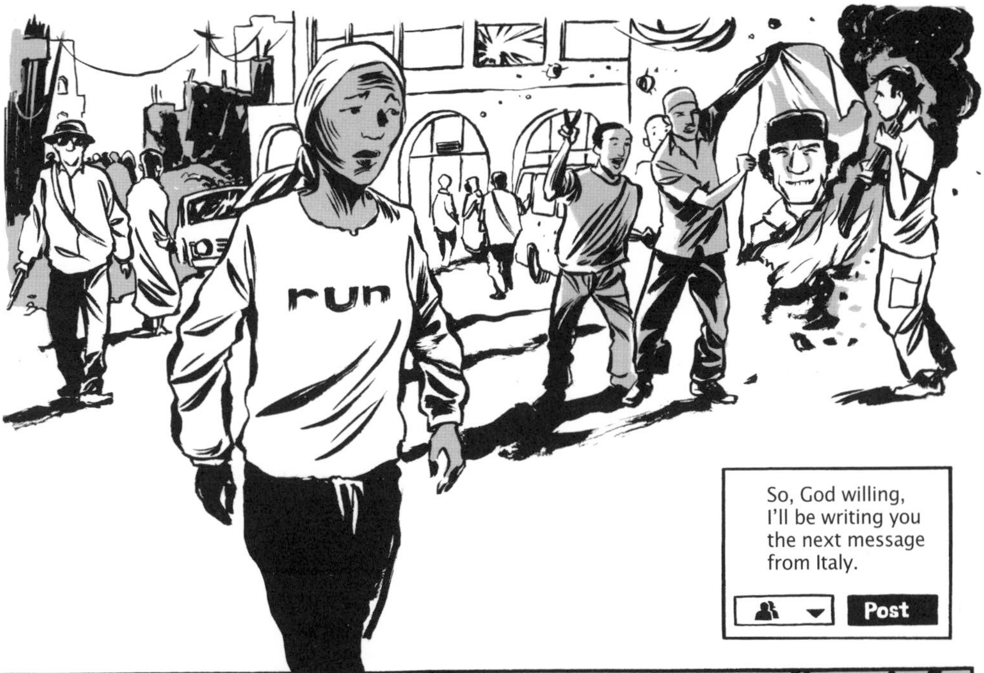
run
So, God willing, I'll be writing you the next message from Italy.
Post

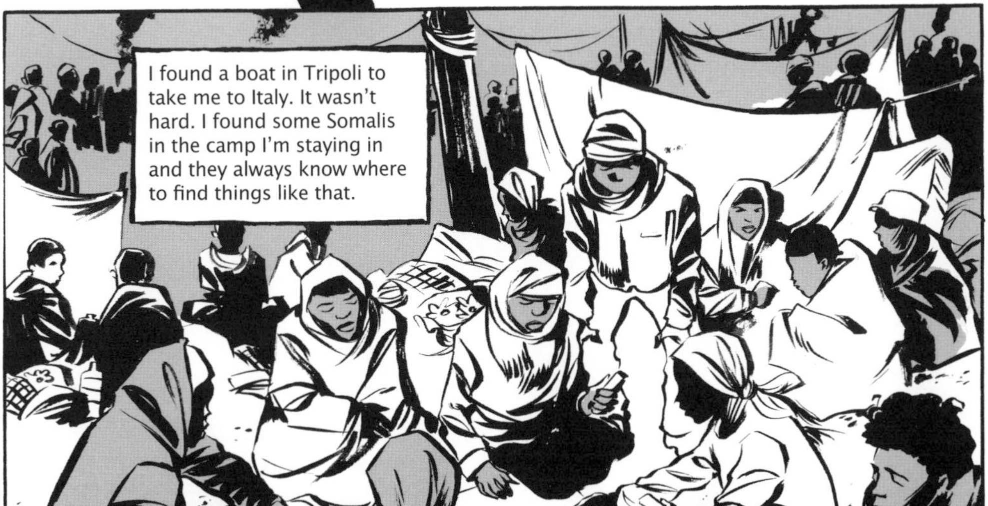
I found a boat in Tripoli to take me to Italy. It wasn't hard. I found some Somalis in the camp I'm staying in and they always know where to find things like that.

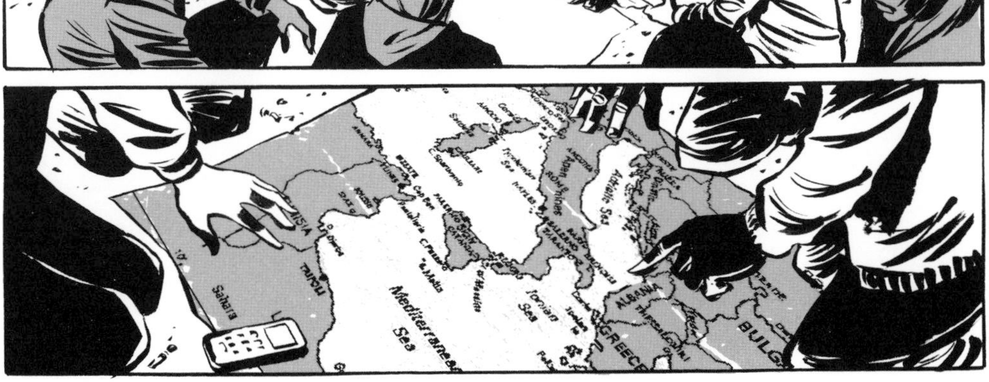
Sahara
Mediterranean Sea
Ionian Sea
Adriatic Sea
ALBANIA
GREECE

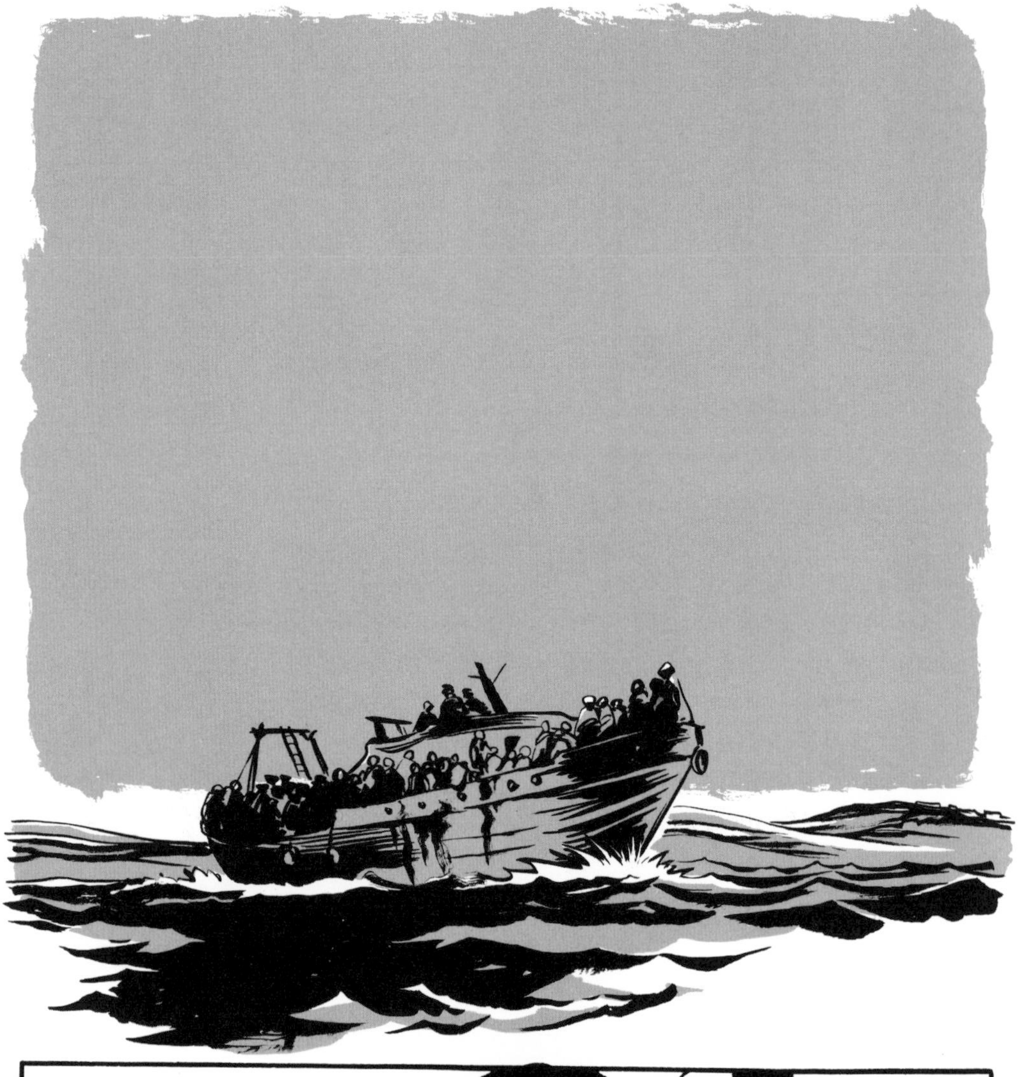

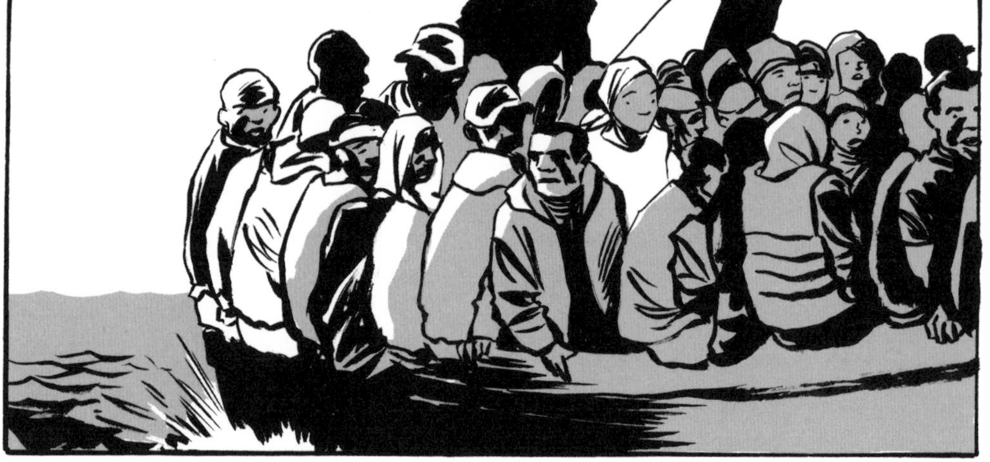

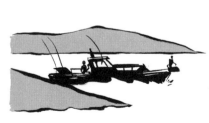

TURN AROUND!!

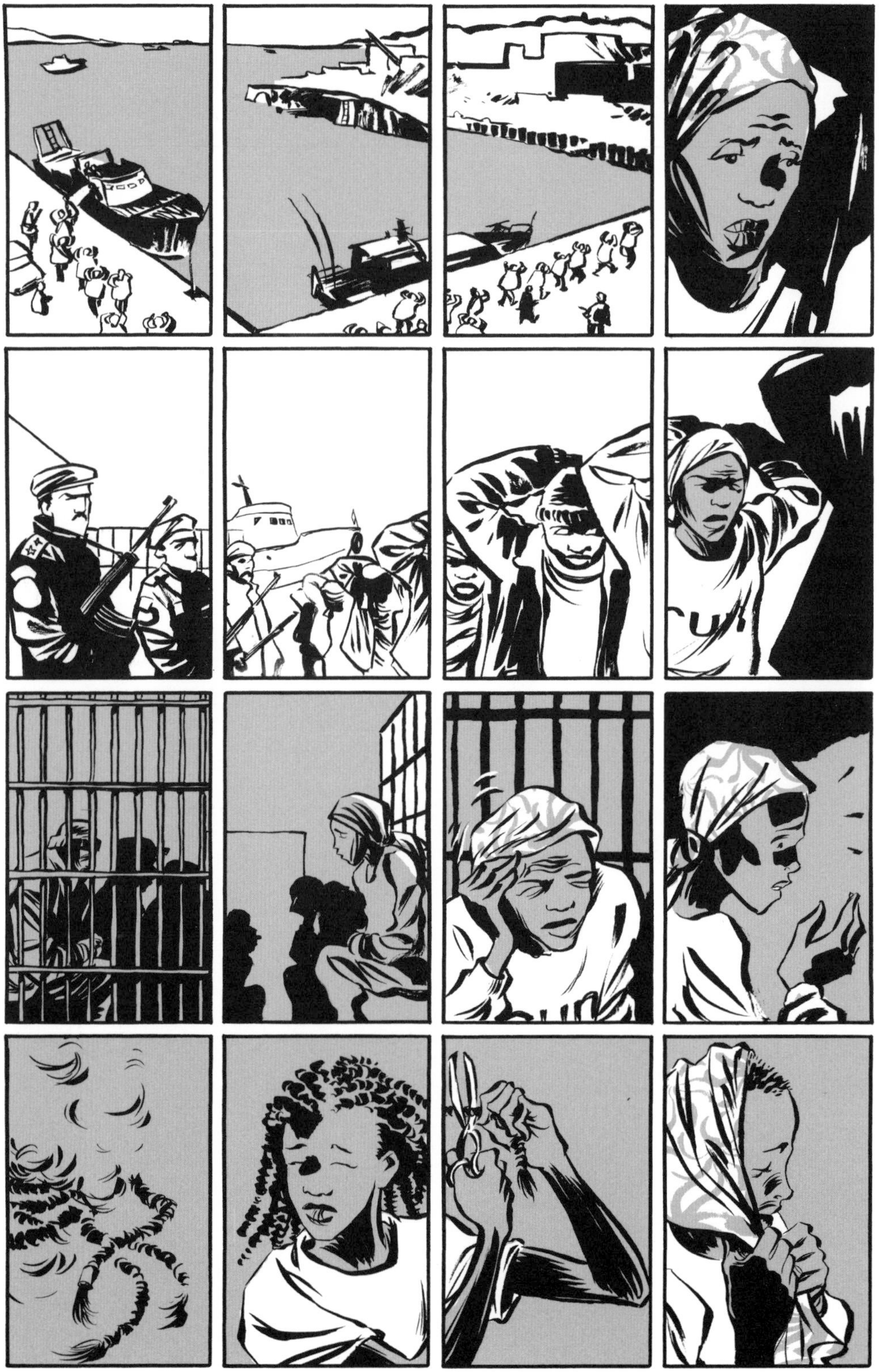

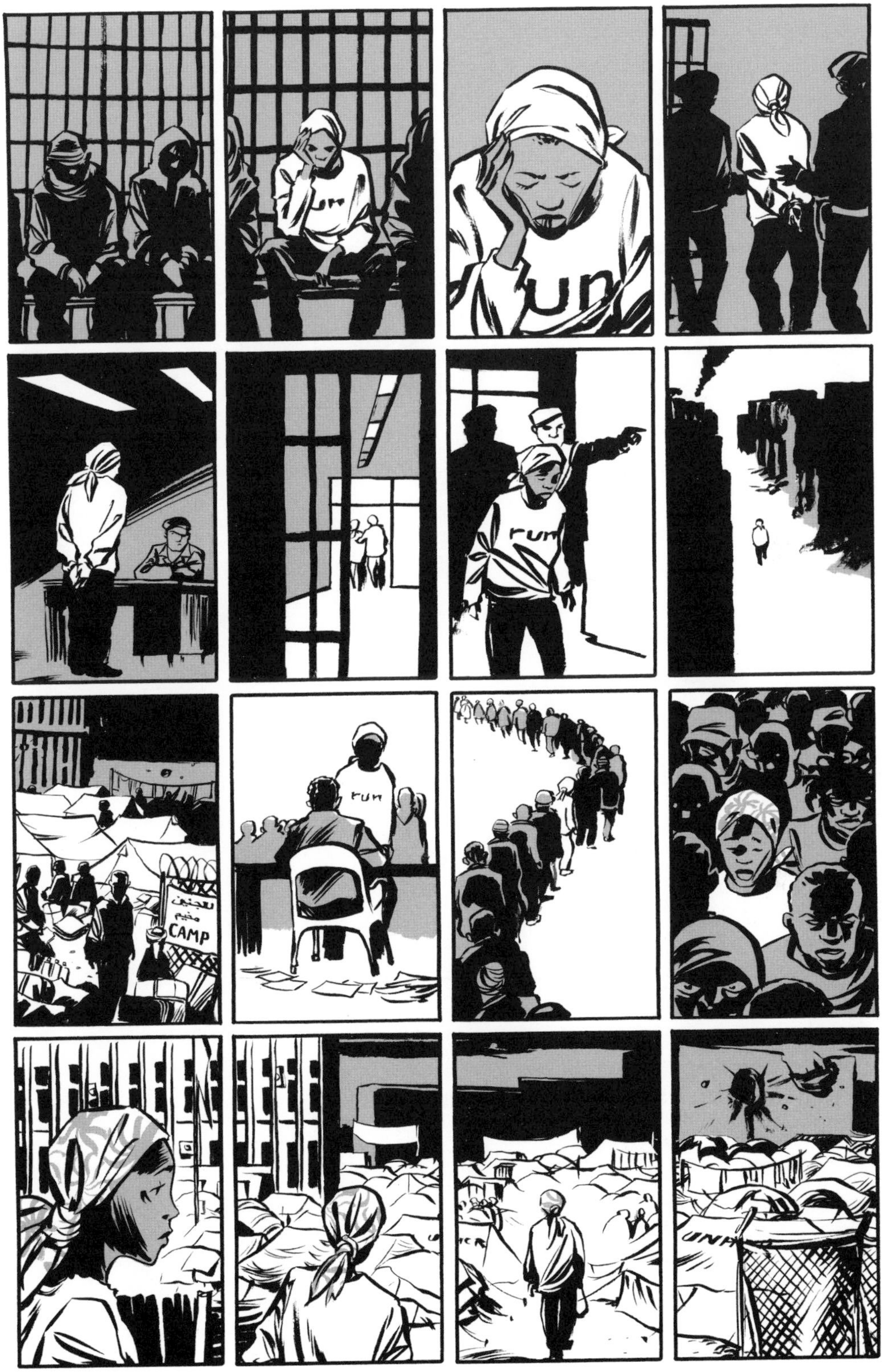
UN
للاجئين
مخيم
CAMP

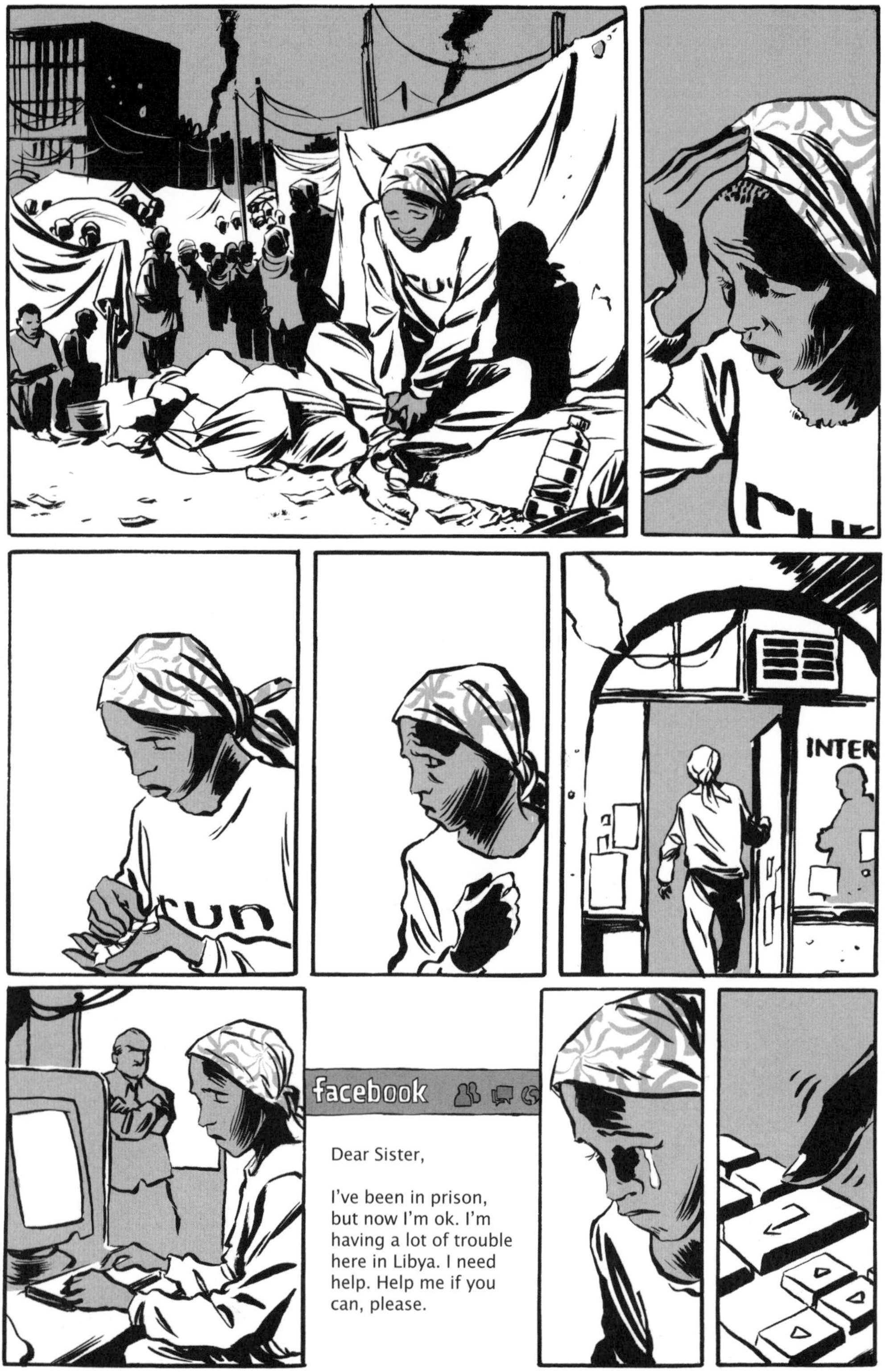
run
run
run
INTER
facebook
Dear Sister,
I've been in prison, but now I'm ok. I'm having a lot of trouble here in Libya. I need help. Help me if you can, please.

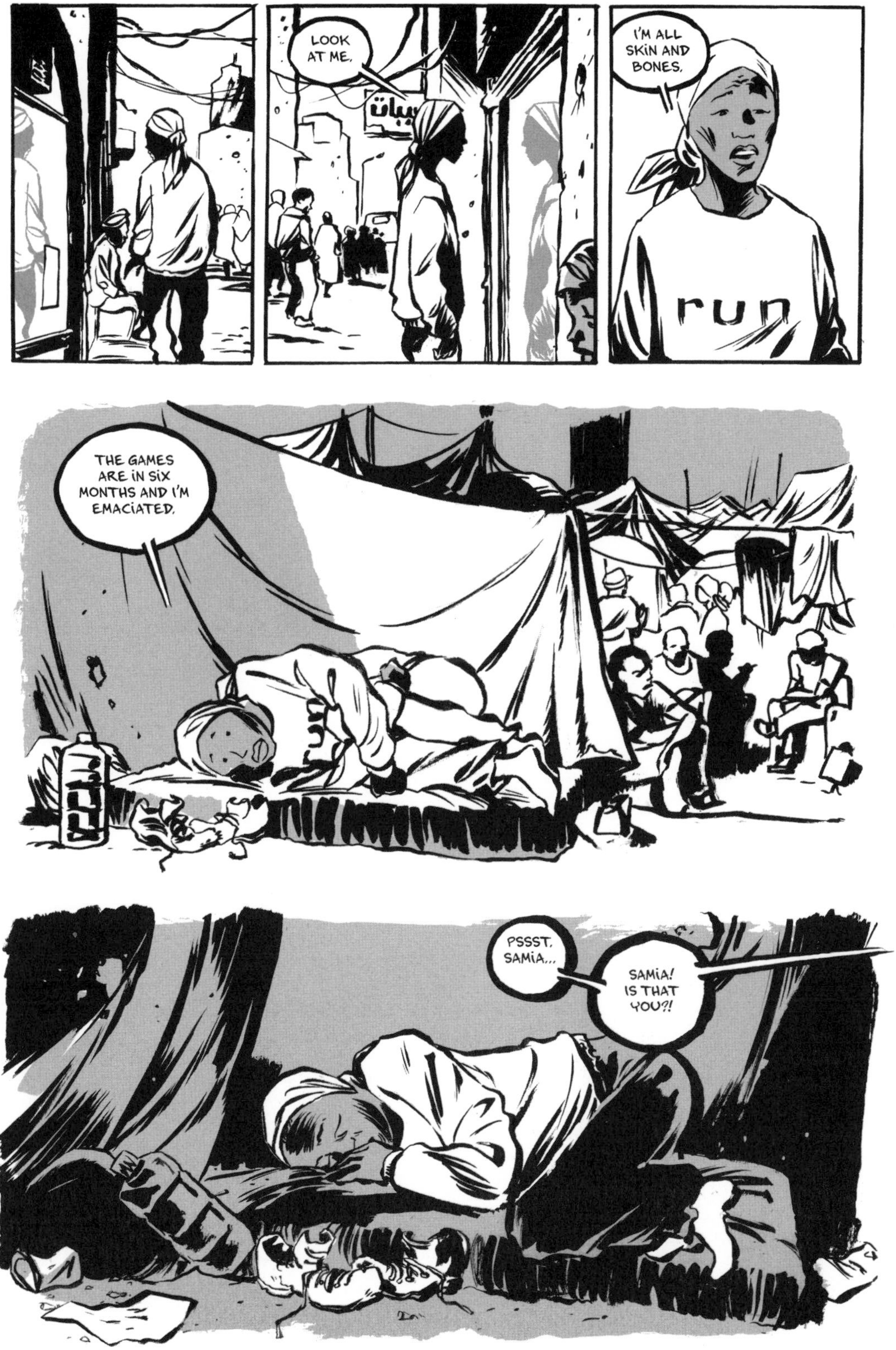
LOOK AT ME.
I'M ALL SKIN AND BONES.
run
THE GAMES ARE IN SIX MONTHS AND I'M EMACIATED.
PSSST. SAMIA...
SAMIA! IS THAT YOU?!

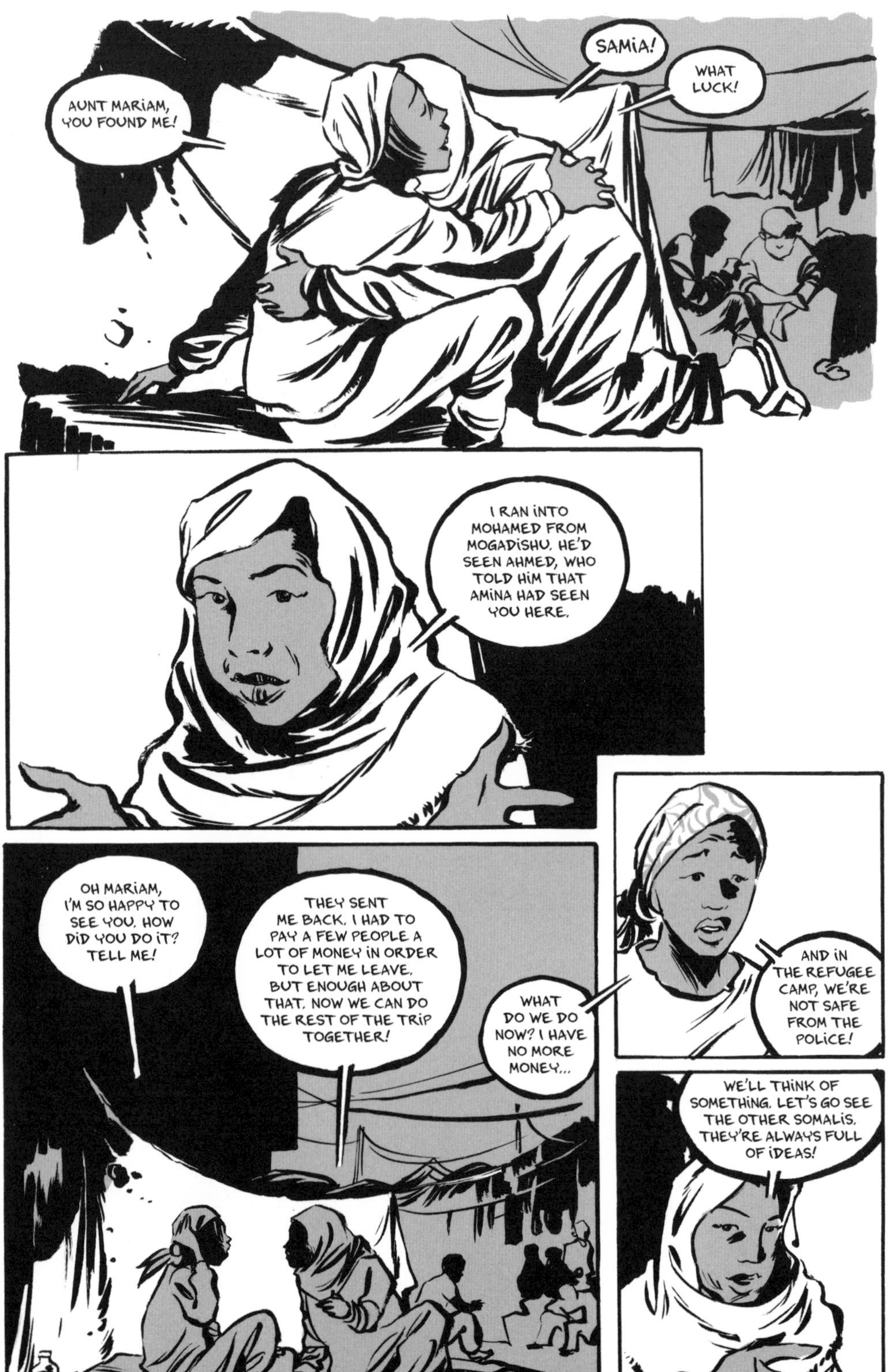
AUNT MARIAM, YOU FOUND ME!
SAMIA!
WHAT LUCK!
I RAN INTO MOHAMED FROM MOGADISHU. HE'D SEEN AHMED, WHO TOLD HIM THAT AMINA HAD SEEN YOU HERE.
OH MARIAM, I'M SO HAPPY TO SEE YOU. HOW DID YOU DO IT? TELL ME!
THEY SENT ME BACK. I HAD TO PAY A FEW PEOPLE A LOT OF MONEY IN ORDER TO LET ME LEAVE. BUT ENOUGH ABOUT THAT. NOW WE CAN DO THE REST OF THE TRIP TOGETHER!
WHAT DO WE DO NOW? I HAVE NO MORE MONEY...
AND IN THE REFUGEE CAMP, WE'RE NOT SAFE FROM THE POLICE!
WE'LL THINK OF SOMETHING. LET'S GO SEE THE OTHER SOMALIS. THEY'RE ALWAYS FULL OF IDEAS!

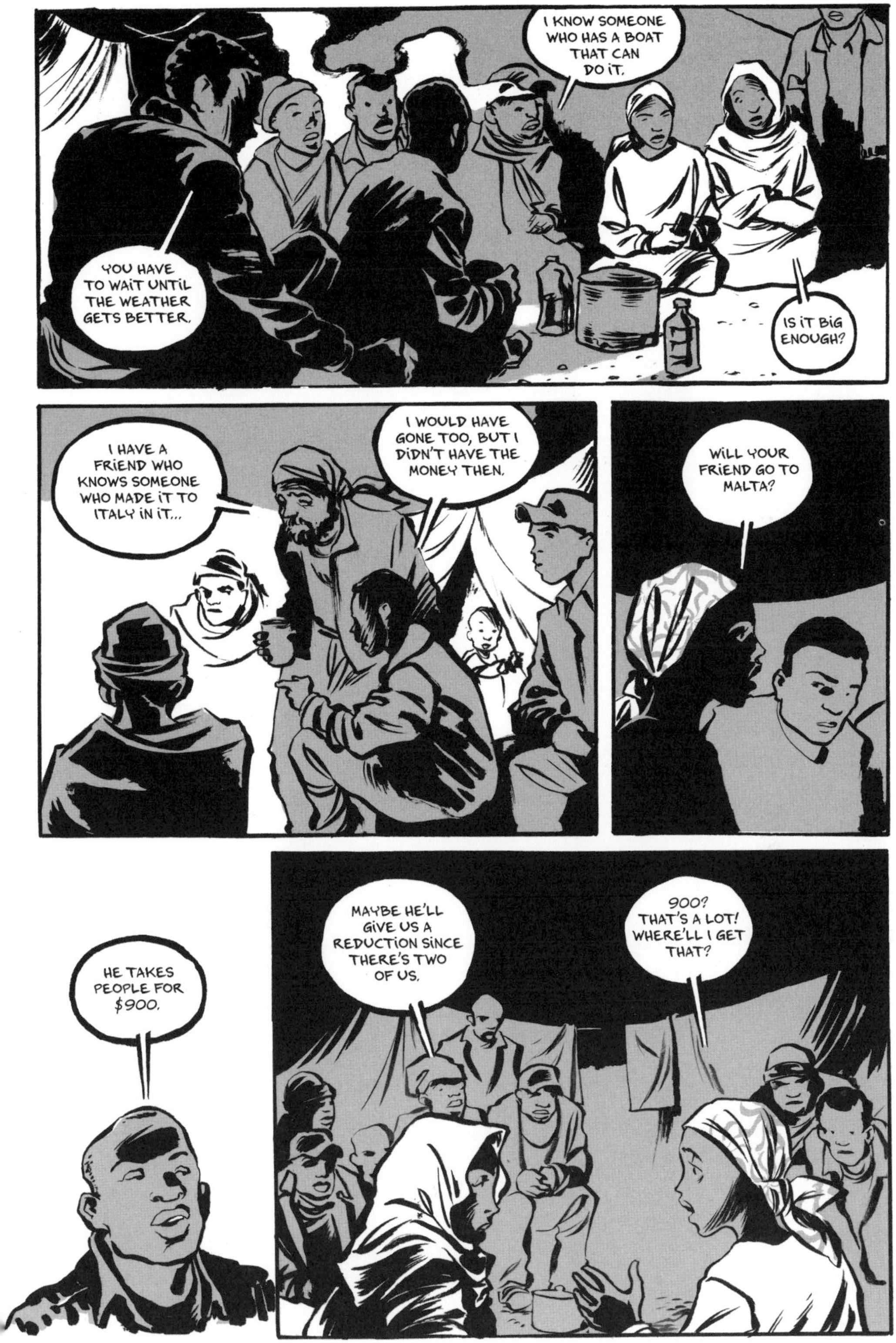
I KNOW SOMEONE WHO HAS A BOAT THAT CAN DO IT.
YOU HAVE TO WAIT UNTIL THE WEATHER GETS BETTER.
IS IT BIG ENOUGH?
I HAVE A FRIEND WHO KNOWS SOMEONE WHO MADE IT TO ITALY IN IT...
I WOULD HAVE GONE TOO, BUT I DIDN'T HAVE THE MONEY THEN.
WILL YOUR FRIEND GO TO MALTA?
HE TAKES PEOPLE FOR $900.
MAYBE HE'LL GIVE US A REDUCTION SINCE THERE'S TWO OF US.
900? THAT'S A LOT! WHERE'LL I GET THAT?

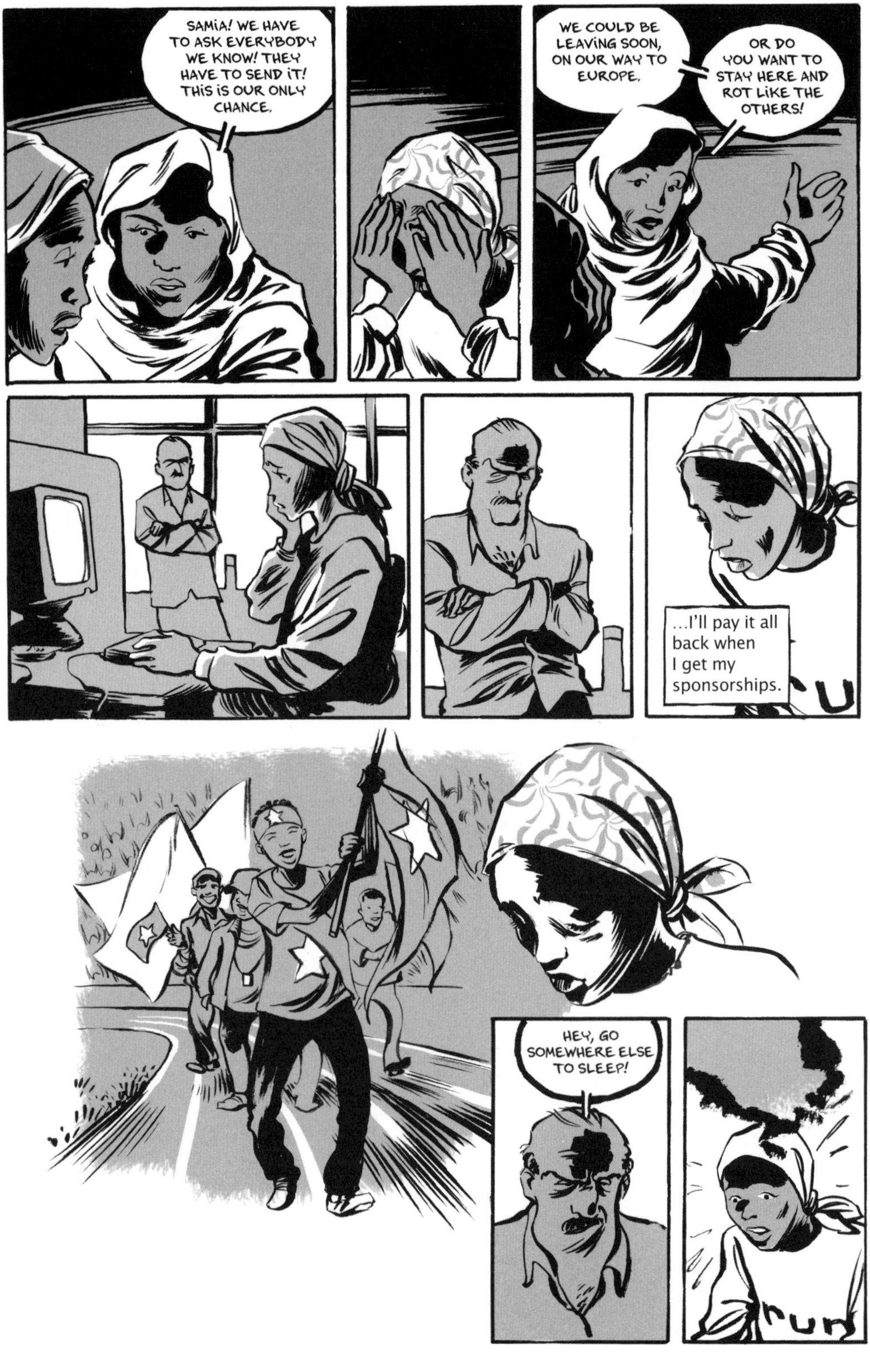
SAMIA! WE HAVE TO ASK EVERYBODY WE KNOW! THEY HAVE TO SEND IT! THIS IS OUR ONLY CHANCE.
WE COULD BE LEAVING SOON, ON OUR WAY TO EUROPE.
OR DO YOU WANT TO STAY HERE AND ROT LIKE THE OTHERS!
…I'll pay it all back when I get my sponsorships.
HEY, GO SOMEWHERE ELSE TO SLEEP!
run

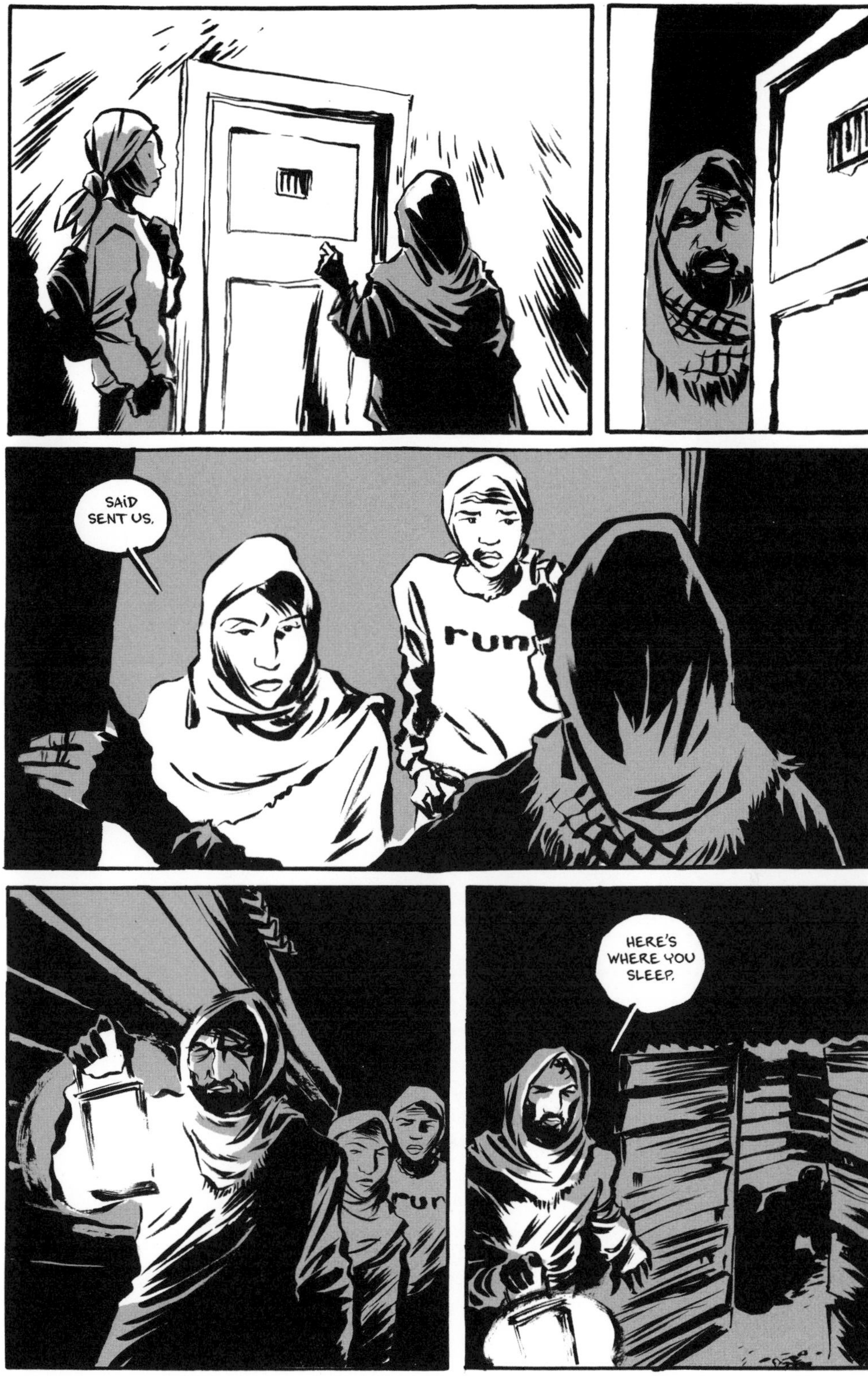
SAID SENT US.
run
run
HERE'S WHERE YOU SLEEP.

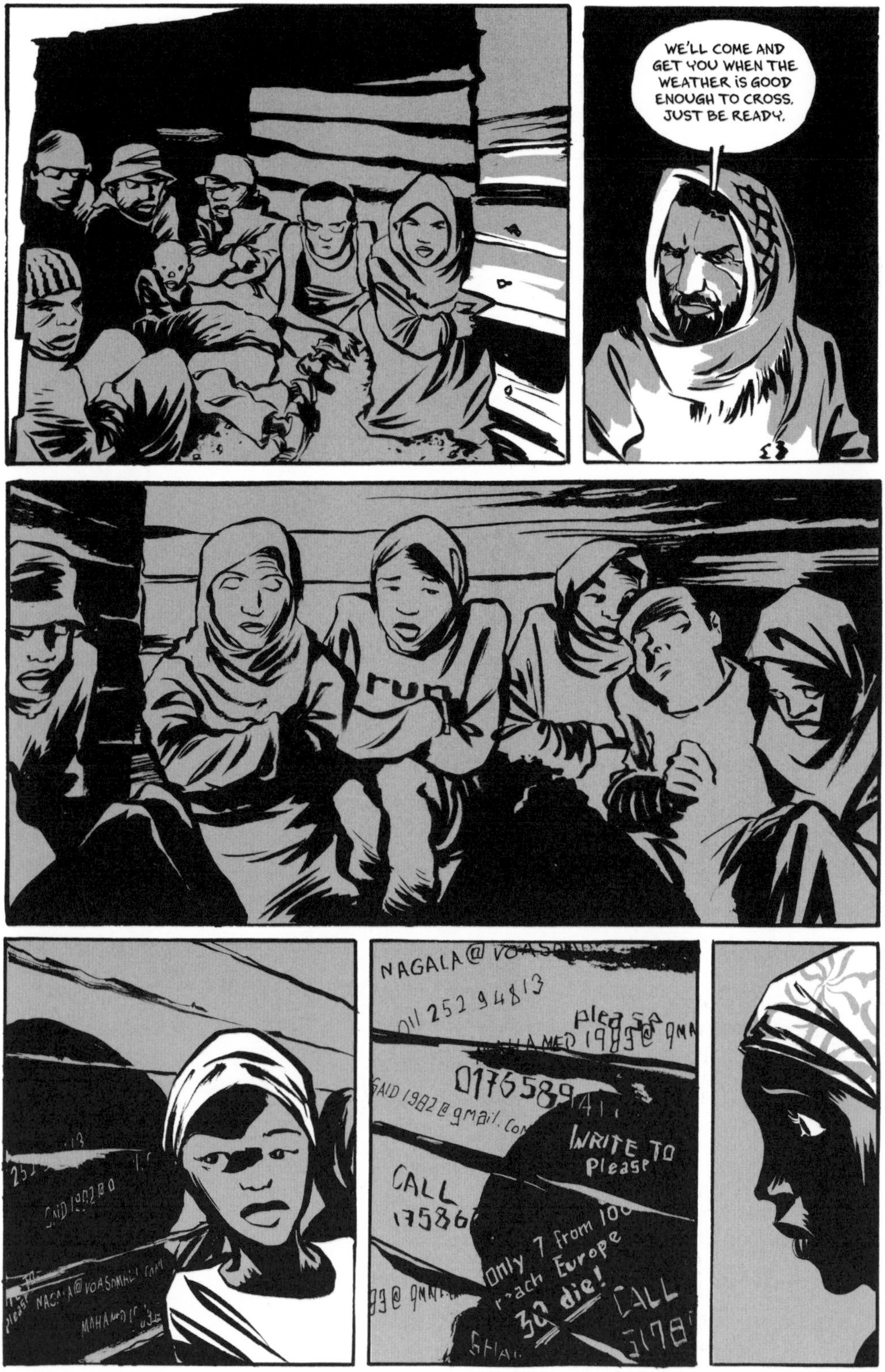
WE'LL COME AND GET YOU WHEN THE WEATHER IS GOOD ENOUGH TO CROSS. JUST BE READY.
run
NAGALA@
011 252 94813
please
0176589
SAID 1982@gmail.com
WRITE TO
Please
CALL
reach Europe
30 die!
CALL

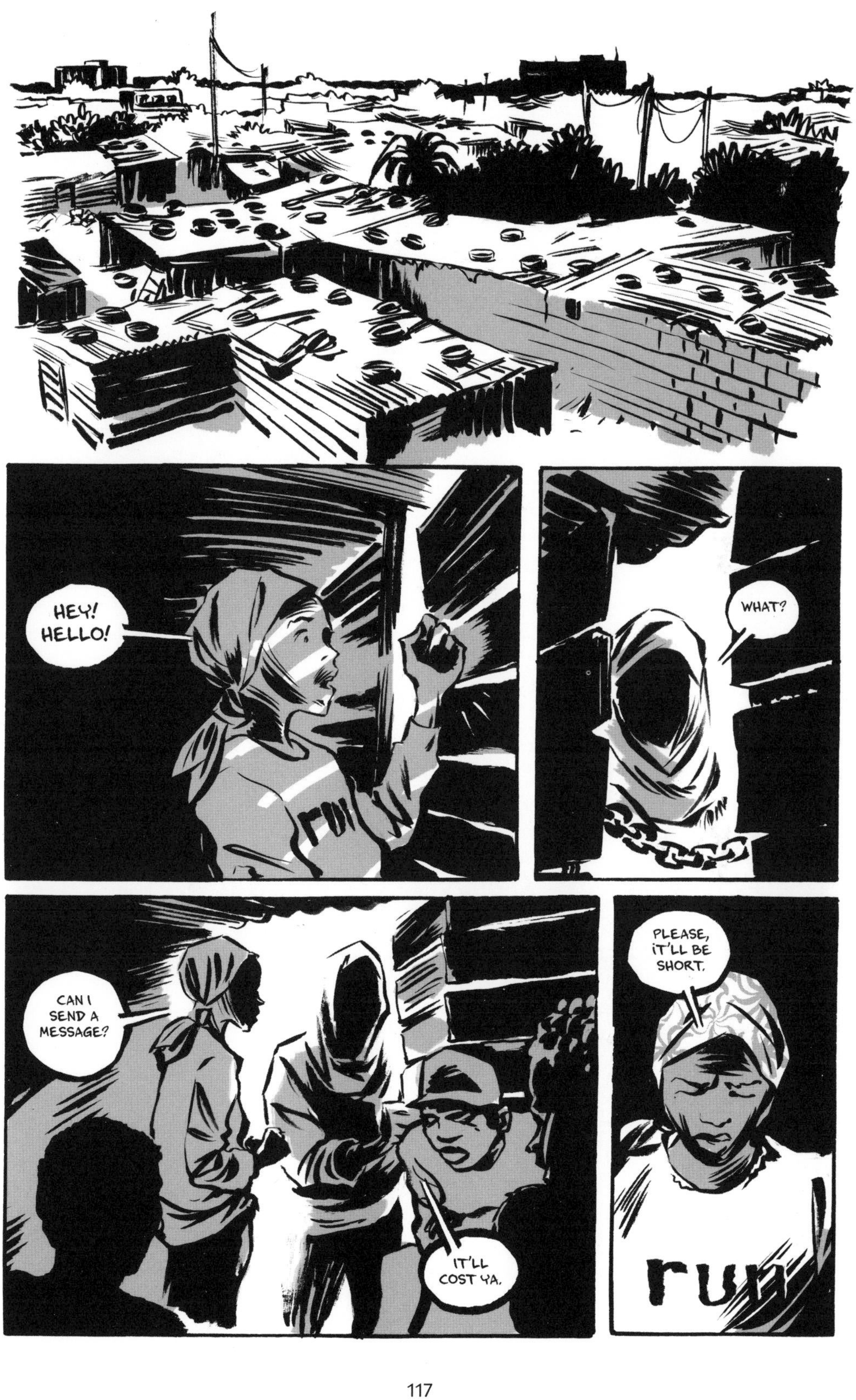
HEY! HELLO!
WHAT?
CAN I SEND A MESSAGE?
IT'LL COST YA.
PLEASE, IT'LL BE SHORT.
run

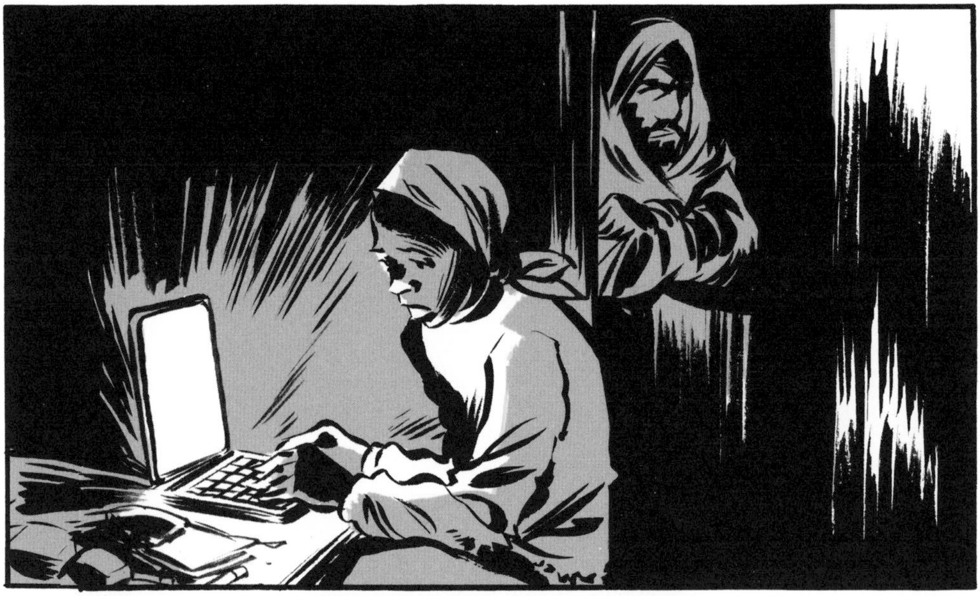

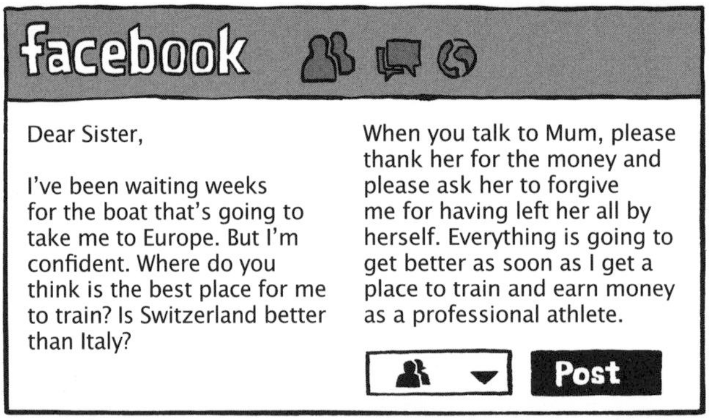
facebook
Dear Sister,
I've been waiting weeks for the boat that's going to take me to Europe. But I'm confident. Where do you think is the best place for me to train? Is Switzerland better than Italy?
When you talk to Mum, please thank her for the money and please ask her to forgive me for having left her all by herself. Everything is going to get better as soon as I get a place to train and earn money as a professional athlete.
Post

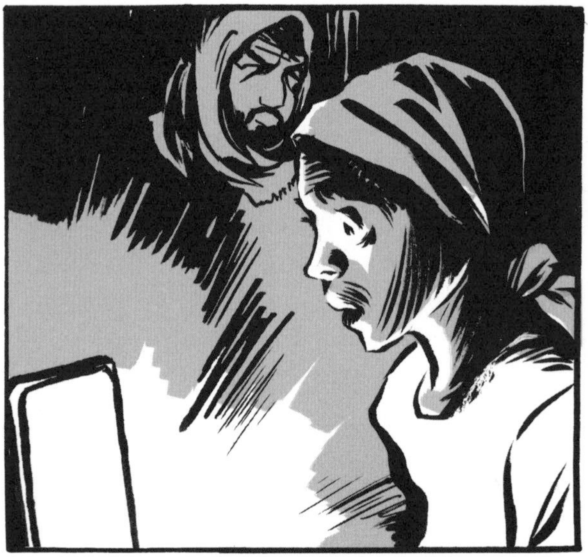

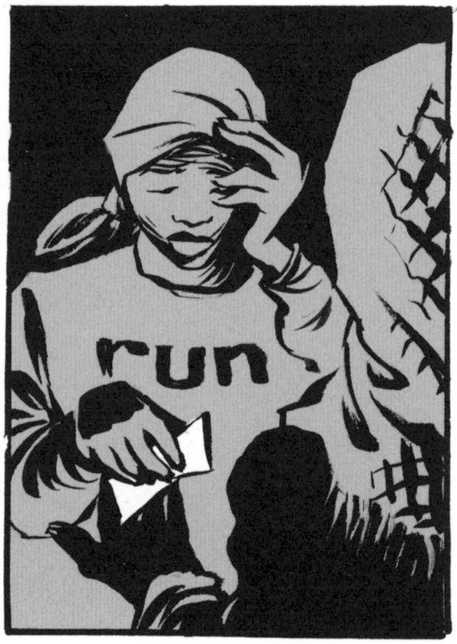
run

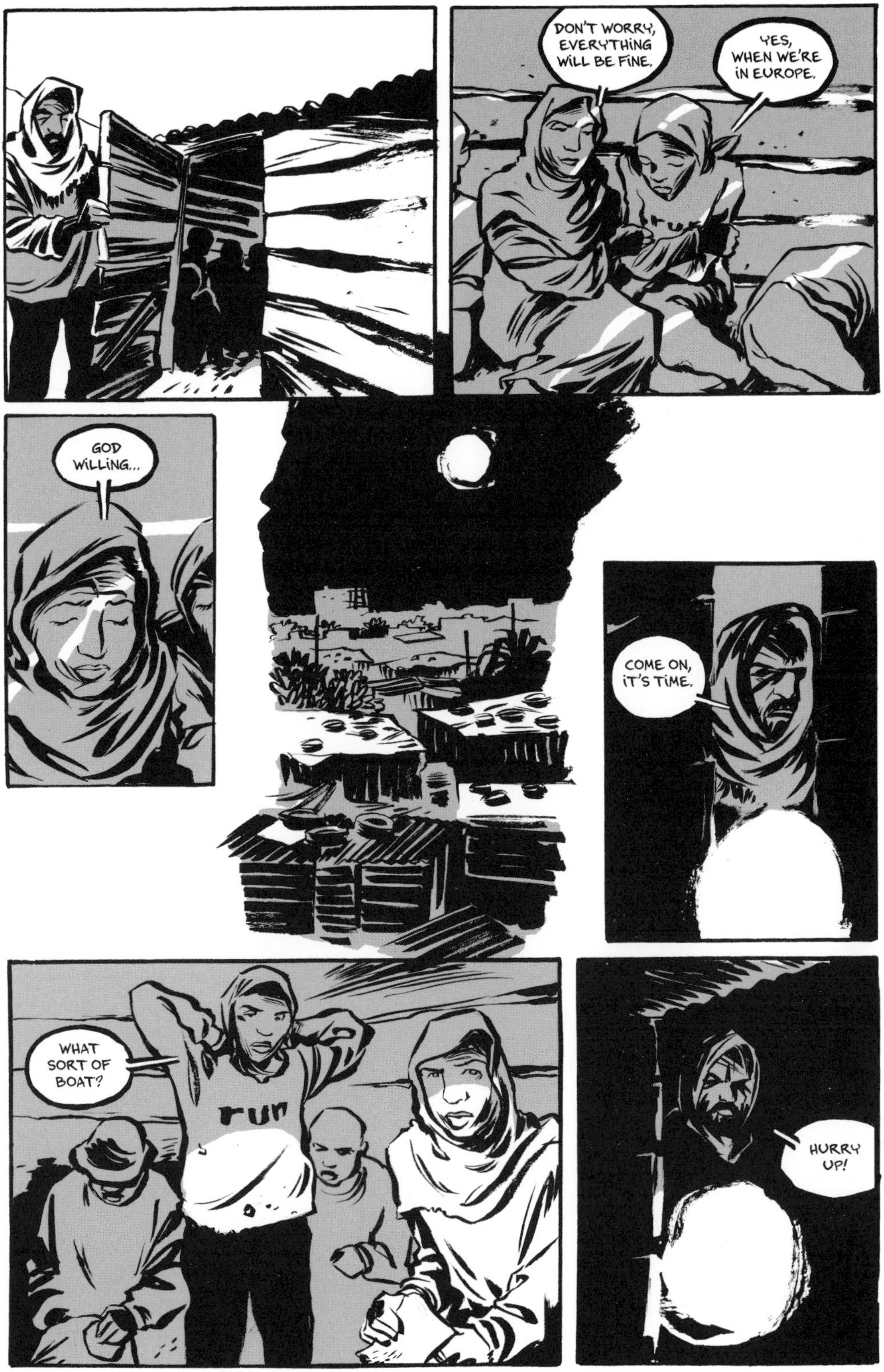
DON'T WORRY, EVERYTHING WILL BE FINE.
YES, WHEN WE'RE IN EUROPE.
GOD WILLING...
COME ON, IT'S TIME.
WHAT SORT OF BOAT?
HURRY UP!

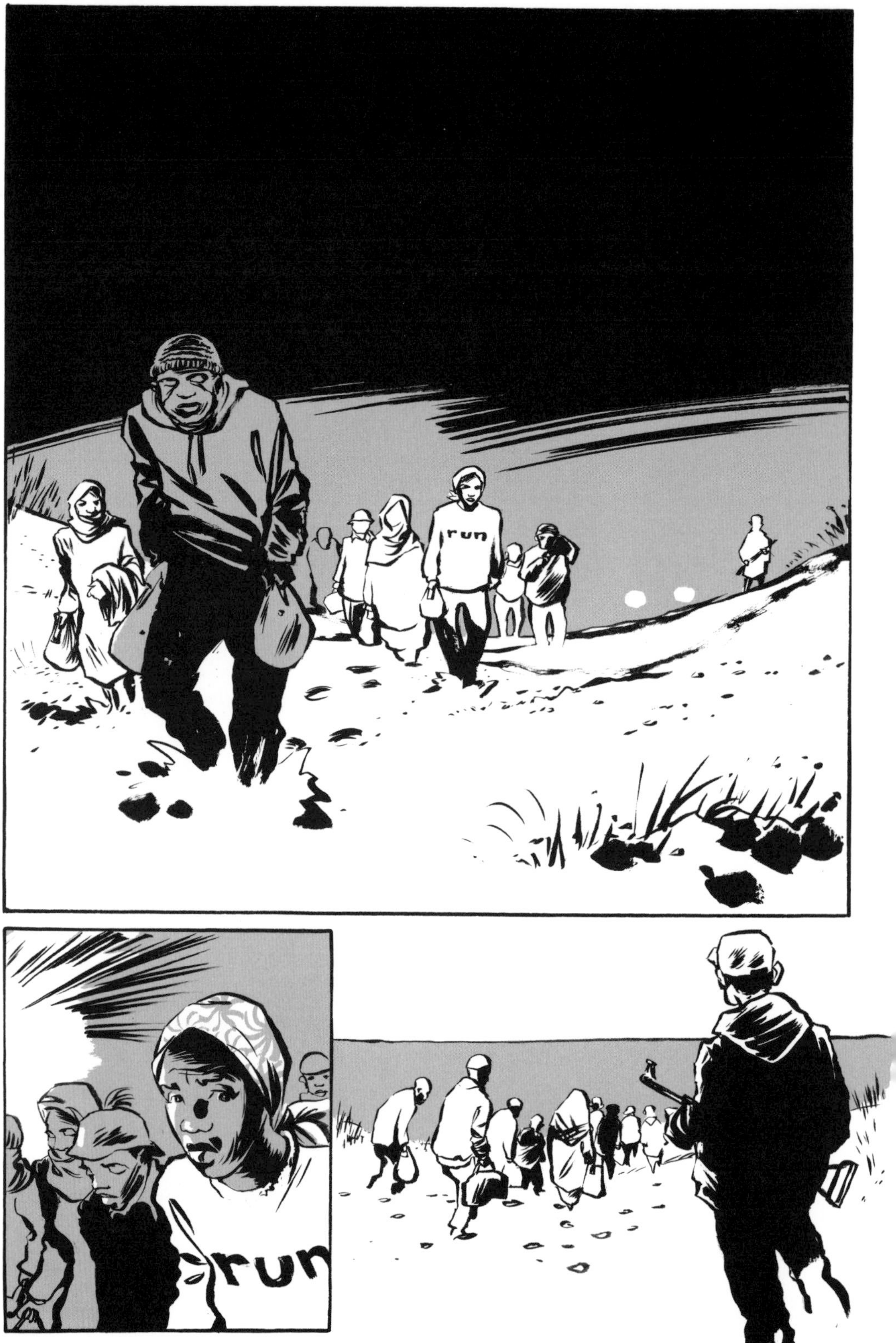
run
run

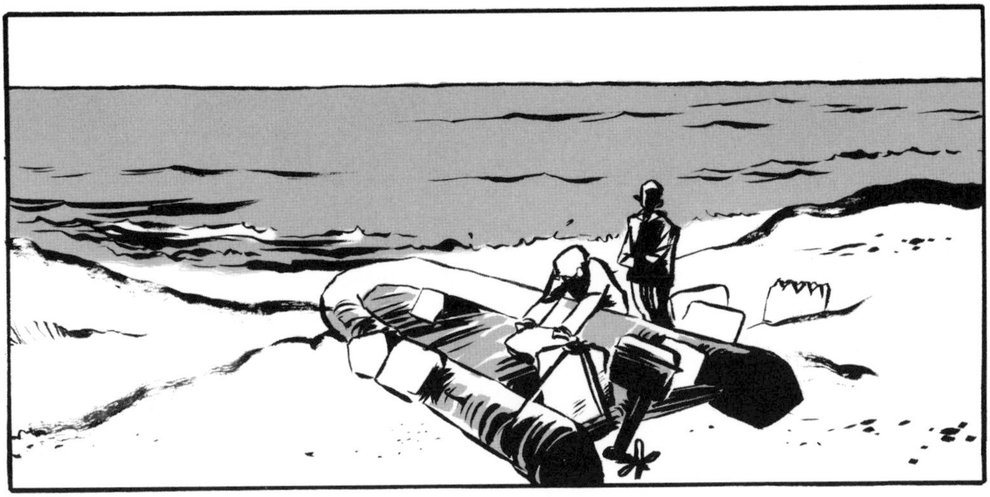

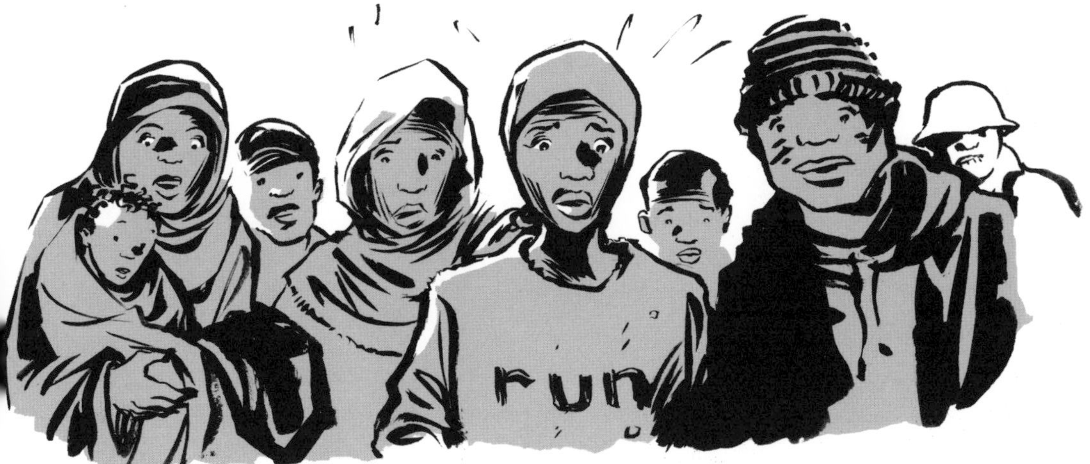
run

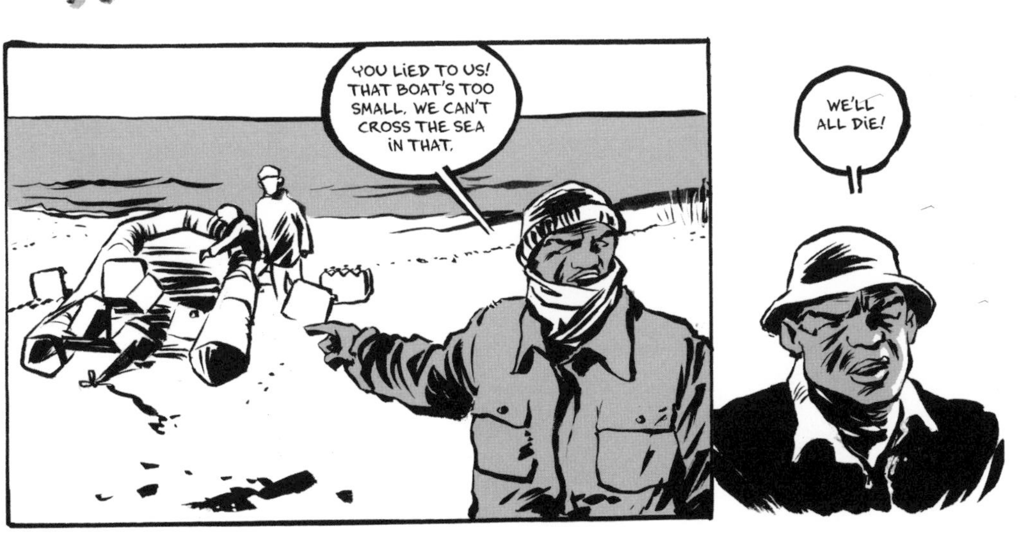
YOU LiED TO US! THAT BOAT'S TOO SMALL. WE CAN'T CROSS THE SEA IN THAT.
WE'LL ALL DiE!

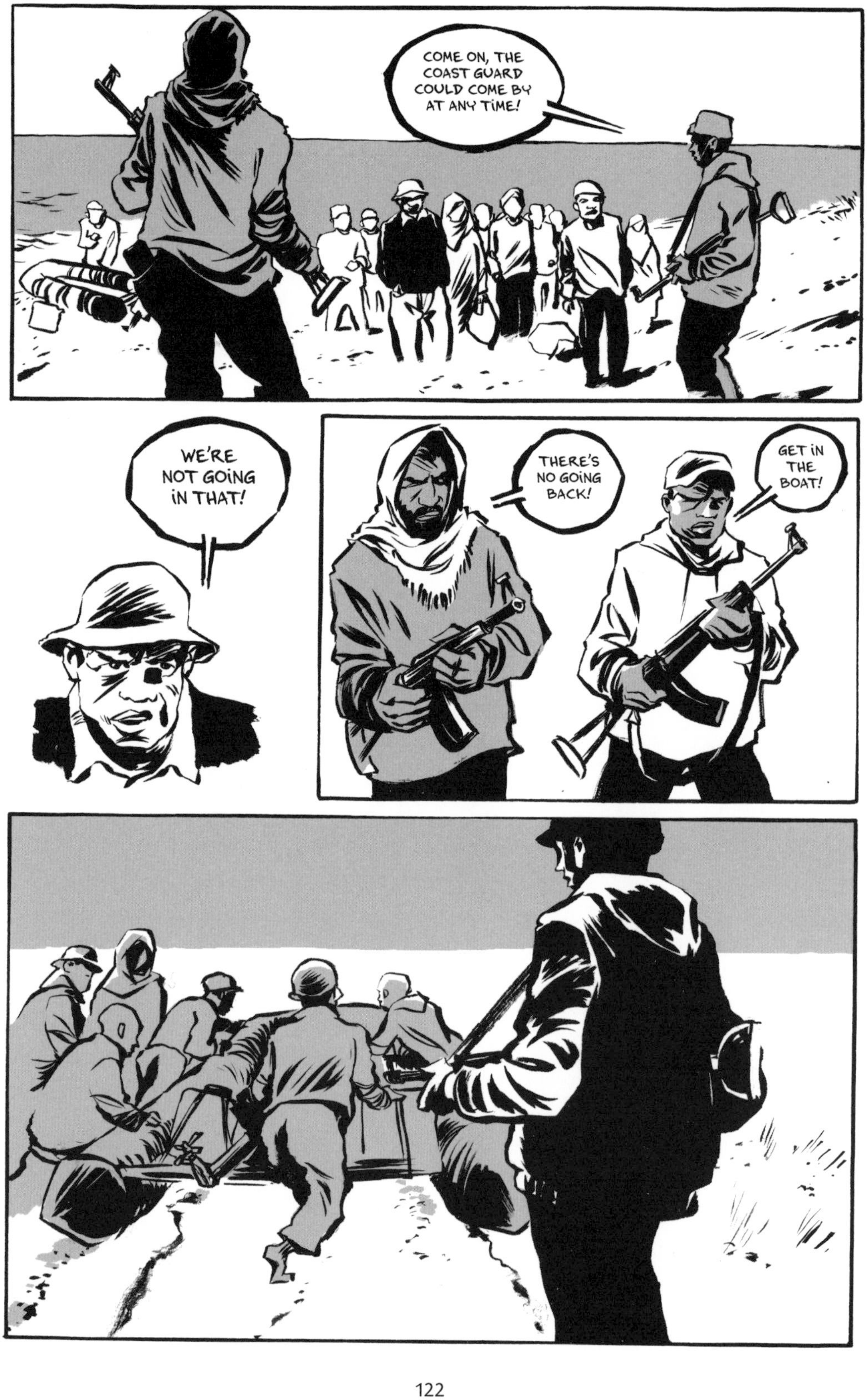
COME ON, THE COAST GUARD COULD COME BY AT ANY TIME!
WE'RE NOT GOING IN THAT!
THERE'S NO GOING BACK!
GET IN THE BOAT!

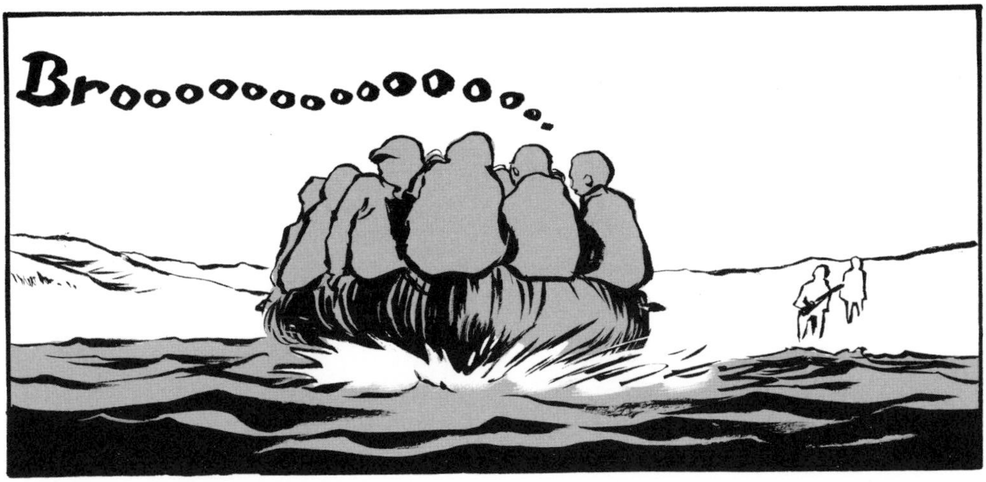
Broooooooooooooo..

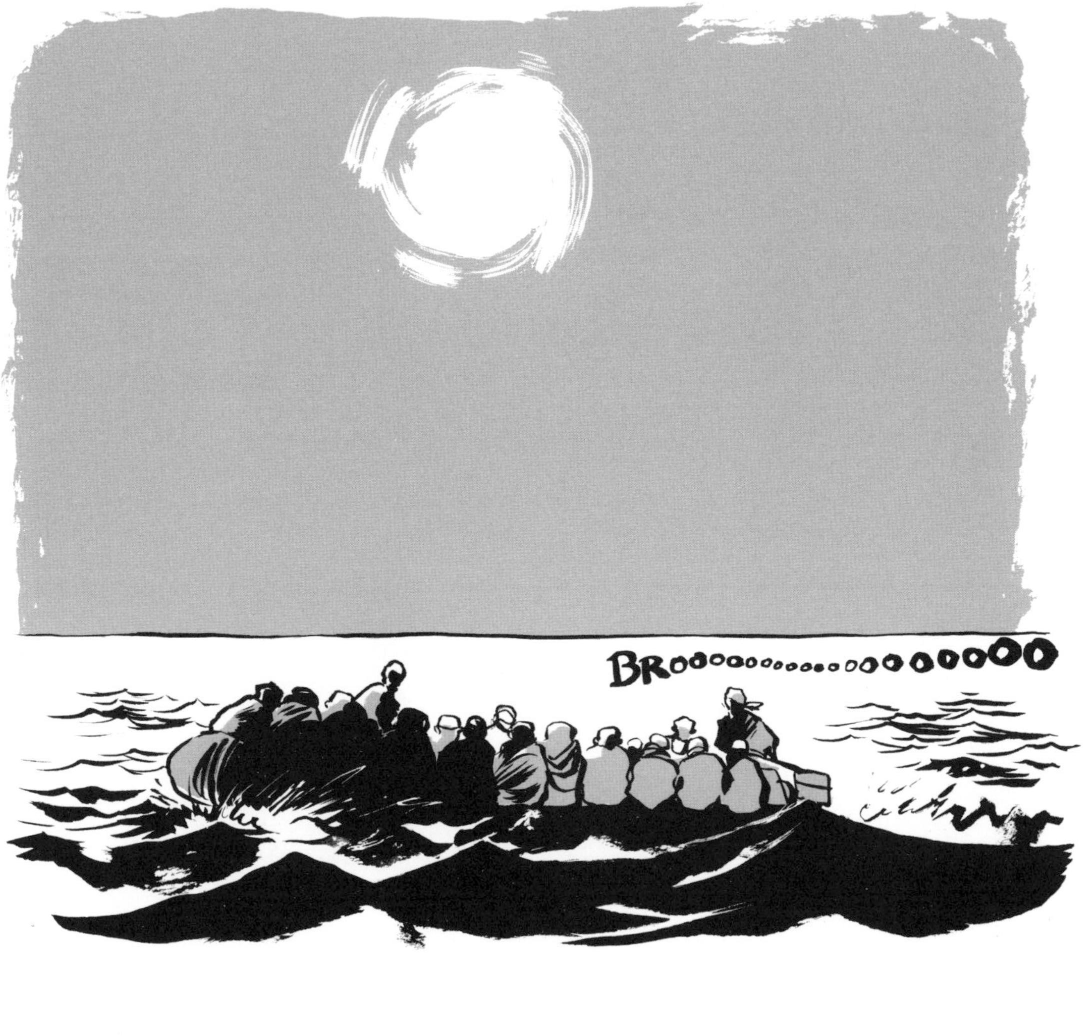
BROoooooooooooooOOOOOOO

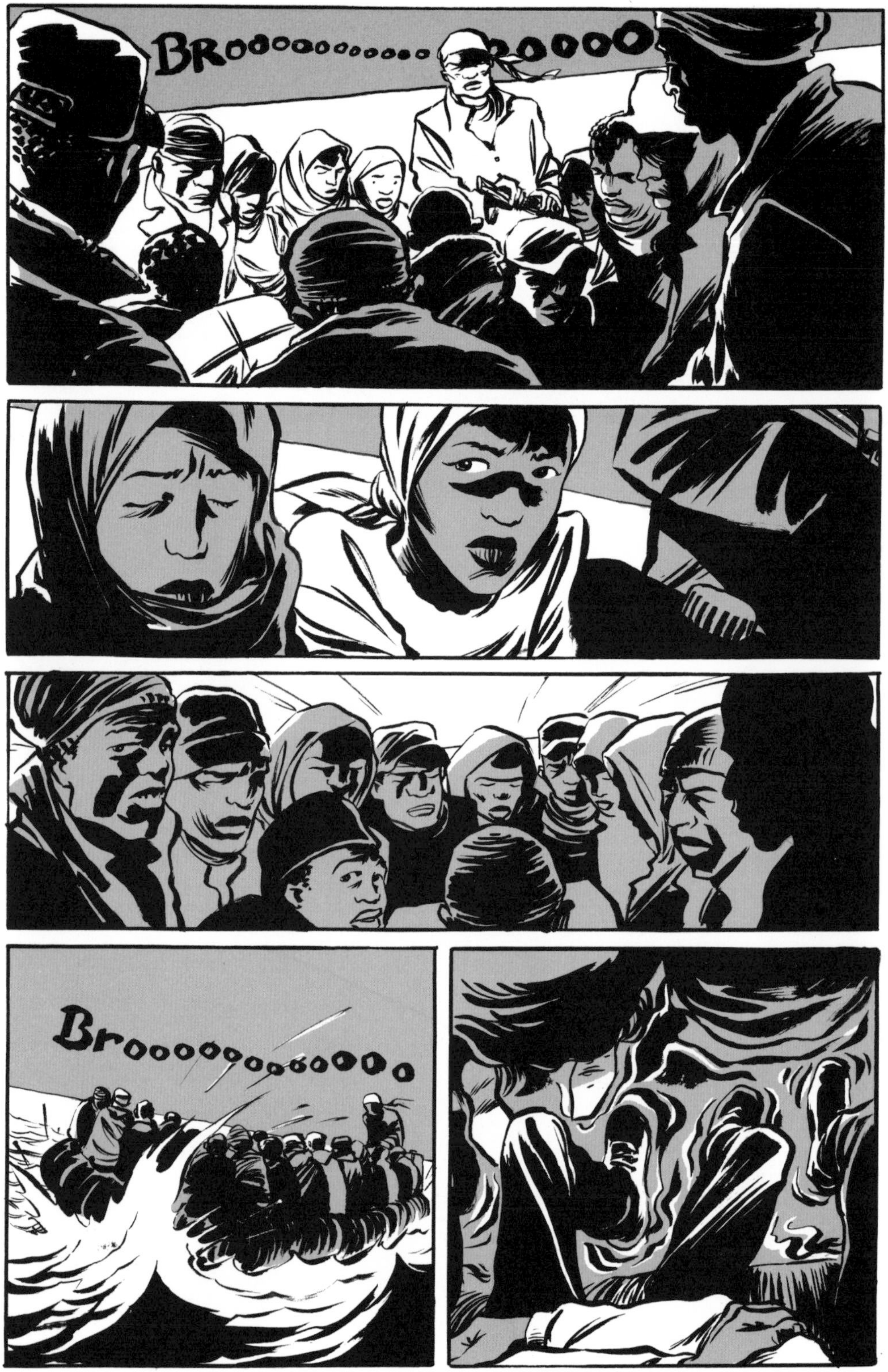
BROOOOOOOOOOOO...OOOOOO
Brooooooooooooo

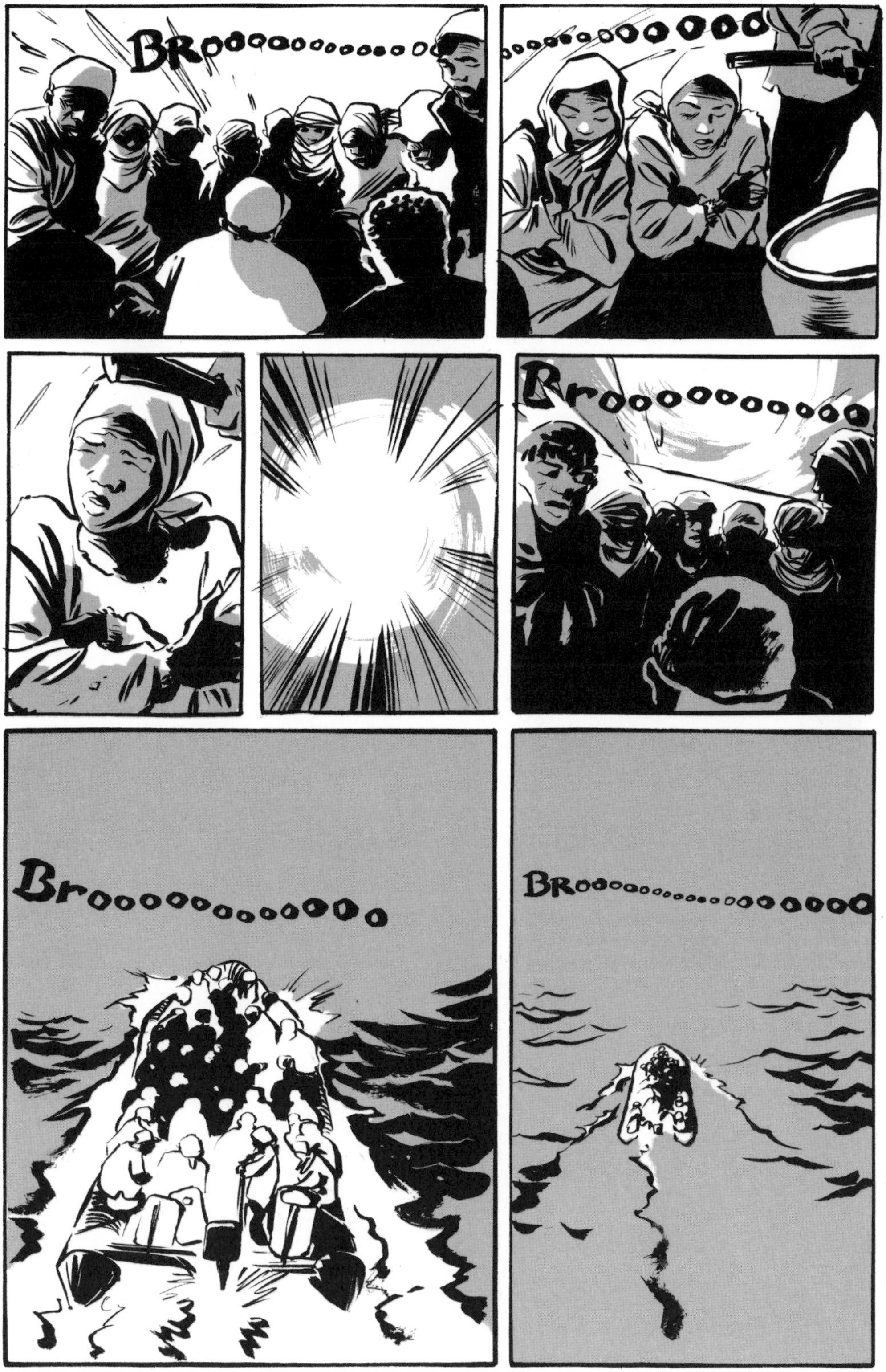
BRoooooooooooooooO
oooooooooOOOOOO
Brooooooooooo
Broooooooooooooo
BRooooooooooooooooooooooO

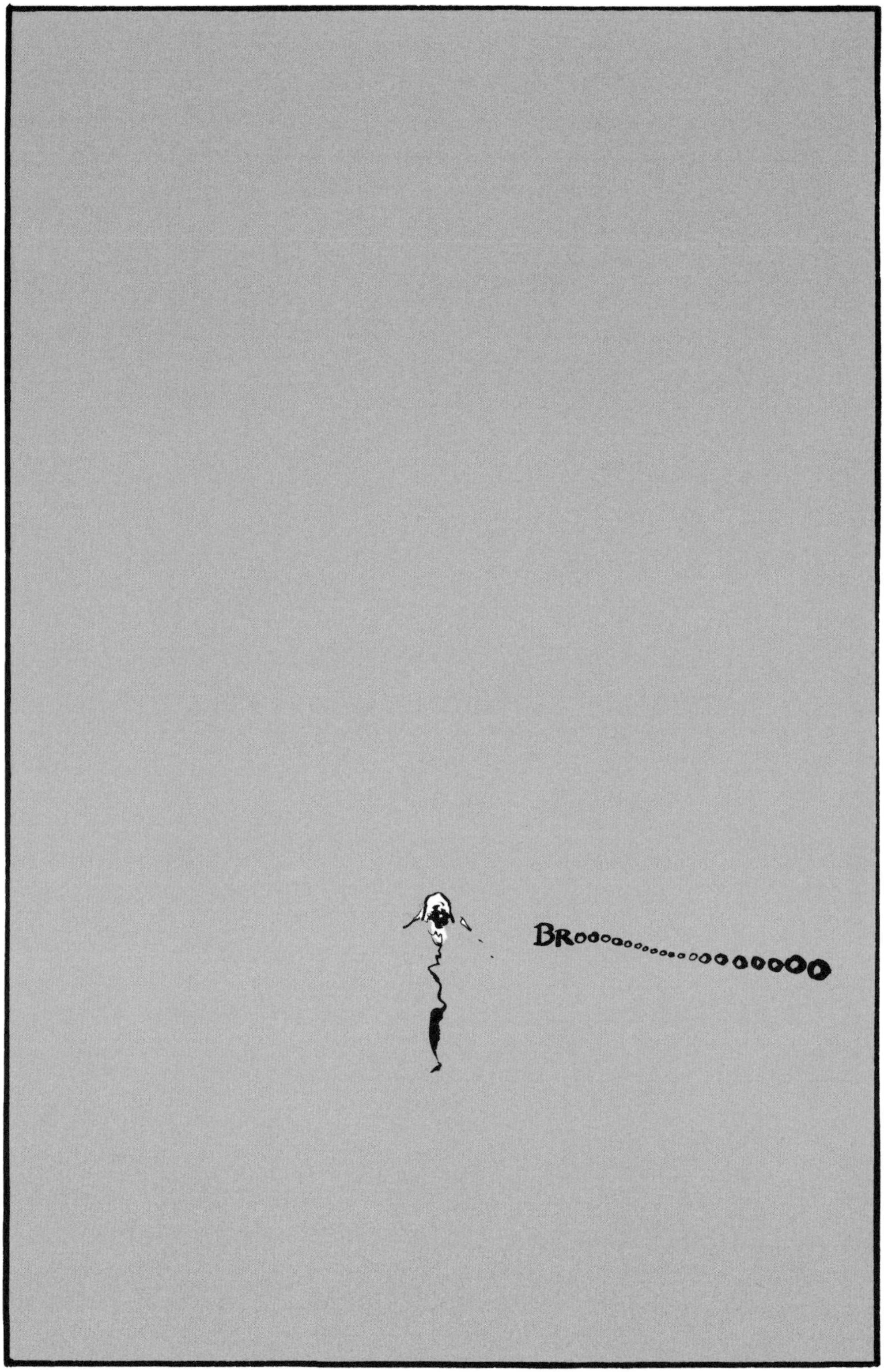
BROooooooooooooOOOOOOOO

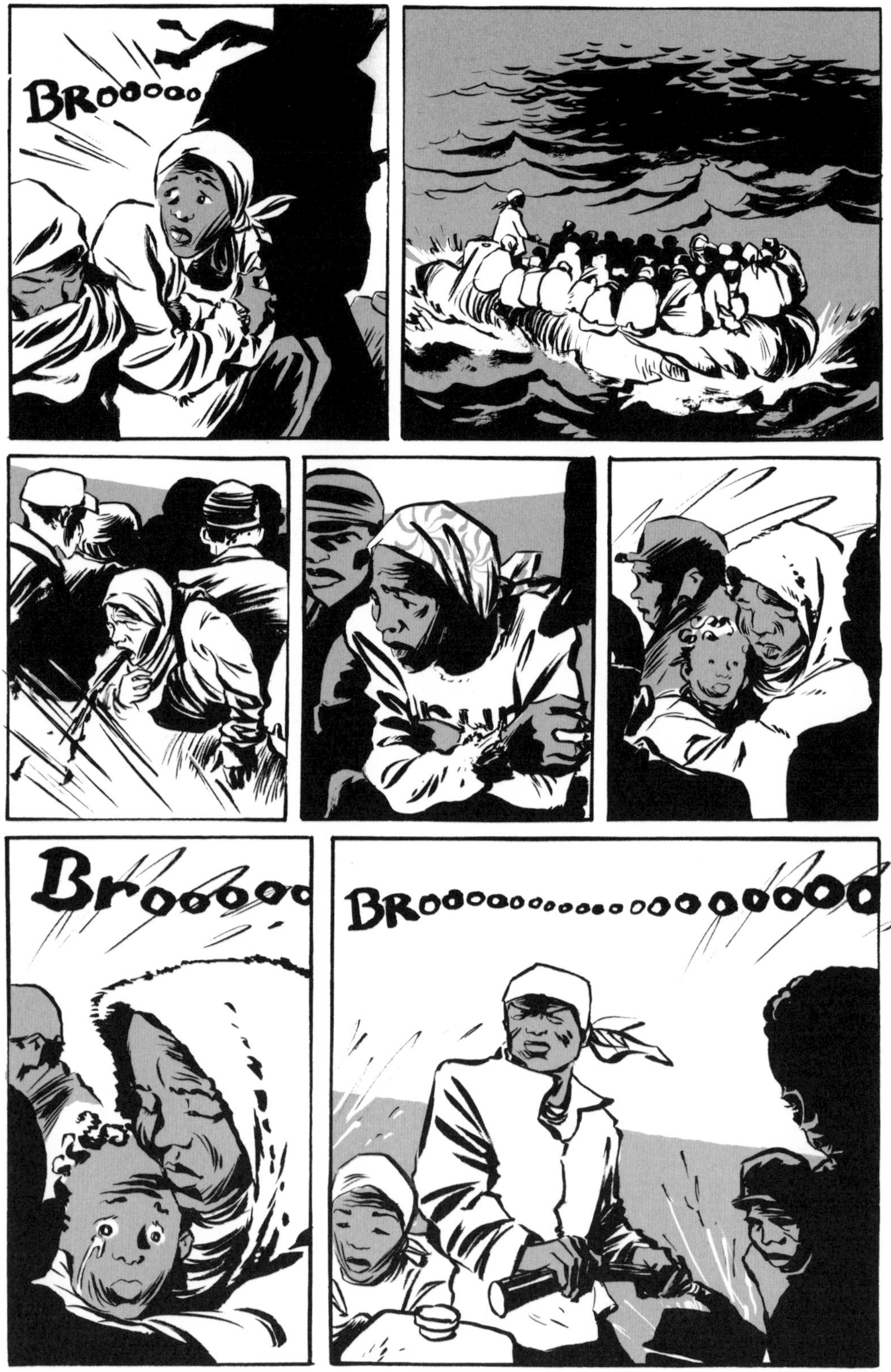
BROooooo
Brooooo
BROoooooooooooooOOOOOOO

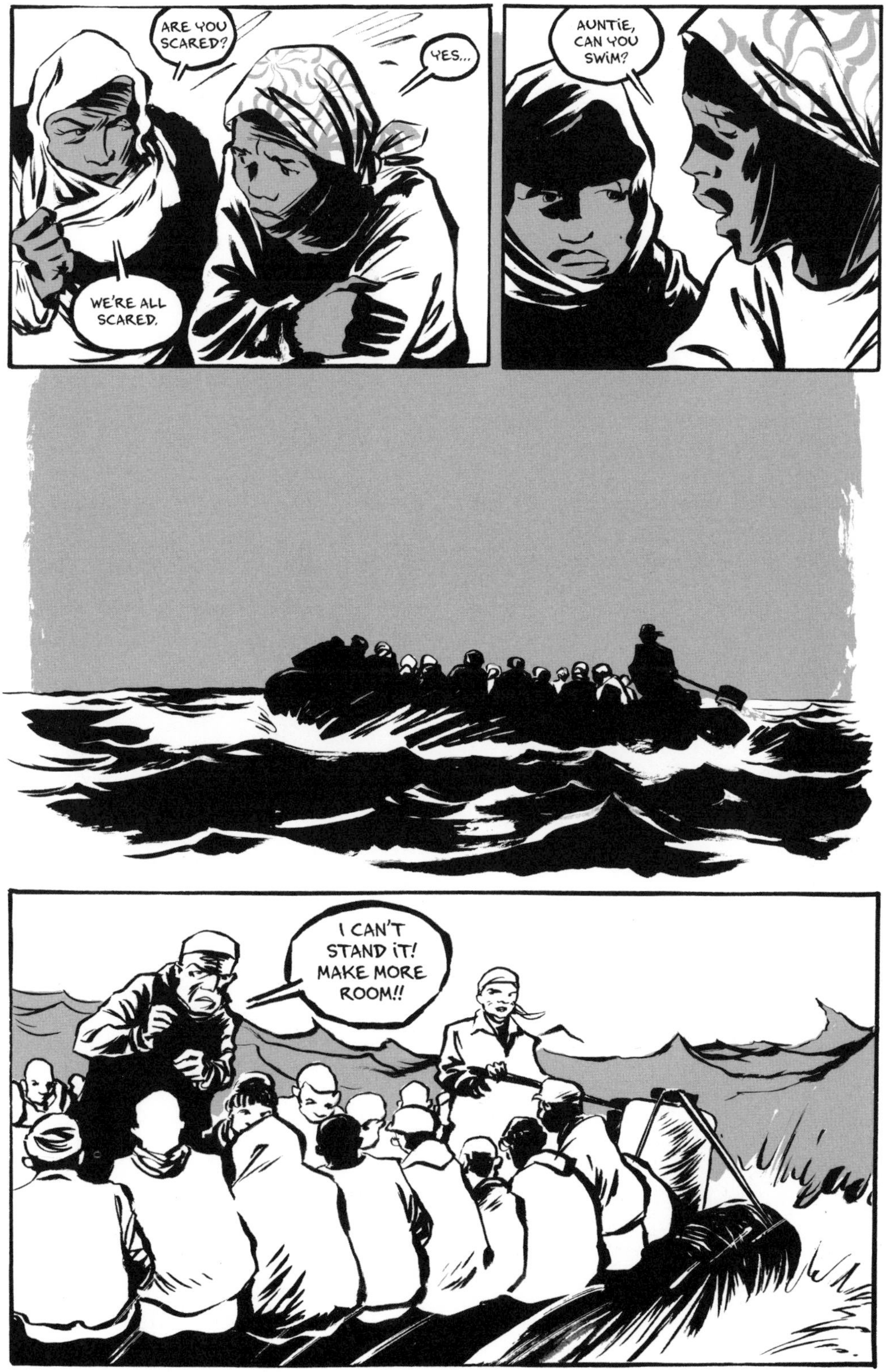
ARE YOU SCARED?
YES...
WE'RE ALL SCARED.
AUNTIE, CAN YOU SWIM?
I CAN'T STAND IT! MAKE MORE ROOM!!

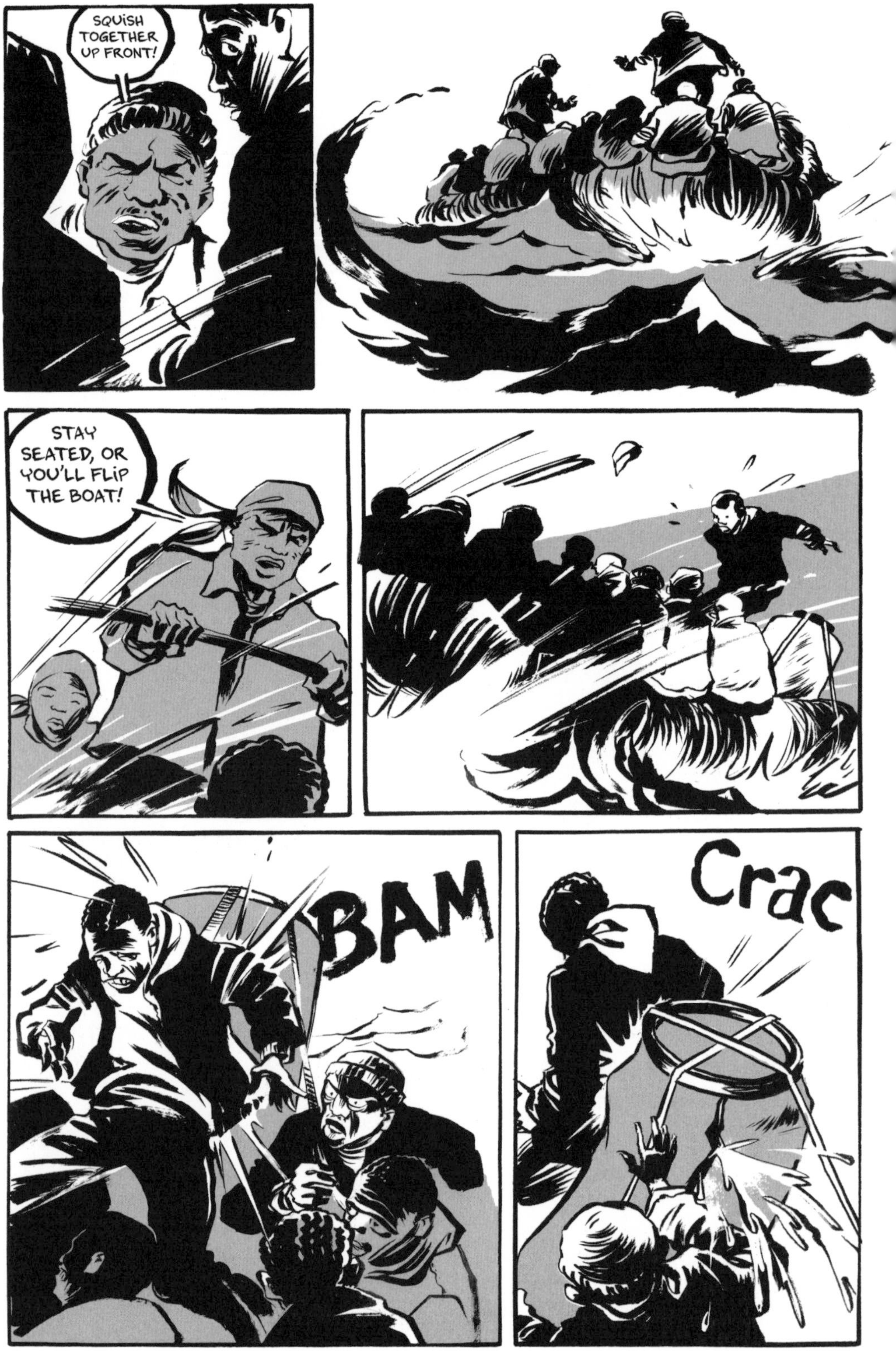
SQUISH TOGETHER UP FRONT!
STAY SEATED, OR YOU'LL FLIP THE BOAT!
BAM
Crac

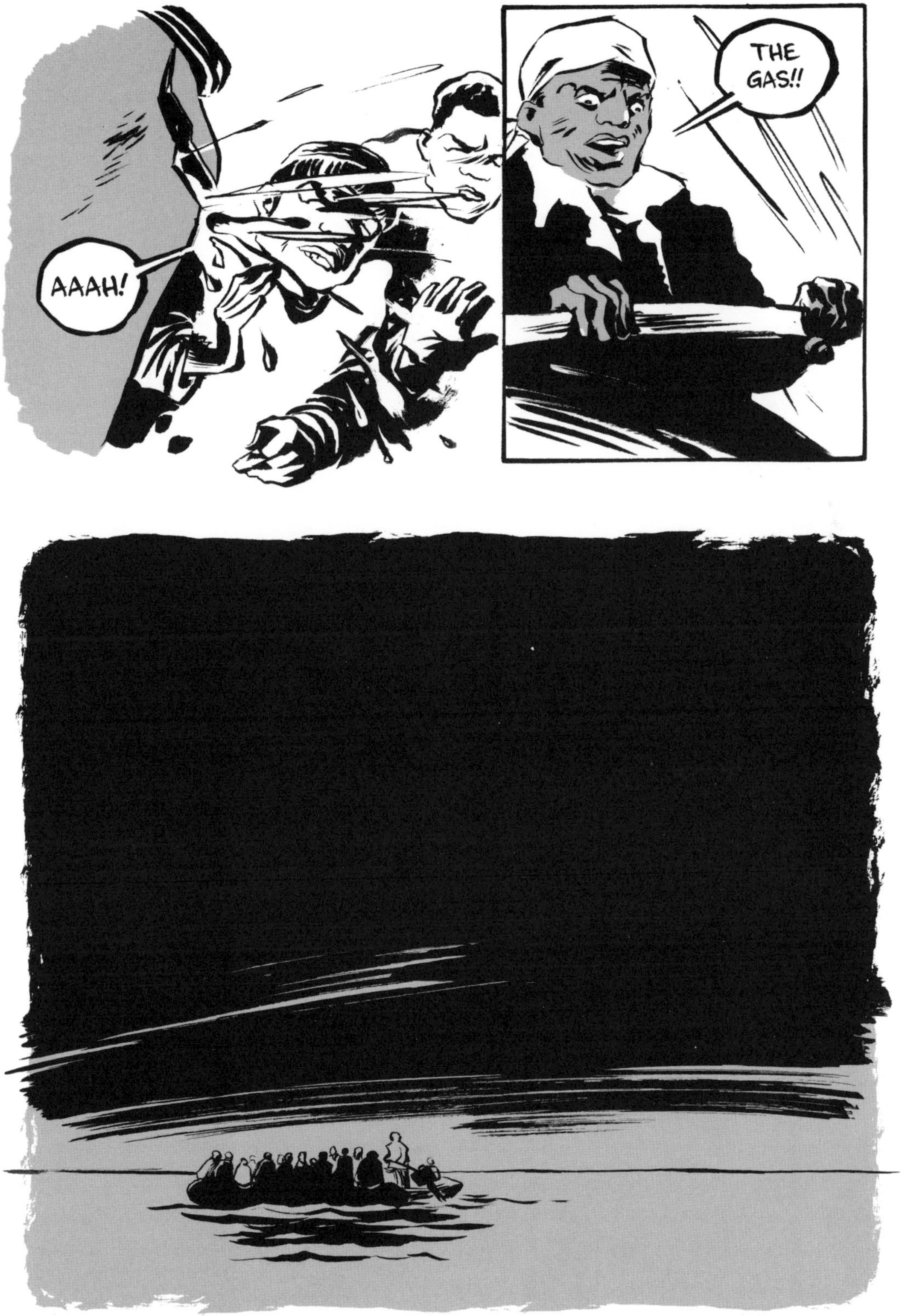
AAAH!
THE GAS!!

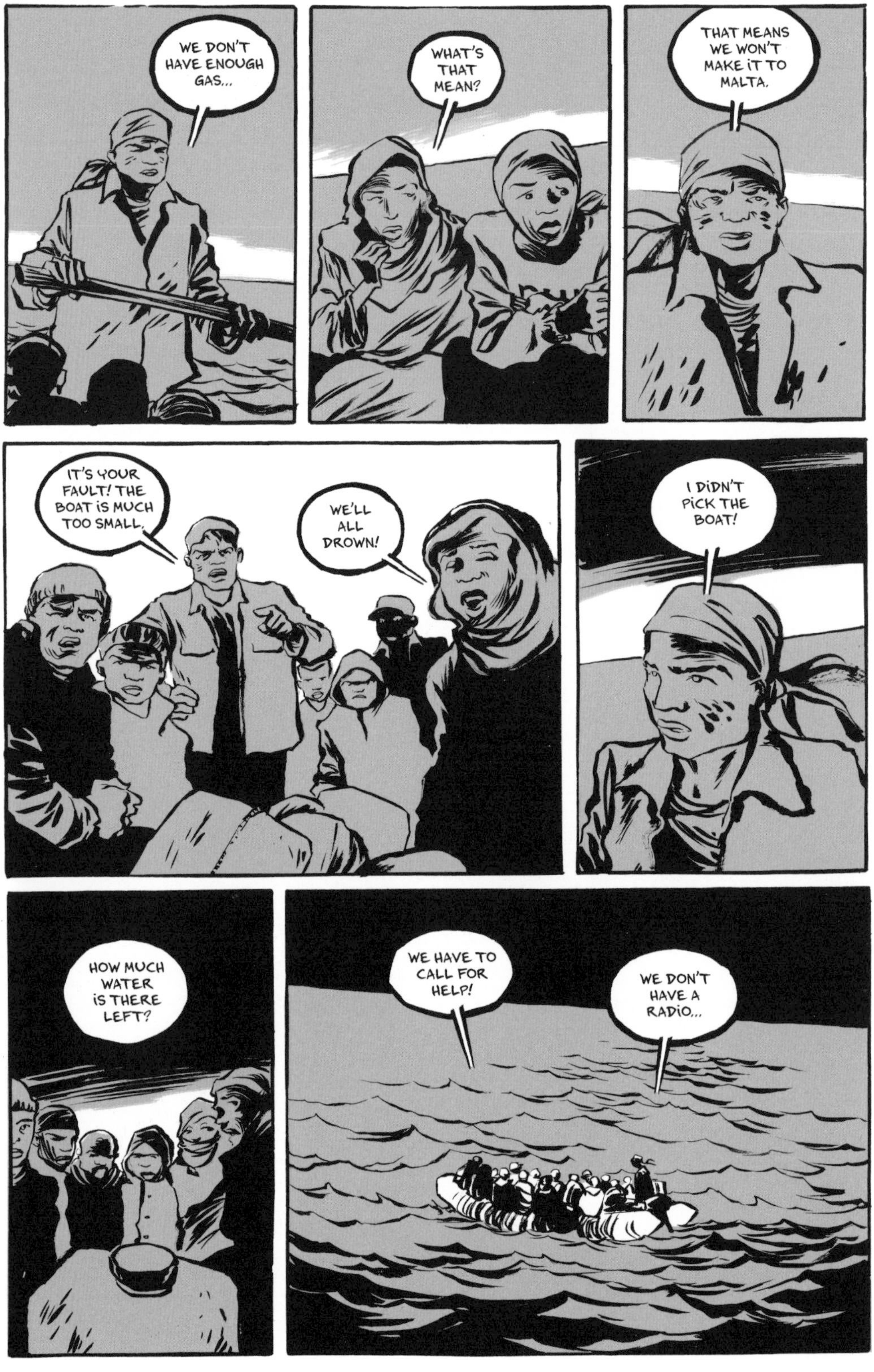
WE DON'T HAVE ENOUGH GAS...
WHAT'S THAT MEAN?
THAT MEANS WE WON'T MAKE IT TO MALTA.
IT'S YOUR FAULT! THE BOAT IS MUCH TOO SMALL.
WE'LL ALL DROWN!
I DIDN'T PICK THE BOAT!
HOW MUCH WATER IS THERE LEFT?
WE HAVE TO CALL FOR HELP!
WE DON'T HAVE A RADIO...

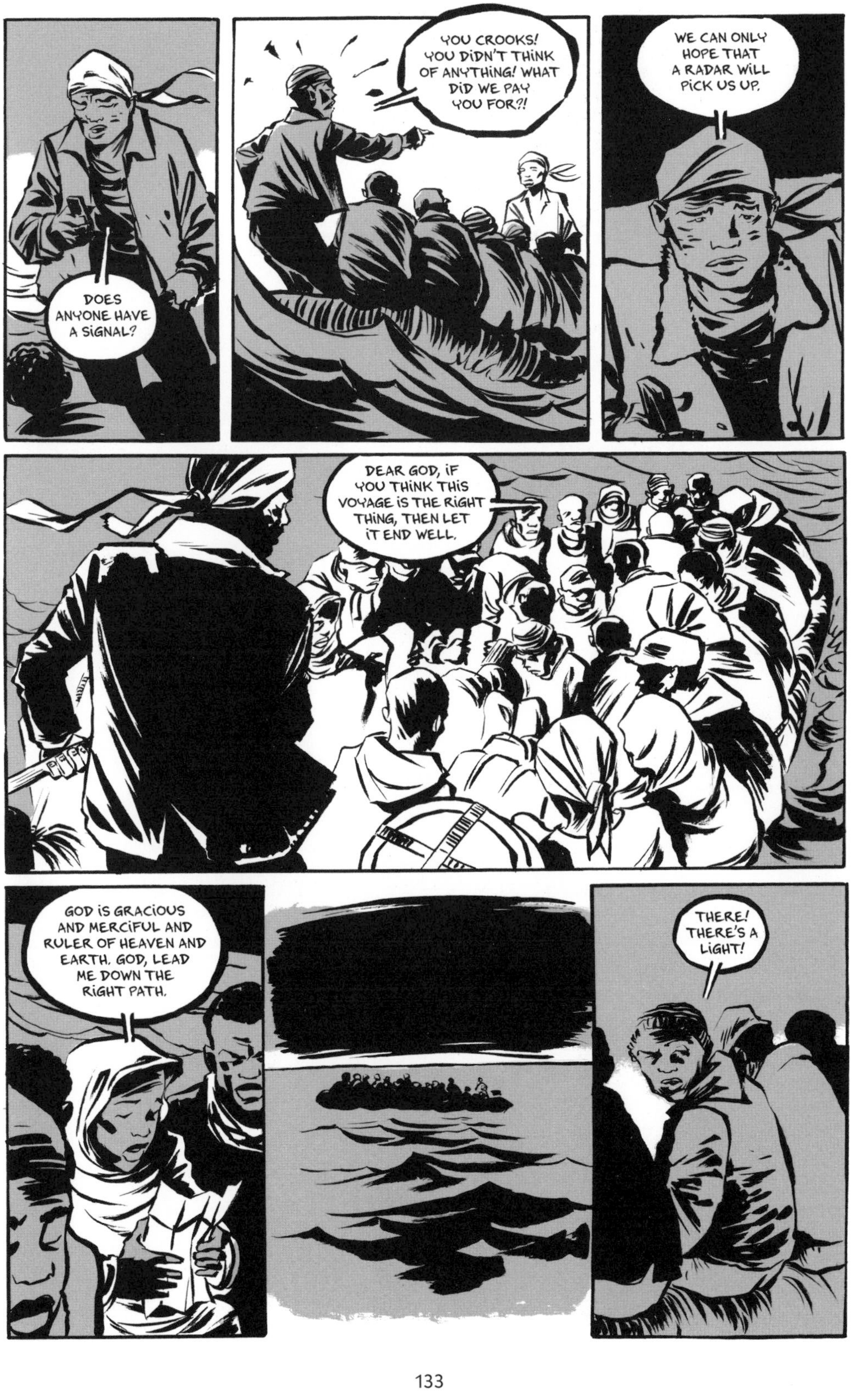
DOES ANYONE HAVE A SIGNAL?
YOU CROOKS! YOU DIDN'T THINK OF ANYTHING! WHAT DID WE PAY YOU FOR?!
WE CAN ONLY HOPE THAT A RADAR WILL PICK US UP.
DEAR GOD, IF YOU THINK THIS VOYAGE IS THE RIGHT THING, THEN LET IT END WELL.
GOD IS GRACIOUS AND MERCIFUL AND RULER OF HEAVEN AND EARTH. GOD, LEAD ME DOWN THE RIGHT PATH.
THERE! THERE'S A LIGHT!

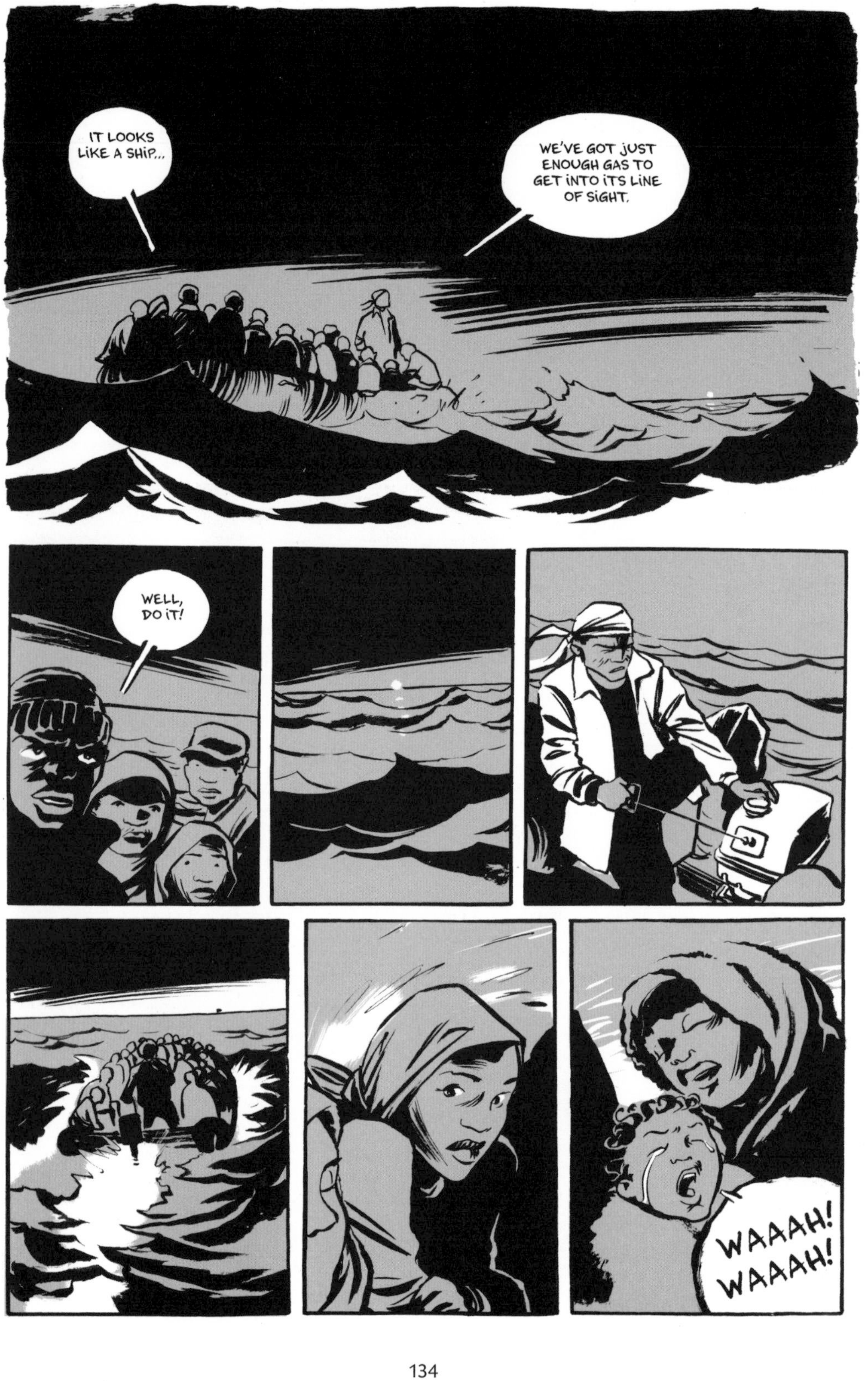
IT LOOKS LIKE A SHIP...
WE'VE GOT JUST ENOUGH GAS TO GET INTO ITS LINE OF SIGHT.
WELL, DO IT!
WAAAH! WAAAH!

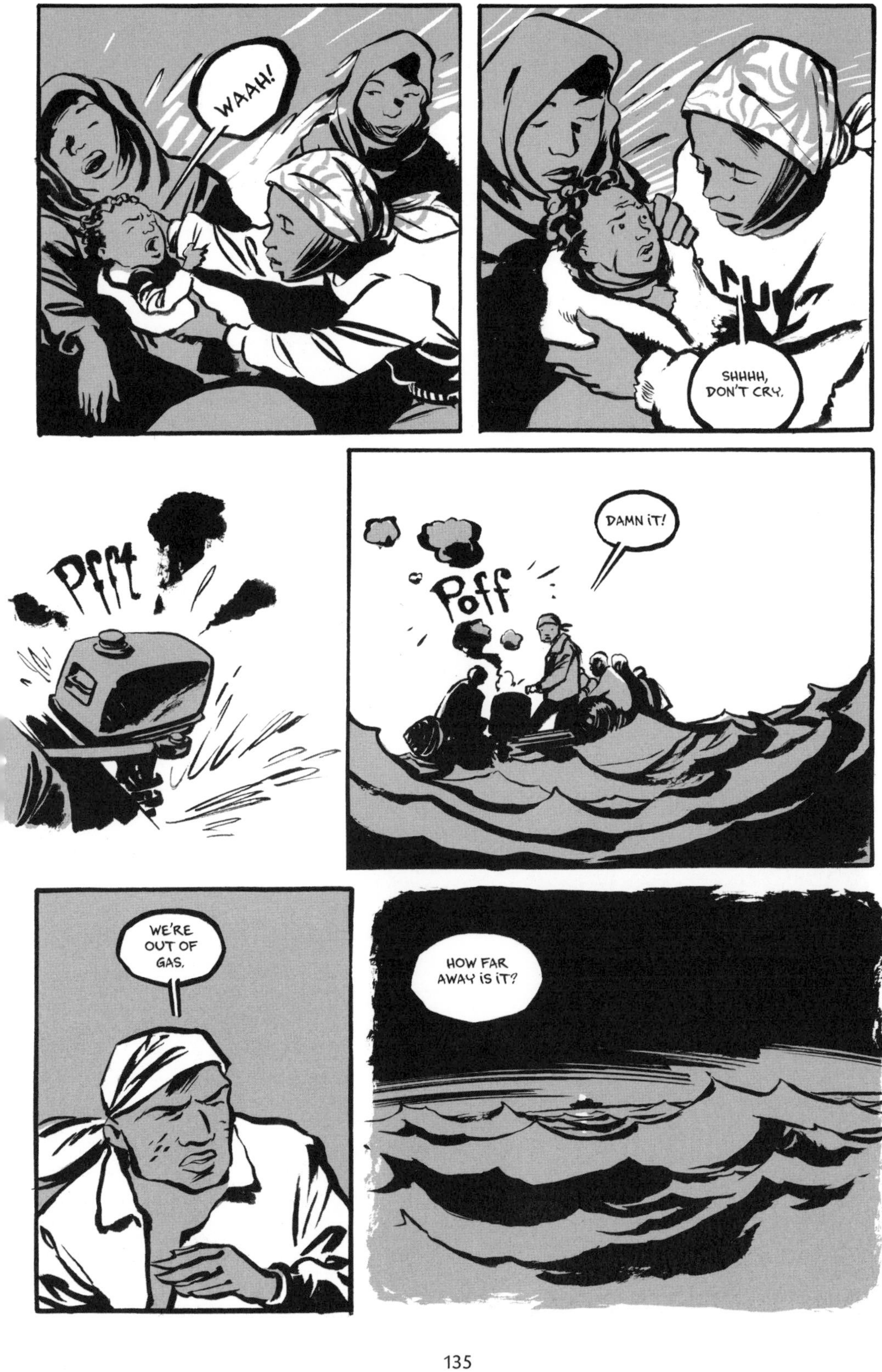
WAAH!
SHHHH, DON'T CRY.
Pffft
Poff
DAMN iT!
WE'RE OUT OF GAS.
HOW FAR AWAY iS iT?

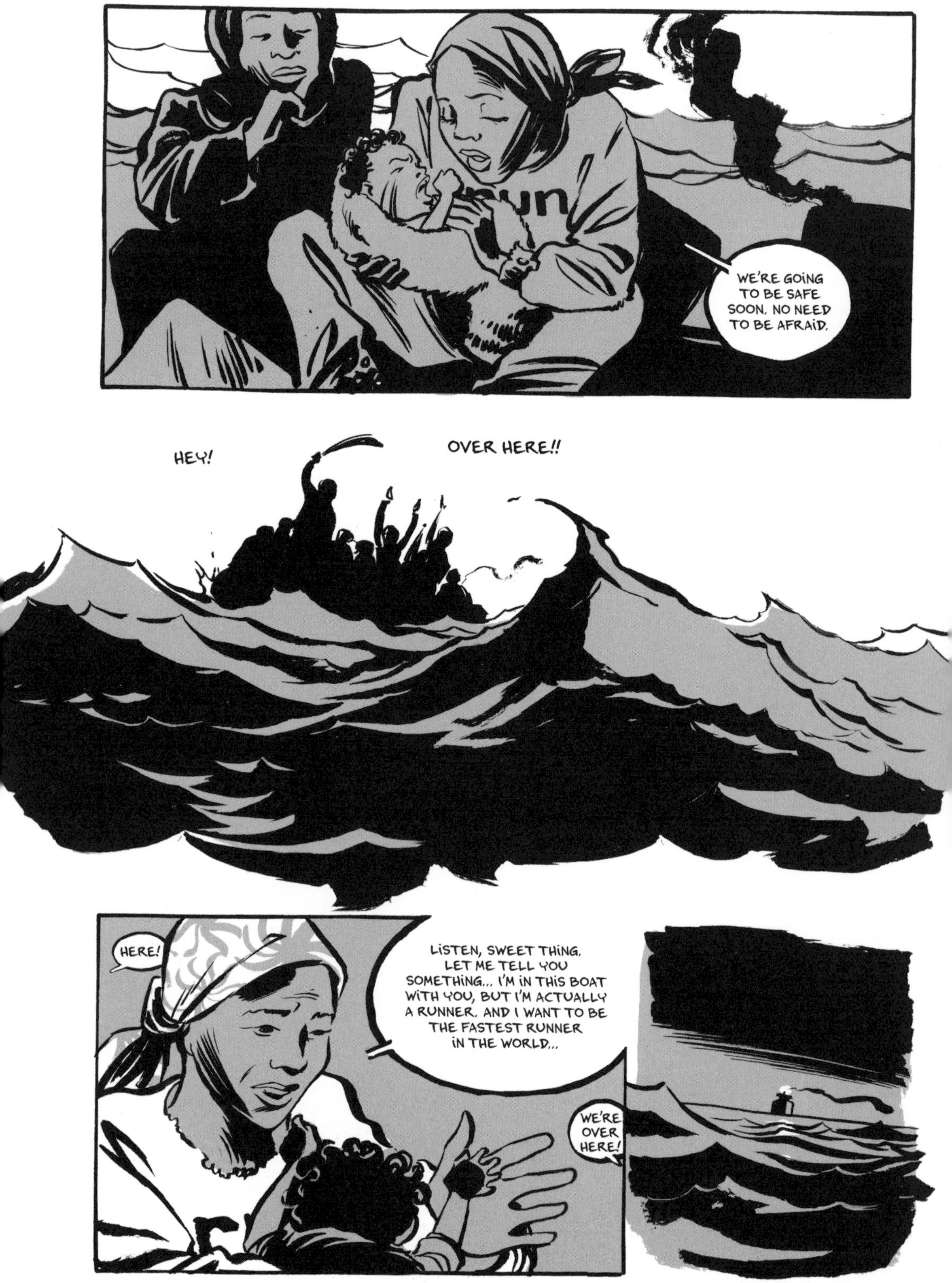
WE'RE GOING TO BE SAFE SOON. NO NEED TO BE AFRAID.
HEY!
OVER HERE!!
HERE!
LISTEN, SWEET THING. LET ME TELL YOU SOMETHING... I'M IN THIS BOAT WITH YOU, BUT I'M ACTUALLY A RUNNER. AND I WANT TO BE THE FASTEST RUNNER IN THE WORLD...
WE'RE OVER HERE!

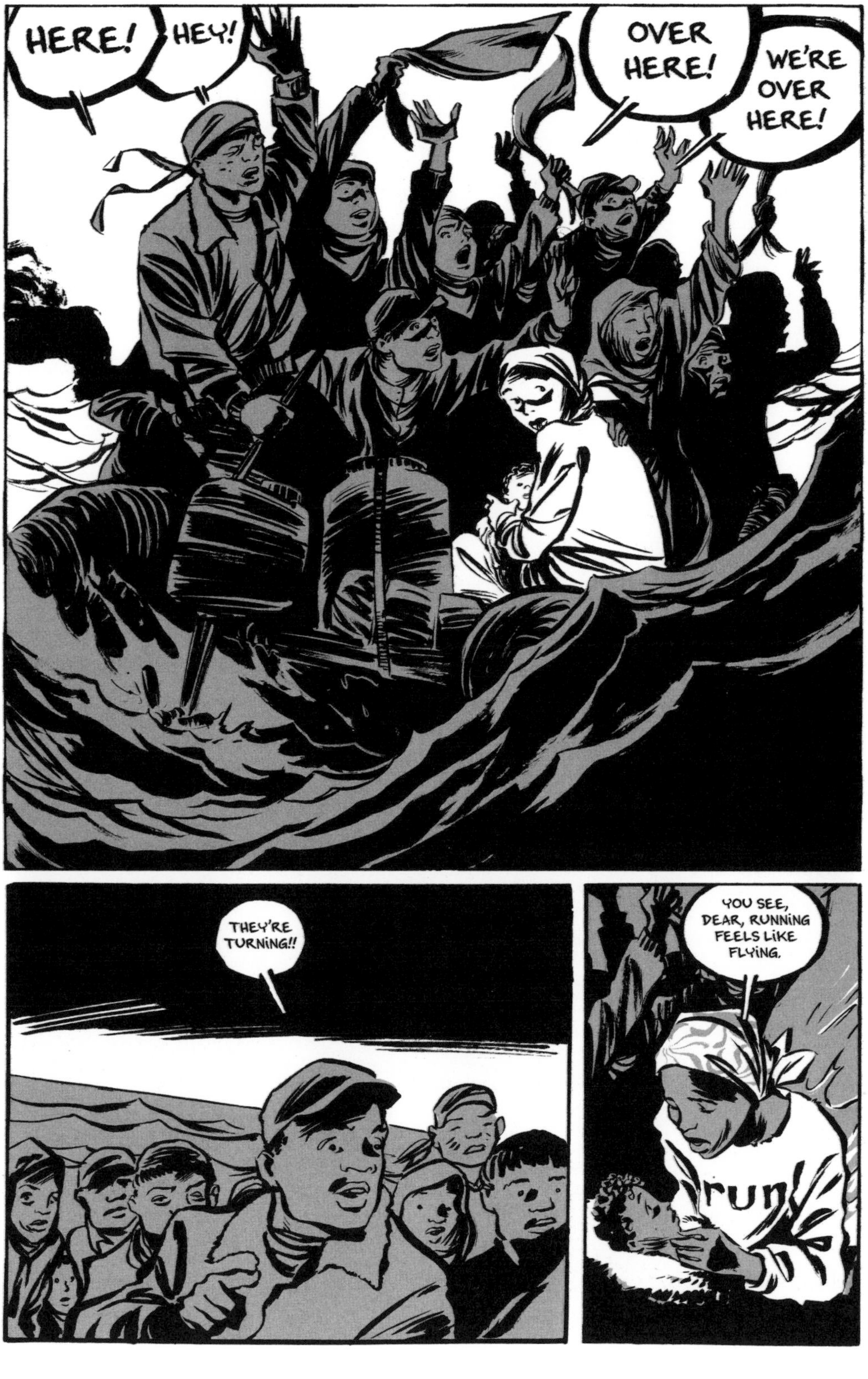
HERE!
HEY!
OVER HERE!
WE'RE OVER HERE!
THEY'RE TURNING!!
YOU SEE, DEAR, RUNNING FEELS LIKE FLYING.
run

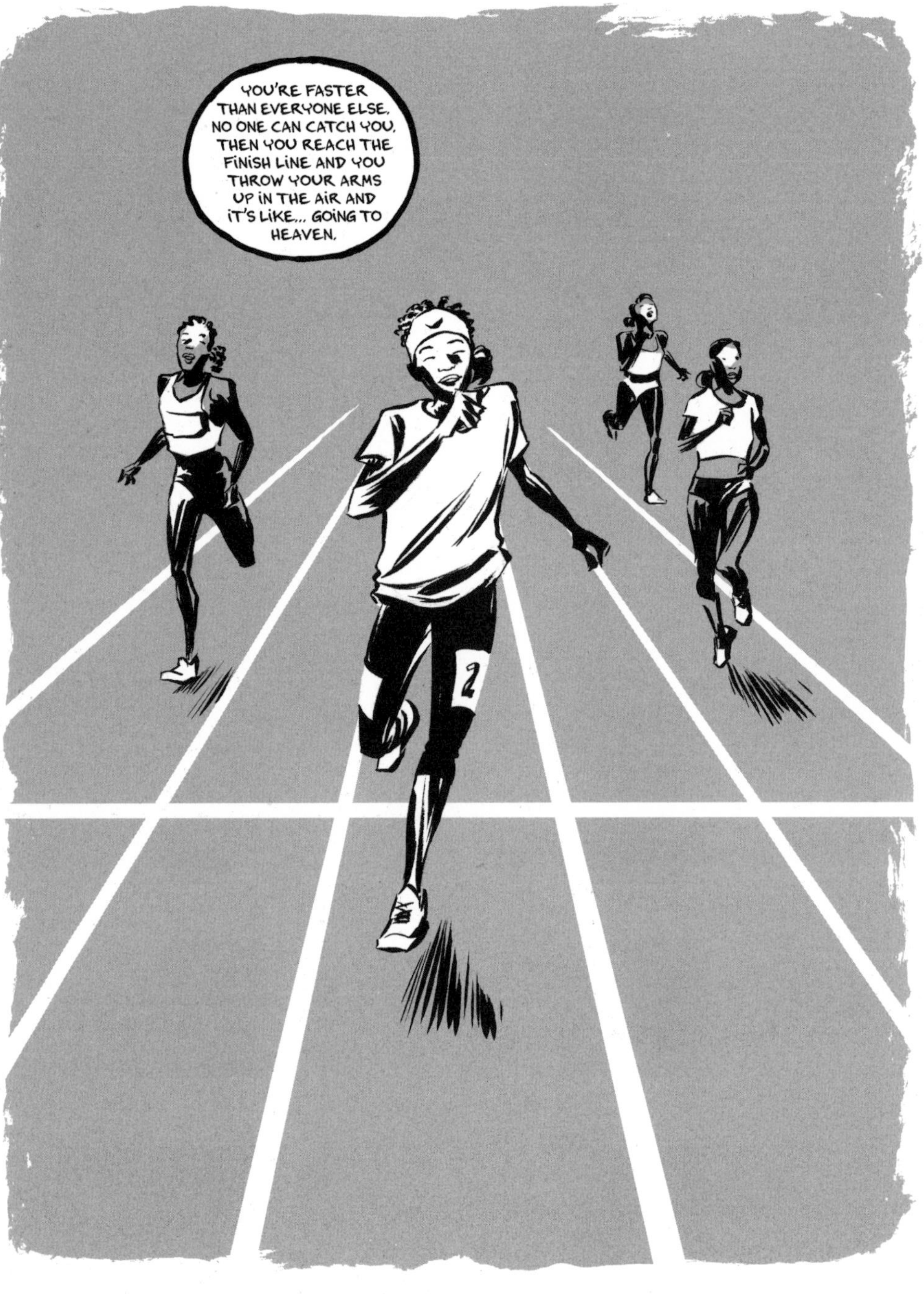
YOU'RE FASTER THAN EVERYONE ELSE. NO ONE CAN CATCH YOU. THEN YOU REACH THE FINISH LINE AND YOU THROW YOUR ARMS UP IN THE AIR AND IT'S LIKE... GOING TO HEAVEN.

YouTube
abdi
WiN a holyday
LIVE
Recommended
abdi bile
abdi bile 1987
abdi bile gold 1989
abdi bile world champion
abdi bile somali runner
abdi bile national hero
abdi bile world cup1500m
abdi bile samia yusuf omar
mar
Cabdi Bile oo ilin ka ti
1 year ago
Somalia Olympian an Ins
1 year ago
HD
Le destin tragique de l'a
abdi bile samia yusuf omar
CABDI BILE
0:00 / 4:08
Cabdi Bile oo ilin ka timit
1,612
1
0
CABDI BILE
I'D LIKE TO END MY SPEECH WITH A LITTLE REMINDER...
...THAT IN THE LAST OLYMPIC GAMES IN BEIJING IN 2008...
...OUR COUNTRY WAS REPRESENTED BY THE YOUNG WOMAN SAMIA AND THE YOUNG MAN IBRAHIM.

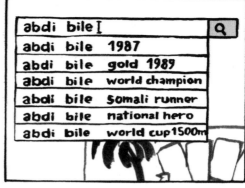

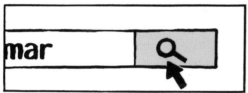

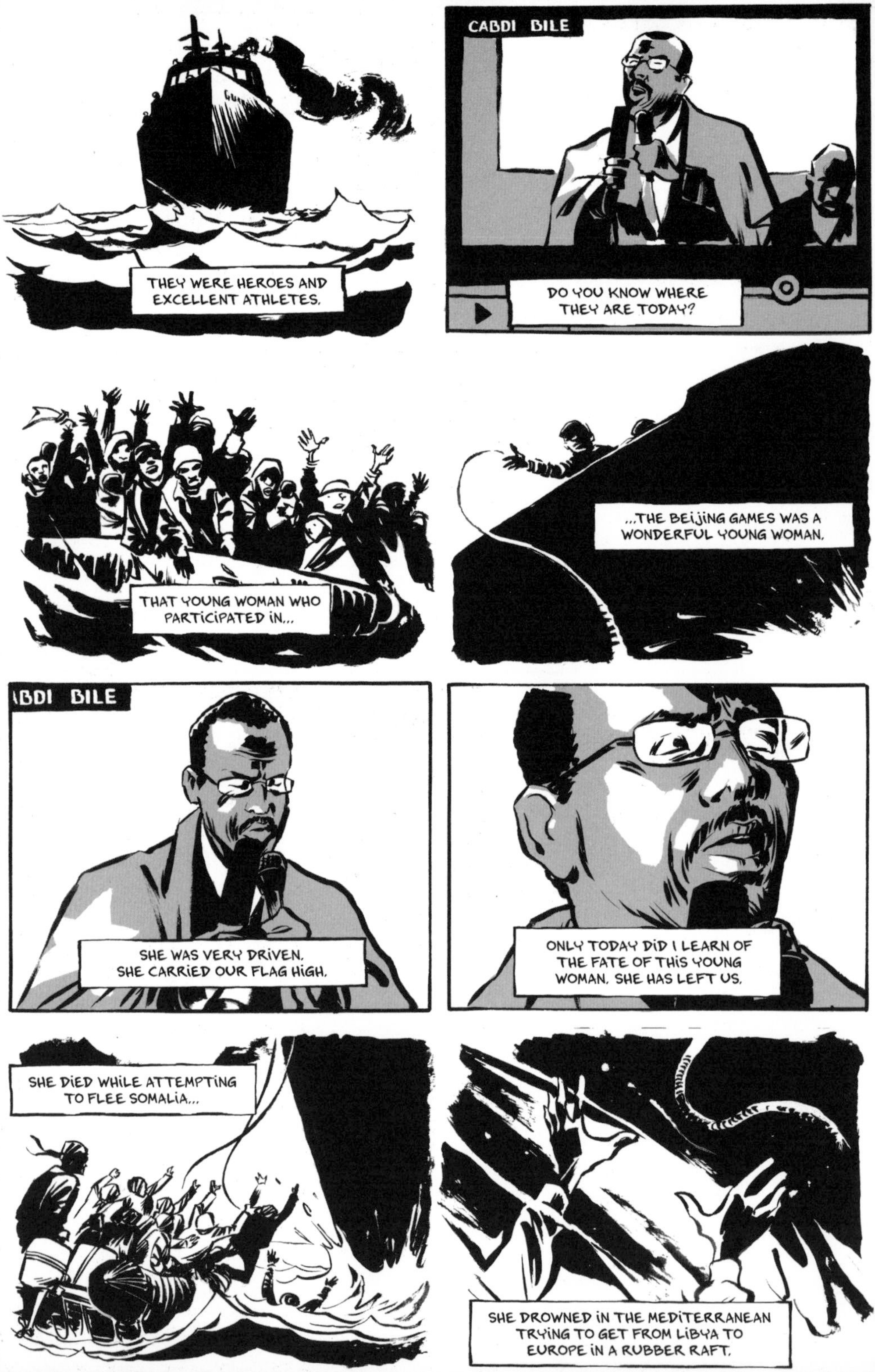
THEY WERE HEROES AND EXCELLENT ATHLETES.
CABDI BILE
DO YOU KNOW WHERE THEY ARE TODAY?
THAT YOUNG WOMAN WHO PARTICIPATED IN...
...THE BEIJING GAMES WAS A WONDERFUL YOUNG WOMAN.
BDI BILE
SHE WAS VERY DRIVEN. SHE CARRIED OUR FLAG HIGH.
ONLY TODAY DID I LEARN OF THE FATE OF THIS YOUNG WOMAN. SHE HAS LEFT US.
SHE DIED WHILE ATTEMPTING TO FLEE SOMALIA...
SHE DROWNED IN THE MEDITERRANEAN TRYING TO GET FROM LIBYA TO EUROPE IN A RUBBER RAFT.

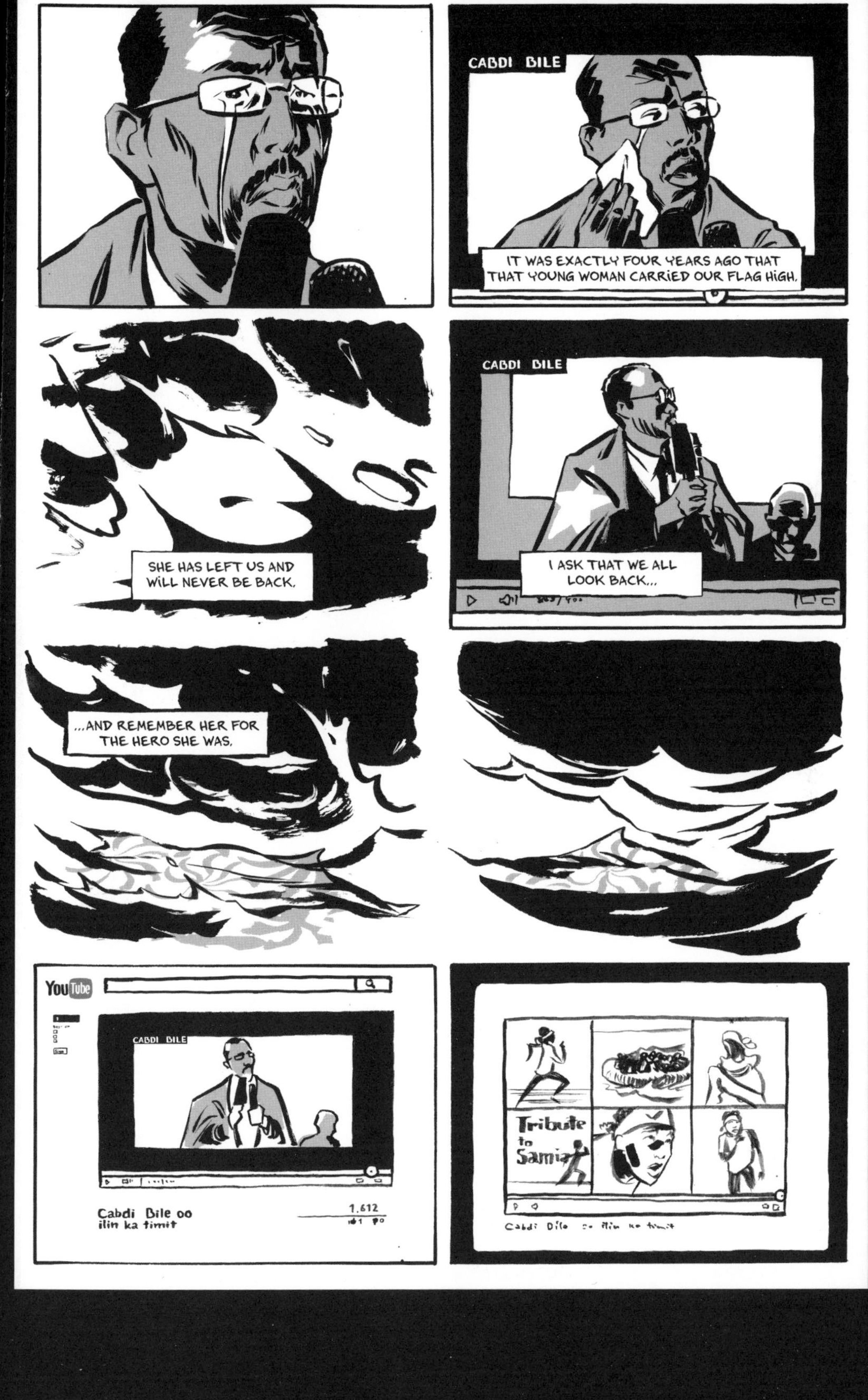
CABDI BILE
IT WAS EXACTLY FOUR YEARS AGO THAT THAT YOUNG WOMAN CARRIED OUR FLAG HIGH.
SHE HAS LEFT US AND WILL NEVER BE BACK.
CABDI BILE
I ASK THAT WE ALL LOOK BACK...
...AND REMEMBER HER FOR THE HERO SHE WAS.
YouTube
CABDI BILE
Cabdi Bile oo
ilin ka timit
1.612
Tribute to Samia

AFTERWORD

In December of 2009, the Omar Yusuf family fled from their two-bedroom home in Mogadishu as the violence spread into their neighbourhood. Against a background of heavy gunfire, and before the sun had even risen, Samia – holding the little hand of a niece or nephew – went down to the unlit area where the buses gathered, walking alongside the family members who remained in Mogadishu: a matriarch, a grown son, two grown daughters and one son-in-law, several grandchildren and Samia's sister and her family. Handing over double the number of shillings required for a usual fare – tickets always went up during peak periods of violence – the group boarded and rode the first bus, headed for an overcrowded camp for displaced Somalis right outside the capital.

As the days stretched into weeks, Samia remained close to their new shelter – a Somali hut stitched together with branches and pastel-colored plastic sacks. Sometimes she talked to others, but mostly she didn't. Because she refused to accept this as her home, she also declined to make friends. Even if she had wanted to, eager to find some way to pass the time, it would have meant disclosing parts of her past – a past that brought her a deep sense of pride, but also now put her family at extreme risk. And so, her neighbours remained in the dark about Samia's identity as an Olympian – something Samia determinedly worked to protect.

* * *

As Samia struggled through the war in the south, I was living in the north in the peaceful region called Somaliland. I was all of 25 years old – someone who had spent the vast majority of my life in rural America, now teaching at a locally run college in Somaliland and trying to carve out a career as a freelance journalist on the side. American editors, I was quickly discovering, were not interested in "peace and stability" pieces when there were peak levels of maritime piracy in the east and aggressive militant rebel groups in the south. So I looked for new ideas to feature – like how well female athletes fared in this conservative society. It was through this research that I came across exactly two articles written about Samia regarding her appearance on the international athletic stage: the BBC provided the run-up to the single 200-metre heat Samia would run in, and Yahoo! provided the details of the actual event – right down to the standing ovation Samia received, despite coming in last. Immediately smitten with the prospect of interviewing her, I spent months tracking her down. She wasn't on Twitter or Facebook, nor was there a fan page with contact information or even a splashy magazine spread that might indicate she was still alive. I admit that it never occurred to me that the quality of her life could have deteriorated to the degree it had. Nor could I have predicted the direction that it would soon take.

When I finally connected with Samia, offering to fly her up to Somaliland if she would let me write about her, I was unprepared for her initial skepticism once she arrived. Ever worried that the wrong person might discover who she really was, the young Somali deflected, redirected and sometimes just ignored my questions. Over a series of months and interviews, in which I also helped her get into Ethiopia, scouted for coaches with her and fielded concerns that the Somalia Olympic Committee had chosen a new girl to represent the team in the London Olympics, I finally broke into the inner fold. It meant I finally became witness to all of the great qualities her other friends and family would mention over the next few years: wit, encouragement, a deep loyalty, passion and – most specially – a very generous soul.

* * *

In August 2014, I travelled to Mogadishu as a guest of Samia's sister, Hodan, for a run sponsored by UNHCR that was held partially in memory of Samia. No longer was her identity tucked away; instead, her death in the Mediterranean Sea had grabbed headlines across the world, inspired works of art across Western Europe and – as in the case of this run – brought her name back to her home country in a big way. In the many interviews I granted immediately following the news that Samia had passed away, journalists insisted that the former Somali Olympian was the new "face of immigration"; despite the thousands of other refugees every year who, like Samia, fled their homes in hopes of finding a safe and stable home elsewhere, those I spoke to hoped that Samia's story might finally be the tipping point that brought about a comprehensive conversation and redress for immigration in Western Europe.

Unfortunately, this has obviously not been the case. When I interviewed Somali refugees on visits to Lampedusa and Sicily in 2013 – just a year after Samia died – I was surprised to find myself being thanked by them simply for giving them a chance to be heard; there was not the media attention you see today. These were not the lives they envisioned for themselves – homeless, unemployed and penniless. They were genuinely surprised that there had been no one to warmly receive them when they finally landed in Europe, after

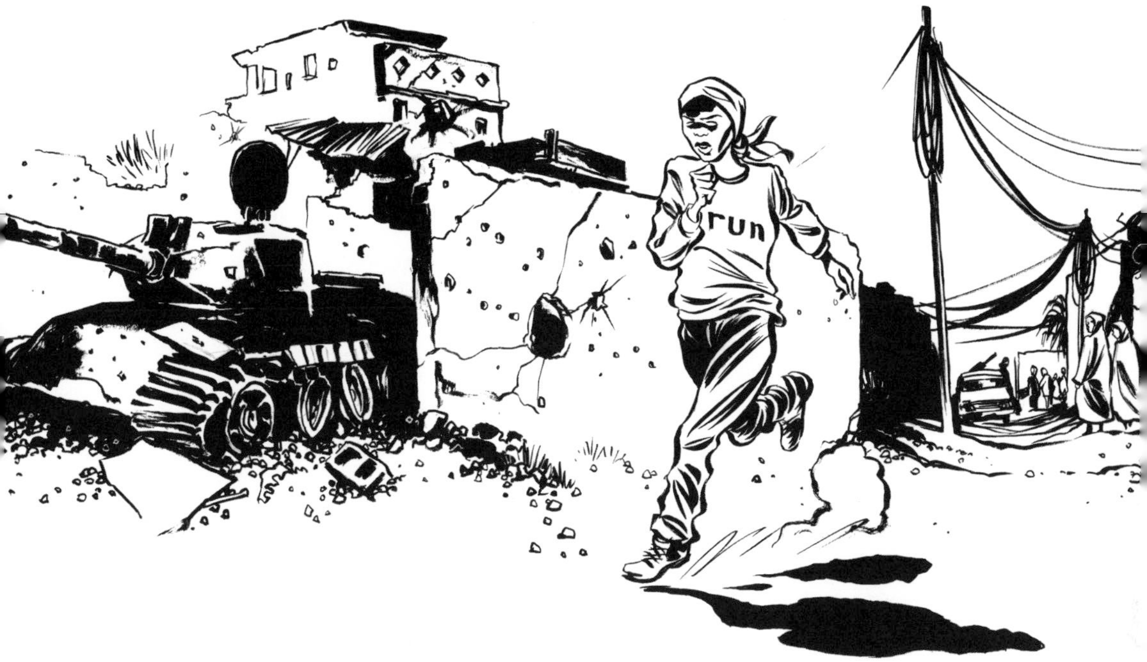
run

having survived starvation, imprisonment, poverty, the punishing desert and the dangerous open sea. Many, in fact, told me they wished they had never made the journey. At least in Somalia they were home.

As the English translation of Reinhard Kleist's beautifully written and illustrated *An Olympic Dream* goes to print, Europe is receiving the highest number of refugees since World War II. The reaction from politicians and citizens in places like Hungary, Germany and the UK has been mixed, and has certainly fluctuated as the number of refugees continues, the media coverage intensifies and the public weighs in.

The issue of immigration is complex and requires action on a number of fronts – from home countries to host countries. It is my hope that at the very least *An Olympic Dream* will remind readers that every refugee they see on TV or in their own area is not a "problem", but rather someone whose life story is just as rich and compelling as Samia's and who deserves just as much compassion and consideration.

BY TERESA KRUG
JOURNALIST

STUDIES OF SAMIA YUSUF OMAR

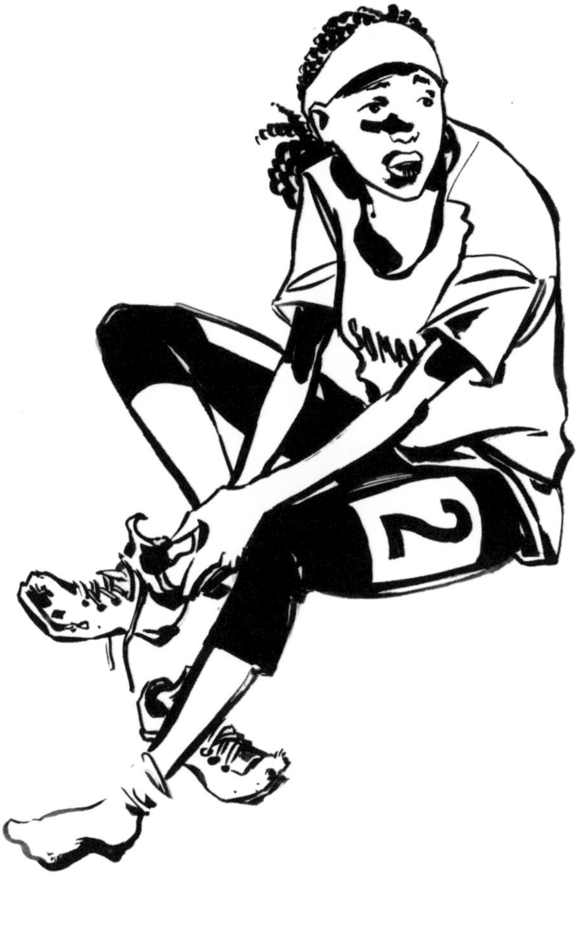
2

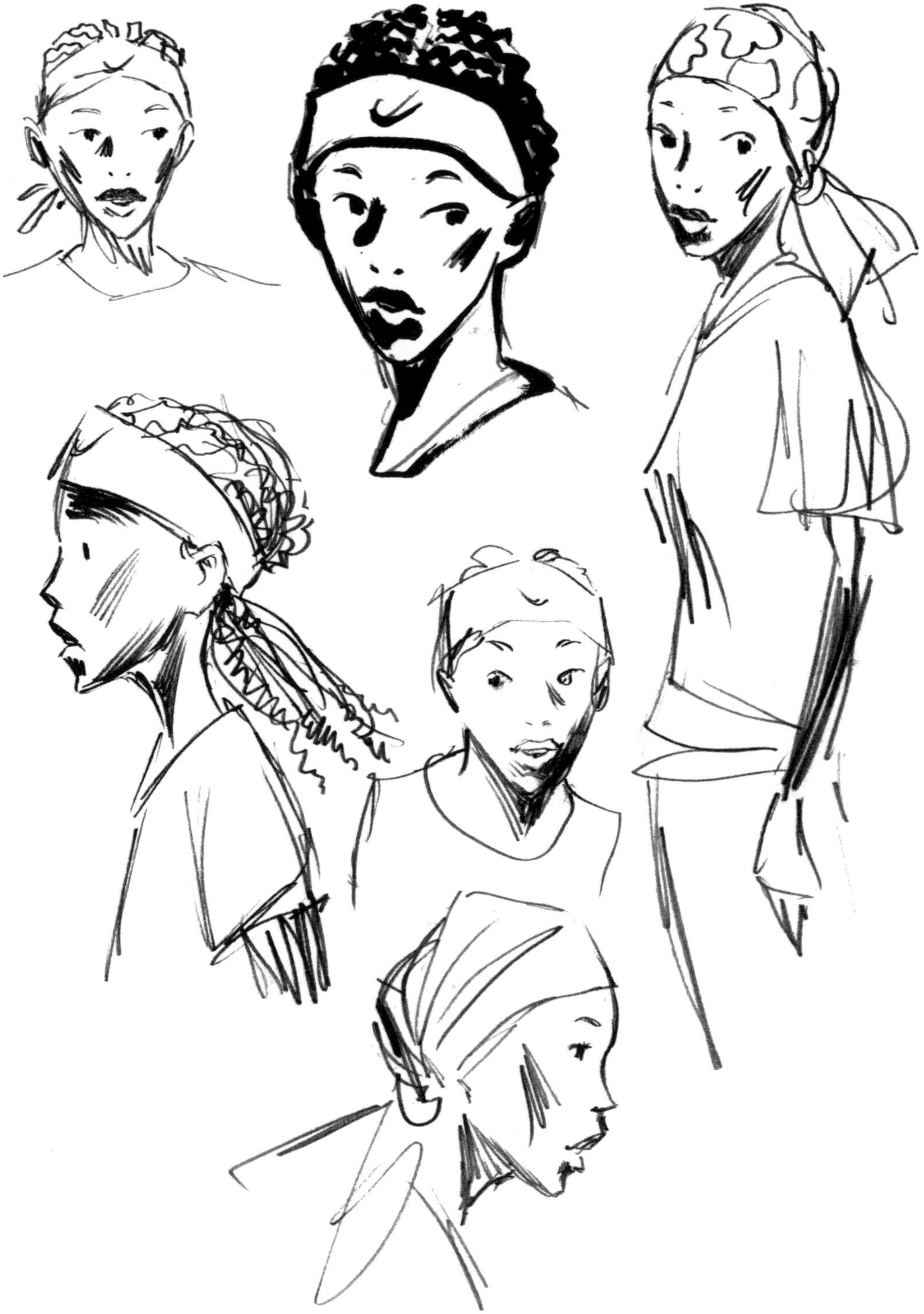